The Future of Entrepreneurship in Africa

This book focuses on entrepreneurial development and the development of small businesses in Africa. The central idea of this book is that entrepreneurial development and small business development are connected. Entrepreneurship is lauded as an engine of growth (economic development and job creation), with small businesses often contributing to new job creation. Also, entrepreneurship and small business development are the heart of many countries' economies. The decision to focus on entrepreneurial development and small business development is that first, there is a consensus that most entrepreneurial activities are aimed at creating small new ventures. Second, countries that give special attention to entrepreneurship stand a chance of industrialization. Third, Africa has been reported as having a rich entrepreneurial landscape as the continent's wealthiest individuals generated their wealth as trailblazing entrepreneurs. Fourth, small-scale entrepreneurs and businesses form the backbone of economic activities across the continent. A motivation to focus on entrepreneurial and small business development is the generally accepted view that start-ups in Africa are growing calling for understanding into how to enhance productivity, efficiencies, and application of new technologies.

The book aims to enhance the understanding of stakeholders (business owners, governments, practitioners) to overturn challenges such as inadequate start-up capital, competition, lack of employees with the right skills, and low use of technology. The ability to develop entrepreneurship in Africa, and the role of small-medium enterprises cannot be underestimated. The promotion of entrepreneurship in Africa is crucial as it creates jobs, provides decent livelihoods, and contributes to GDP. Most entrepreneurial initiatives in developing economies entail identifying opportunities and new venture creation. It is worth recognizing that most new ventures created take the form of small businesses and the entrepreneurial processes involve entrepreneurs' knowledge and skills, identifying opportunities, involvement in setting up a business and managing the business.

The various aspects of this book focus on many entrepreneurial activities that are undertaken on the African continent. This book is focused on African countries since there is a reason to be optimistic about the prospects for growth and entrepreneurship. To achieve entrepreneurial success in African countries, the African Development Bank (2021) proposes that there must be a link between macro and firm-level characteristics that will serve as the mix of entrepreneurship in societies.

This book, therefore, considers some macro-level factors such as education, training, and skills development, technological developments, government programs, and entrepreneurial challenges and opportunities. At the firm-level, this book focuses on entrepreneurial initiatives such as branding and marketing.

The Future of Entrepreneurship in Africa

in Africa

Cross-Sectoral Perspectives Post COVID-19

Edited by
Robert E. Hinson, Doreen Nyarko Anyamesem Odame,
Kojo Kakra Twum, Patient Rambe, Paul Agu Igwe,
David Gamariel Rugara

Routledge
Taylor & Francis Group

A PRODUCTIVITY PRESS BOOK

First published 2024
by Routledge
605 Third Avenue, New York, NY 10158

and by Routledge
4 Park Square, Milton Park, Abingdon, Oxon, OX14 4RN

Routledge is an imprint of the Taylor & Francis Group, an informa business

ISBN: 978-1-032-29848-1 (hbk)
ISBN: 978-1-032-29847-4 (pbk)
ISBN: 978-1-003-30233-9 (ebk)

DOI: 10.4324/9781003302339

Typeset in Garamond
by Deanta Global Publishing Services, Chennai, India

Contents

Preface

The global economy has witnessed a dramatic turn over the years creating a trade imbalance. Many countries have implemented domestic and regional policies to enhance the economic development and social well-being of their citizens. Notwithstanding this, developing countries have been at the weaker end of global trade due to challenges such as the fall in commodity prices, weakening local currency and the high cost of doing business. Despite Africa being home to more than 1 billion people and having diverse human and natural resources, the continent has not fully utilised the potential of its resources. The expectation is that policymakers must formulate and implement policies that promote growth through productivity and jobs creation.

Mindful of the numerous economic and social challenges that Africa is confronted with, the key question is what policies must be formulated and what actions should be undertaken to put the continent on the path to prosperity. It has been commonly accepted that entrepreneurship and free trade in Africa are the major catalysts for a new era of economic prosperity. As such, entrepreneurship can serve as a vehicle through which policies to enhance productivity and create jobs can be executed. Therefore, entrepreneurship must be at the centre of all efforts to transform the fortunes of the African continent. The activities of starting and running a business, which are entrepreneurial activities, are vital in promoting economic growth and development.

The African Continental Free Trade Area (AfCFTA) which has become operational in 2021 must serve as a major boost to entrepreneurship on the continent. The role of entrepreneurs in ensuring the success of the free trade agreement is to forge new value chains and exploit new investment opportunities. With the biggest free trade area, the continent has the capacity to create a new economic path by exploiting its resources. This new journey by Africa demands academics to provide a clear understanding of how to use the AfCFTA to promote entrepreneurship.

Building entrepreneurship requires the conduct of cutting-edge research to scrutinise theoretical and practical frameworks that work best in and for Africa. This edited book focuses on the three entrepreneurship domains, namely the African entrepreneur, the entrepreneurial firm and the macro-socio-economic conditions. It is worth noting that entrepreneurship research in Africa acknowledges the unique African culture, diversity and economic conditions. This edited book documents how entrepreneurship policies can be positioned to achieve desired outcomes such as SME financing, internationalisation, gender-based entrepreneurship and small business marketing. Scholars and practitioners focusing on entrepreneurship development will benefit from the perspectives shared by contributors across Africa.

This book underscores the importance of understanding the nuances of entrepreneurship from an African perspective. The contribution of scholarship to promoting entrepreneurship necessitates taking drastic actions especially in contexts where there are dire economic and social conditions. Building the understanding of students, scholars and practitioners on pertinent entrepreneurship and small business development issues in Africa offers inspiration and interesting insights into entrepreneurship. The appreciation of entrepreneurial practices, marketing strategies, mitigating small business challenges, internationalisation and gender-based entrepreneurship approaches will serve as a teaching and learning guide for students, academics and practitioners.

This edited book has chapters that address four main themes. The themes span the challenges of sustaining businesses in Africa (Theme 1), the internationalisation of small businesses in Africa (Theme 2), the marketing strategies adopted by small businesses in Africa (Theme 3) and a gender-based perspective on entrepreneurship (Theme 4).

The introductory chapter makes a case for using entrepreneurship to turn around the economic fortunes of the African continent. The chapter contains sections on the potential of AfCFTA to propel entrepreneurship in Africa through the creation of an enabling environment for start-ups and the enhancement of their value creation processes. The chapter also introduces the need to enhance marketing capabilities, strategise for internationalisation and eliminate gendered disparities. This book proposes that marketing capabilities must focus on enhancing customer-focused strategies. The book provides a way to promote the internationalisation agenda by finding ways to eliminate barriers to ensuring the global participation of firms. Chapter 1 proposes that the gender dynamics of doing business can affect the competitive positioning of African businesses.

The first theme of the book focuses on the entrepreneurial realities experienced during COVID-19 and the challenges and prospects of informal entrepreneurs. Chapters 2 and 3 of the book investigate the management and financial challenges faced by small businesses in Ghana.

The second theme of the book focuses on the internationalisation of small businesses. Chapter 4 discusses the legal, economic and financial, social and cultural, and technological barriers that have a significant effect on internationalisation. Therefore, this chapter provides empirical results on the relationship between barriers and internationalisation. Chapter 5 uses the PESTEL framework to analyse environmental factors that enable the internationalisation of firms on the African continent.

The third theme of the book is on marketing capabilities of small businesses. Chapter 6 of the book focuses on the use of marketing strategies, innovativeness and environmental dynamism to promote small businesses. This chapter makes a case for an interface between entrepreneurship and marketing.

The fourth theme of the book focuses on the gender perspective on entrepreneurship. Specifically, the role of women in entrepreneurship in Africa is carefully discussed. Chapter 7 discusses the role of female entrepreneurs in the tourism industry. Chapter 8 analyses the role of formal and informal institutions in assisting women in SME. Chapter 9 addresses the issues of women's access to finance.

The final chapter of the book presents some implications of the various themes discussed in this book for theory, policy and practice. The book provides some lessons on challenges faced by small businesses in navigating the entrepreneurship terrain. The chapter concludes with lessons on marketing strategies to use and the need to pursue internationalisation on a wider scale.

Notes on Contributors

Kwame Adom is an Associate Professor of Business at Burman University in Canada. His research draws experience from Africa in general and Ghana in particular, to inform theoretical and practical developments in entrepreneurship. His recent publications are on the role of culture and gender stereotypes in women entrepreneurship, indigenous knowledge for sustainability and informalisation of enterprises.

Gloria Kakrabah-Quarshie Agyapong is the Head of the Department for Marketing and Supply Chain Management at the University of Cape Coast, Ghana. She is a Senior Lecturer, a marketing scholar and has published many research articles in reputable journals. Her research focuses on public sector marketing, service marketing and entrepreneurship.

Francis O. Boachie-Mensah is a Professor of Marketing in the Department of Marketing and Supply Chain at the University of Cape Coast in Ghana. His research interests span supply chain management and firm performance, social media marketing and marketing strategy.

Rebecca C. Emeordi holds a Master of Philosophy degree in Management from the University of Lincoln, England. She also holds a Master's degree in International Business. She is an accounting and finance enthusiast determined to work to enhance the use of accounting information by firms.

Robert E. Hinson is a Professor of Marketing and Pro Vice- Chancellor of the Ghana Communication Technology University. He holds a DPhil in Marketing from the University of Ghana and a PhD in International Business from the Aalborg University Business School. He also holds several visiting and honorary professorships across some European and South African Universities.

Paul Agu Igwe is a Senior Lecturer in Strategy and Enterprise at the University of Lincoln, England. He serves as project lead for research on innovation and entrepreneurship for higher education in Africa. He has published in quality journals on promoting entrepreneurship in Nigeria.

Nnamdi Madichie is a Professor of Marketing and Entrepreneurship. His academic work is currently at the University of Kigali, Rwanda; Coal City University, Nigeria; and Nnamdi Azikiwe University, Nigeria. He has experience working for Bloomsbury Institute London and has worked on projects for UNCTAD. He is an extraordinary researcher with many publications on innovative technologies, women entrepreneurship, cultural issues in entrepreneurship, corporate social responsibility, consumer behaviour and entertainment marketing.

Ratakane Maime is a Lecturer at the Central University of Technology, Free State in South Africa. He holds a Doctor of Business Administration (DBA). His teaching is focused on financial and management information systems. His research is on developing frameworks to enhance the financial benefits of implementing web technologies.

Gertrude Mensah is a marketing academic interested in the marketing of small businesses. She holds a Master of Philosophy in Marketing from the University of Ghana Business School in Ghana. She has served as a research and teaching assistant at the University of Ghana Business School.

Atsu Nkukpornu is a Lecturer in Entrepreneurship at Cape Coast Technical University in Cape Coast, Ghana. He holds a PhD from the University of Ghana Business School. He is a serial entrepreneur, and his research interest is in the area of entrepreneurship in Africa. He has published research articles and book chapters on entrepreneurial development in Ghana.

Etse Nkukpornu is Lecturer in Finance in the Department of Accounting and Finance, Christian Service University College. He holds a Master of Science in Economics from Kwame Nkrumah University of Science and Technology, Ghana, and a Master's degree in Finance from the Kwame Nkrumah University of Science and Technology, Ghana.

Doreen Nyarko Anyamesem Odame is a Lecturer at Ghana Communications Technology University, Accra, Ghana. Her research interests span social development, public sector management, African business development and health systems management. She has published articles in internationally recognised journals such as the *Journal of International Development*. She is a co-author of a book on social media and the public sector in Africa.

Kenny Odunukan holds a PhD in International Business, Management and Strategy at the University of Lincoln, England, where he teaches International Entrepreneurship. He has over ten years of working experience in multinational companies. He has published research articles in high-quality journals. He has made academic contributions to firm internationalisation, strategic management and digital entrepreneurship.

Oyedele Martins Ogundana is a Senior Lecturer in Accounting and Finance at Nottingham Business School in the UK. He has many years of experience as a senior accountant with government institutions in Nigeria. His recent publications are in women entrepreneurship in developing economies, entrepreneurial competencies and the performance of SMEs.

Patient Rambe is a Research Professor in Entrepreneurship in the Faculty of Management Sciences at the Central University of Technology, Free State in South Africa. He has published research articles in high-quality journals on innovation and competitiveness and the adoption of technology to promote small business development in Africa.

David Gamariel Rugara is the Head at the International Executive Office of Lincoln International Business School, UK. His research interest is in international business and higher education management. His research has been published in high-quality journals.

Amon Simba is a Senior Lecturer in Entrepreneurship, Innovation and Strategy at Nottingham Business School, UK. He has published in internationally recognised journals including *The Journal of Entrepreneurship and Innovation Management* and *The International Journal of Small Business and Entrepreneurship*. One of his major research interests is women entrepreneurial development in Africa.

Kojo Kakra Twum is a Senior Lecturer in Marketing and Head of the Department of Business Administration at the Presbyterian University, Ghana. He has co-authored books on Responsible Management, Social Media Marketing and Public Sector Marketing Communications. He has published research articles in quality journals, focused on public sector marketing, services marketing, corporate social responsibility, marketing analytics and innovative technologies.

Ugbede Umoru is a Senior Lecturer in the Department of Management at Nottingham Business School, UK. He holds a PhD from Nottingham Trent University. His PhD research focused on institutional factors influencing the internationalisation of emerging market telecommunication firms. He is a lead facilitator in international business for postgraduate programmes. He also served as a coordinator for placement programmes between his university and companies such as Verizon, Rolls Royce and Liverpool Football Club.

Chapter 1

Introduction to Africa's Entrepreneurial Landscape

Paul Agu Igwe, Robert E. Hinson, David Gamariel Rugara,
Doreen Nyarko Anyamesem Odame, Kojo Kakra Twum
and Patient Rambe

Contents

Apart from the health sector, the COVID-19 pandemic has also greatly affected the economic sector in Africa (Lone & Ahmad, 2020). Some of the challenges have manifested in the fall of commodity prices, reduced tourism, weakening of local currencies, increasing cost in maintaining health outcomes as well as high cost of managing the pandemic. These are factors that impact macro-economic growth and stability negatively. As the world repositions the global economy following the COVID-19 pandemic, international entrepreneurship and international trade dominate major scholarly and policy discussions. This adds urgency and scale to the collective and regional responses to economic, health, social and environmental challenges concerning bilateral relationships, regional security, trade integration and governance (Igwe, Ochinanwata & Madichie, 2021). This book provides timely and intriguing discussions about the interactions between marketing, internationalisation and gender in the development and growth of small- and medium-scale enterprises (SMEs) in Africa as the continent strives to revive from the effects of COVID-19.

Among the many strategies and protocols to control the pandemic was the closure of borders and restrictions of cross-border movements. As it stands now, the border restrictions and

DOI: 10.4324/9781003302339-1

closures have aggravated the already existing economic challenges and difficulties on the continent (Sucheran, 2021). Policies targeted at border closures and restrictions led to increased transaction costs, increased household expenses, shortage of supplies among others, with these negative outcomes more pronounced among small-scale traders, agricultural workers, unskilled workers and populations engaged in the informal sector. Several empirical studies in this book have highlighted how these challenges impact on business growth and sustainability. Earlier in January 2012, the Africa Continental Free Trade Area (AfCFTA), also referred to as Agenda 63 was adopted. The signage of the agenda was a remarkable and significant event to mark the second decade of the 21st century in Africa. The AfCFTA was anticipated to be the largest trade agreement after the World Trade Organization and was aimed at creating a single continental market for goods and services and facilitating the free movement of business and business activities (Aniche, 2020). In this book, we argue that African countries are lagging behind innovative strategies for business growth and sustainability. The continent also seems to have less capacity when compared with the Western and Asian regions concerning globalisation of markets, technological innovations, market development, digital economy and industrial development. Asiedu (2018) educates that AfCFTA was constituted for four major reasons:

I. Enhance intra-African trade through comprehensive and mutually beneficial pacts with member states
II. Improving Africa's trade position by reinforcing the continent's presence on the international market
III. Reduction in tariffs to foster business growth expansion
IV. Improve the manufacturing sector by increasing output of services and goods on the continent

The aims of the AfCFTA were geared toward improving entrepreneurship in Africa through the creation of an enabling environment to foster the enactment and growth of entrepreneurship in Africa. Though each of the countries of the African continent has its peculiar challenges that mitigate business growth and economic expansion, one major challenge common to all the countries in Africa is the relegation of services to the final stages of the market lifecycle, and advocates against this old paradigm have pushed for a deeper and broader integration which embraces services, investments, manufacture and competition (Ennew, Waite & Waite, 2013). This cycle has been described as the sure and most effective way to address national-level economic challenges and constraints. Prideaux et. al. (2020) asserts that the main engine for such economic transformation is entrepreneurship. In this regard, innovative policies and strategies that have the capability of addressing the different facets of entrepreneurship cannot be overemphasised. It is only by so doing that we can realise the full benefits and potential of entrepreneurship for sustainable economic development. In the subsequent section, we present the entrepreneurial dynamics and differences of the various Sub-Saharan Africa (SSA) regions.

Africa's Entrepreneurship Policy and Development Climate

The importance of examining the drivers and challenges of entrepreneurship at the regional level is highlighted by the nature and scale of the fundamental changes in the global environment (Ortega-Argilés, 2022). During the last three decades, the world economy has changed almost out of recognition, and new opportunities and challenges have emerged and affected regions differently

(Ortega-Argilés, 2022). Industry 4.0, the Internet of Things, Big Data, Artificial Intelligence, digital platforms and Robotics and, recently, COVID-19 have provided new opportunities and challenges that impact markets and economic development. This is one of the expectations of the significant role of AfCFTA in the long term. It is envisioned that the free trade area will lead to increased competition, innovation and prosperity for Africa's people (World Economic Forum, 2019).

Entrepreneurship has been discovered as a critical driver of growth in SSA. Empirical evidence reveals that for every ten successful businesses, there is a potential of an estimated 1.4 billion dollars increase in gross domestic product (GDP) per capita and up to about 2,400 job opportunities (Ariker, 2022). Though the North African region has good economic prospects, it is yet to tap into its full entrepreneurship potential. A persistent challenge that mitigates entrepreneurial growth and development in the region has been challenges with start-up and early-stage businesses (Aljuwaiber, 2020). Though the majority of the population are believed to have entrepreneurial potential, they are confronted with these start-up challenges. Some of these challenges manifest in product value chain, business discontinuity and gender disparities. There is an urgent call for entrepreneurship education and policy awareness on supportive and dynamic ecosystems that foster entrepreneurial start-ups and sustainability (Oukil, 2007).

The Economic Community of West African States (ECOWAS) comprises two main regional blocks. One is the West African Economic and Monetary Union (WAEMU), which constitutes the French-speaking countries within ECOWAS. The second block is the West African Monetary Zone (WAMZ), which is made up of all the English-speaking countries within the region (Musila, 2005). The influence and the dictates of colonisation had different economic paths for each of the blocks. While the anglophone WAMZ block focused on strategies for economic development and national integration, the francophone block focused on trade centralisation. In effect, while the British had specific control structures and mechanisms for countries like Gambia, Ghana, Sierra Leone and Nigeria, France sought after policies that unified Senegal, Mali, Guinea, Burkina Faso, Benin, Cote d'Ivoire and Niger (Augustin, 2010).

There were different entrepreneurial directions among the two blocks that led to a lack of collaboration and different economic outcomes. For instance, Akisik et al. (2020) find that while both blocks compete closely on revenue generation and mobilisation, anglophone countries receive better business outcomes than their francophone counterparts. Again, due to the regional collaboration that exists among francophone countries, their businesses have better and regular business engagements. This signifies the existence of policies that focus on easing business regulatory issues that for instance facilitate easy business start-ups and cross-border initiatives. Aside from these differences, economic growth and sustainability in both blocks are driven by unskilled labour, subsistent agriculture and extraction of natural resources (Morris & Fessehaie, 2014). This does not favour economic growth and sustainability. Countries must therefore seek efficient and innovative means of production.

South Africa is noted for a mixed economy, characterised by high poverty rate, relatively low GDP per capita and high-income inequalities. In 2011, the G20 entrepreneurship barometer reported that the slow entrepreneurial development in South Africa can be attributed to the sophisticated financial sector and is still counted as a major cause of poor economic growth in the region. Akinemi and Adejumo (2018) confirm that the South African region is still confronted with start-up challenges, which have been attributed to regulatory issues, skill shortages and ultimately unemployment. Access to funding, for instance, is a major challenge in South Africa, which in turn affect entrepreneurial start-ups negatively (Skinner & Watson, 2021).

Apartheid policies and legacies also had a major role to play in the South African situation; present populations of European, Indian and Asian descent play a better position for business start-ups than the black populations. Apartheid policies also led to low education and training of the black population in South Africa, which fuelled low entrepreneurship among the black popu-lation (Spreen & Vally, 2010). In response to this, successive governments in South Africa have embarked on policies aimed at facilitating and enabling start-ups of entrepreneurial activities in South Africa. Some of these policies include the National Development Plan (NPD) and the New Growth Path Strategy, which set out to develop five million jobs by 2020 (Hendriks, 2013). Other interventions in the strategy included reducing unemployment by 6% by 2030.

Entrepreneurial Development in Africa: Enhancement of Marketing Capabilities and International Entrepreneurship

Picking from the trends and experiences of the various African regions, there are three main themes that run across entrepreneurial development in Africa: enhancement of marketing capabilities, strategising for international entrepreneurship and eliminating gendered disparities. Simply put, marketing capabilities refer to a firm's strategic position to respond appropriately and efficiently to customer needs in relation to time, cost and place. The marketing capability of a firm therefore is determined by the firm's focus on customer needs, competitor offerings and business dynamics that can enable you to deliver to meet customer needs (Buccieri et. al., 2020). Establishing mar-keting capabilities can be in two folds: creating avenues for economic empowerment of African businesses that will enable consumers to patronise domestic products. The second revolves around expanding the export market base to generate significant revenue for a robust economy.

Though Africa is noted for some level of participation in the international market, the region still contends with the effects of colonial legacies which are manifested in ineffective economic and trade policies. This notwithstanding, the dynamics that pertains to Africa is a good indication of fertile grounds for entrepreneurial development (Chang & Mendy, 2012). Entrepreneurship has high success tendencies given the right product mix, pricing and distribution strategies. Entrepreneurial development in Africa, therefore, requires appropriate and adequate awareness of local resources, socio-cultural dynamics, domestic knowledge and an understanding of how these characteristics can be integrated into the global markets. This will foster African relevant opportu-nities for long-term sustainable entrepreneurial and socio-economic development in Africa.

International trade, single market, regional integration and governance of treaties and poli-cies remain contentious areas. In West Africa's large market, countries leveraging their compara-tive advantages will improve regional trade integration, growth, and development (AfDB, 2018). AUC/OECD (2022) predicted that the entry into force of the AfCFTA in January 2021 creates new opportunities to accelerate productive transformation by developing regional production net-works. According to the report, regional production of processed and semi-processed goods has much room to grow, currently at a mere 2.7% of Africa's participation in global value chains (AUC/OECD, 2022). Also, the report recommends two policy priorities: (i) the digitalisation of intra-African trade and production and (ii) a focus on national industrialisation strategies (Table 1.1). Trade has much room for improvement, but the main barrier to more intra-African trade comes from nontrade barriers – both political and economic (AfDB, 2018).

Strategising for International Entrepreneurship

In the subsequent chapters of this book, we stress the need for an appreciation of local dynamics in Africa for sustainable entrepreneurial development. The diversity of the population and culture in Africa requires innovative strategies that can respond to different consumer needs. Developing

Table 1.1 Policy Recommendations to Develop Selected Value Chains in African Regions

Region	Value Chain	Policy Recommendations
Southern Africa	Automotive	Improve the business environment and encourage investment from global lead firms
		Actively support firms to maintain production and financial liquidity during the pandemic
		Adopt accommodative trade policies by removing tariffs and other trade barriers
Central Africa	Wood	Improve the business environment through stable macroeconomics, harmonising business laws and liberalising import markets
		Invest in transport and logistical infrastructure
		Work with local communities and the private sector to develop processing capacity
East Africa	Agri-food	Review the East African Community's Common External Tariff and reduce non-tariff barriers
		Co-ordinate national industrial strategies and promote interactions between industrial clusters across countries in the region
		Expand the One Network Area roaming initiative to other countries beyond the East African Economic Community (EAC)
North Africa	Energy	Improve the business environment and target industrial clusters to attract global lead firms
		Establish training and research centres to build the relevant skills in the workforce
		Facilitate intra-regional trade in raw materials and intermediate goods for the sector
		Invest in transport links and develop plans for intra-regional energy interconnection
West Africa	Agri-food	Improve access to finance, and provide technical and financial assistance to co-operatives
		Facilitate digitalisation and climate-smart practices by smallholders and informal producers Enhance implementation of Economic Community of West African States (ECOWAS) agreements on trade facilitation and quality standards
		Target cross-border special economic zones to attract investment and increase competitiveness

Source: AUC/OECD (2022, p. 20).

international platforms for African markets is crucial in establishing sustainable entrepreneurial growth in Africa. Most importantly because African markets cannot rely on domestic demands alone as a factor to grow local businesses. In fact, export is noted to be positively correlated with improved economic performance and poverty alleviation. Kenya for instance is known to enjoy about 5% increase in revenue from the exportation of cut flowers, which creates employment opportunities for the rural population, especially women (Sultanuzzaman et al., 2019; Rangasamy, 2009). The discussion in this book points to the fact that entrepreneurial development in Africa will remain insignificant with sole dependence on just domestic market. Export market and international mix, therefore, remain crucial for significant business and entrepreneurial growth.

International entrepreneurship opportunities can provide ways to achieve socio-economic prosperity for Africa. Sustaining exportation and participation in global markets, however, is challenged by complicated regulations and unfavourable labour practices. Exportation of local products and natural resources from Africa over the years has been cited as the cause of economic impoverishment in Africa, characterised by boom-and-bust cycles, limited multiplier effects and royalties that do not trickle down to the indigenous populations. This has resulted in civil strife in several parts of Africa, aggravating the poverty menace in the region. This is for instance manifested in the misallocation of oil revenue in the Niger Delta region of Nigeria and other parts of Africa. These notwithstanding, there are tremendous export market opportunities in Africa (Fossati, Rachinger & Stivali, 2021). With the enactment of policies such as Agenda 2063 and the AfCFTA, local producers can target customers from other African countries. However, as it stands now, this potential progress is challenged by infrastructural difficulties, low levels of education, corruption and neo-colonial misconceptions. Dealing with these challenges will require structural economic transformation that moves labour from low-skilled parts of the economy to high-skilled, higher-paying ones (AfDB, 2018). Reducing inequality will require structural economic transformation moving labour from low-skilled parts of the economy to high-skilled, higher-paying ones. Also, economic transformation will require providing enabling environment and resources to enable SMEs to compete favourably in the local markets as well as internationalise and access the global market and attract foreign investments.

To compete with other regions, African government must prioritise investing in digital technology to make trading easier, thereby promoting digital, financial and social inclusion. With the world's largest free trade area and a 1.2-billion-person market, Africa is creating an entirely new development path, harnessing the potential of its resources and people. However, Africa's economic growth path was abruptly interrupted by COVID-19 pandemic control measures that restricted the movement of goods and persons to contain the pandemic. Under current projections, it will take African countries more than five years to regain their pre-COVID share (about 5%) of the world's gross domestic product (AUC/OECD, 2022). The various discussions in this book suggest that futuristic agenda for African economic prosperity will require high-quality entrepreneurial growth and the implementation of policies that will set the stage for a sustainable recovery and growth.

Ideas presented in this book point to the informal sector as a prominent and effective means to establishing the international market base. By its (informal sector) characteristics, it employs most of the population, and is robust in curving significant economic threats. The informal sector has a large industry knowledge repository and has stronger socio-cultural bonds due to its high tendency of hiring local and indigenous people (Suryanto, Adianto & Gabe, 2020). These characteristics satisfy contractual bonds and agreements among partners, which is crucial in cross-border business relationships. This book provides innovative and effective recommendations that draw on the specific dynamics of the African region: the social, cultural, political and economic factors that contribute to entrepreneurial development.

Strategising Gender Dynamics for Entrepreneurial Growth of Africa

Discussions about the economic growth and competitive positioning of African businesses on the global market cannot be complete without an appreciation of the gender dynamics in Africa. The potential of women in entrepreneurship is characterised as one of the many unexplained areas of the African economy that inhibit growth in the 21st century. Though women contribute a major portion of the growth revenue of Africa, the full potential of their productivity is generally hampered due to the widespread inequalities in areas like education, land acquisition and business inputs in general (Manda & Mwakubo, 2014). Other factors such as uneven distribution of time burden, unrecognised domestic duties and high birth rate also reduce women's ability to fully participate in economic activities in Africa. The interaction between gender and entrepreneurship can manifest in three main categories – *women making up the majority of the informal sector, legal and institutional regularities that affect men and women differently* and *gendered disparities that affect women negatively, limiting their growth potential.*

In most of the Sub-Saharan African countries, women are disproportionately represented in the informal sector than their male counterparts, making up about 92% (Omri, 2020). In places like Accra, Lagos and Nairobi, urban markets are more dominated by women than men. The dynamics that exist in the informal sector, however, tend to position women as victims and not significant participants in trade and business. Though it may be argued that informal jobs offer privileges like the employment being closer to home and job flexibility, the sector remains a poverty trap for women as it does not provide equal opportunities for participation for men and women. Women are unequally treated in areas like access to capital and social security (Bonnet, Vanek & Chen, 2019).

Within the legal regulatory environment, there are yet several factors that affect men's and women's economic participation differently. Some of these include property rights, labour laws and personal security, among many others. Though other factors such as age and size of enterprise also pose constraints to businesses, gender inequality is found to play a major role in business growth and sustainability. Indeed, it is worthy of note that, the severity and magnitude of the constraints outlined may be experienced as much among men as in women, across the different regions in Africa. Research has shown that for factors that women indicate as major or severe obstacles, men also indicate same. Examples were cited as access to funds, competition and business regulation. However, factors such as lower levels of confidence, lack of role models and fear of failure do not allow women to enter entrepreneurship in the first place. The discussion in this book brings to light important issues and recommendations that affect business start-ups and ownerships.

Structure of the Book

This book is structured into three main themes: to discuss critical issues, provide recommendations for business start-ups and sustainability for businesses in Africa. The trends and experiences of various African regions show three main themes that run across entrepreneurial development in Africa: *enhancement of marketing capabilities, strategising for international entrepreneurship* and *eliminating gendered disparities.* The empirical findings and ideas presented in this book point to the informal sector as a prominent and effective means to establishing the international market base. The informal sector has a large industry knowledge repository and has stronger socio-cultural bonds due to its high tendency of hiring local and indigenous people (Suryanto, Adianto & Gabe, 2020). These characteristics satisfy contractual bonds and agreements among partners, which is crucial in cross-border business relationships. This book provides innovative and effective recommendations that draw on the specific dynamics of the African region: the social, cultural, political and economic factors that contribute to entrepreneurial development.

The first part of the book focuses on the challenges of sustaining businesses in Africa, especially in crisis situations, with COVID-19 as a case study. In Chapter 2, Astu Nkukpornu and Este Nkupkornu discuss the realities of challenges in operating businesses, with a focus on COVID-19. The chapter explains the already existing challenges that confront businesses and entrepreneurship in Africa, with COVID-19 presenting new dynamics of challenges, highlighting micro-entrepreneurs and sports entrepreneurs as the hardest hit. Among the many strategies and protocols to control the spread of the virus was restriction of movement and closure of almost all large gatherings. This aggravated the already existing business challenges in Africa. The major challenge that COVID-19 left for sports entrepreneurs was funding and sustenance of not just main sports clubs, but other subsidiary businesses that are related to sports. The chapter ends with a recommendation to sports entrepreneurs to develop innovative business strategies that can keep them in business during challenging times. Gertrude Mensah in Chapter 3 discusses the challenges that informal entrepreneurs and business owners are confronted with and suggests appropriate strategies that can keep them in business. Findings from this study revealed that entrepreneurs operating in the informal sector usually feel trapped to remain in the sector because they lack the necessary tools and skills to move them into the formal sector, such as education. This is manifested in their inability to for instance cope with procedural and taxation processes. The fact cannot be disputed, however, that just like the formal sector, the informal sector is very lucrative with a lot of prospects. In view of this, the author recommends clearly outlined policies from government that can serve as a guide to entrepreneurs within the informal sector.

The second theme of the book focuses on the dynamics of market internationalisation in entrepreneurial development in Africa. In Chapter 4, Kenny Odunukan uses a case study from Nigeria to give an empirical lens to the challenges that rural businesses encounter in the quest to go beyond local borders. Some of the challenges were listed as cultural barriers and differences, improper record keeping and limited capital, explaining that these challenges create complexities for internationalisation. The author uses qualitative approaches to develop structural models that provide a theoretical basis for understanding rural enterprises' transition onto international markets. The model provides an understanding and guidance to policymakers and business owners about internationalisation of rural and small-scale businesses in Africa. Patient Rambe and Ratakane Maime explored the potentialities and limits of high-tech family-owned start-ups in Africa in Chapter 5. The authors observe that these small tech firms venture into international markets without adequate knowledge of the dynamics. The chapter therefore provides an understanding of the dynamics that exists as well as the complexities that play out in the transition. The chapter ends with theoretical as well as practical guidelines for pulling through such challenges and complexities. In Chapter 6, Gloria Agyapong, Francis O. Boachie-Mensah and Kojo Kakra Twum examine how marketing strategies impact on customer satisfaction to improve business performance by exploring marketing strategies and performance of second-hand spare part dealers in Ghana. The findings from this study revealed that, even amid challenges, having the appropriate marketing strategies will enhance customer satisfaction and business growth. The authors show there is a mediating relationship between environmental variables, marketing strategies and performance, recommending that innovative management of this interaction will yield improved performance and business growth.

The third theme of the book focuses on how gender dynamics interacts with business development and entrepreneurial growth. In Chapter 7, Kwame Adom explores the gendered dynamics of entrepreneurial opportunities within the tourism industry with a demonstration that, though females dominate the tourism industry, their participation is limited to the hospitality sub-sector, to the neglect of other yet lucrative sub-sectors like transportation and communication. The author proposes for implementation of strategies that will motivate female entrepreneurs into other sub-sectors of the tourism industry. In Chapter 8, Oyedele Martins Ogundana, Amon Simba and Ugbede Umoru examine the gendered perspectives of SMEs in Africa. The chapter highlights that there is a mixed relationship for women in the business environment, as women encounter hindrances as much as they are provided with opportunities. The author recommends that women should be well represented at the policy table to better articulate and present their issues for appropriate policy decisions. An assessment of women's access to financial capital and high-growth enterprises is carried out by Rebecca C. Emeordi, Paul Agu Igwe and Nnamdi O. Mandichie in Chapter 9. The chapter lists some major challenges that women encounter as bureaucratic regulatory procedures, discrimination and gender inequalities, highlighting that these challenges not only affect business growth but national development.

References

AfDB. (2018). *African Development Bank Report on West African Economic Outlook 2018*. https://www.afdb.org/fileadmin/uploads/afdb/Documents/Publications/2018AEO/African_Economic_Outlook_2018_West-Africa.pdf

Akinyemi, F. O., & Adejumo, O. O. (2018). Government policies and entrepreneurship phases in emerging economies: Nigeria and South Africa. *Journal of Global Entrepreneurship Research*, 8(1), 1–18.

Akisik, O., Gal, G., & Mangaliso, M. P. (2020). IFRS, FDI, economic growth and human development: The experience of Anglophone and Francophone African countries. *Emerging Markets Review*, 45, 100725.

Aljuwaiber, A. (2020). Entrepreneurship research in the Middle East and North Africa: Trends, challenges, and sustainability issues. *Journal of Entrepreneurship in Emerging Economies*, 13(3), 380–426.

Aniche, E. T. (2020). African continental free trade area and African Union Agenda 2063: The roads to Addis Ababa and Kigali. *Journal of Contemporary African Studies*, 16(1), 1–16

Arıker, Ç. (2022). Massive open online course (MOOC) platforms as rising social entrepreneurs: Creating social value through reskilling and upskilling the unemployed for after COVID-19 conditions. In *Research Anthology on Business Continuity and Navigating Times of Crisis* (pp. 607–629). IGI Global.

Asiedu, M. (2018). *The African continental free trade agreement (AfCFTA)*. Global Political Trends Center (GPoT).

Austin, G. (2010). *African economic development and colonial legacies. International Development Policy 1*, 11–32. Institut de hautes études internationales et du développement.

AUC/OECD. (2022). *Africa's Development Dynamics 2022: Regional Value Chains for a Sustainable Recovery*. AUC, Addis Ababa/ OECD Publishing. https://doi.org/10.1787/2e3b97fd-en

Bonnet, F., Vanek, J., & Chen, M. (2019). Women and men in the informal economy: A statistical brief. International Labour Office, Geneva, 20.

Buccieri, D., Javalgi, R. G., & Cavusgil, E. (2020). International new venture performance: Role of international entrepreneurial culture, ambidextrous innovation, and dynamic marketing capabilities. *International Business Review*, 29(2), 101639.

Chang, C. C., & Mendy, M. (2012). Economic growth and openness in Africa: What is the empirical relationship?. *Applied Economics Letters*, 19(18), 1903–1907.

Ennew, C., Waite, N., & Waite, R. (2013). *Financial services marketing: An international guide to principles and practice*. Routledge.

Fossati, R., Rachinger, H., & Stivali, M. (2021). Extent and potential determinants of resource misallocation: A cross-sectional study for developing countries. *The World Economy, 44*(5), 1338–1379.

Hendriks, S. (2013). South Africa's National Development Plan and New Growth Path: Reflections on policy contradictions and implications for food security. *Agrekon, 52*(3), 1–17.

Igwe, P.A., Ochinanwata, C., & Madichie, N.O. (2021). The "Isms" of regional integration: What do underlying interstate preferences hold for the ECOWAS union? *Politics Policy, 49*, 280–308. https://doi.org/10.1111/polp.12396

Lone, S. A., & Ahmad, A. (2020). COVID-19 pandemic – an African perspective. *Emerging Microbes & Infections, 9*(1), 1300–1308.

Manda, D. K., & Mwakubo, S. (2014). Gender and economic development in Africa: An overview. *Journal of African Economies, 23*(suppl_1), i4–i17.

Morris, M., & Fessehaie, J. (2014). The industrialisation challenge for Africa: Towards a commodities based industrialisation path. *Journal of African Trade, 1*(1), 25–36.

Musila, J. W. (2005). The intensity of trade creation and trade diversion in COMESA, ECCAS and ECOWAS: A comparative analysis. *Journal of African Economies, 14*(1), 117–141.

Omri, A. (2020). Formal versus informal entrepreneurship in emerging economies: The roles of governance and the financial sector. *Journal of Business Research, 108*, 277–290.

Ortega-Argilés, R. (2022). The evolution of regional entrepreneurship policies: "No one size fits all". *The Annals of Regional Science, 69*, 585–610. https://doi.org/10.1007/s00168-022-01128-8

Oukil, M. S. (2007). The development of entrepreneurship in the Middle East and North Africa: An overview of constraints and perspectives. In A. Allam (Ed.), *Business excellence and competitiveness in the Middle East and North Africa* (pp. 309–318). Interscience Enterprises Ltd.

Prideaux, B., Thompson, M., & Pabel, A. (2020). Lessons from COVID-19 can prepare global tourism for the economic transformation needed to combat climate change. *Tourism Geographies, 22*(3), 667–678.

Rangasamy, L. (2009). Exports and economic growth: The case of South Africa. *Journal of International Development: The Journal of the Development Studies Association, 21*(5), 603–617.

Skinner, C., & Watson, V. (2021). Planning and informal food traders under COVID-19: The South African case. *Town Planning Review, 92*(3), 301–307.

Spreen, C. A., & Vally, S. (2010). Prospects and pitfalls: A review of post-apartheid education policy research and analysis in South Africa. *Comparative Education, 46*(4), 429–448.

Sucheran, R. (2021). Preliminary economic impacts of the COVID-19 pandemic on the hotel sector in South Africa. *African Journal of Hospitality, Tourism and Leisure, 10*(1), 115–130.

Sultanuzzaman, M. R., Fan, H., Mohamued, E. A., Hossain, M. I., & Islam, M. A. (2019). Effects of export and technology on economic growth: Selected emerging Asian economies. *Economic Research-Ekonomska istraživanja, 32*(1), 2515–2531.

Suryanto, M. E., Adianto, J., & Gabe, R. T. (2020). Accommodating the informal economy in public space. *Urbani Izziv, 31*(1), 89–100.

World Economic Forum. (2019). Africa is creating one of the world's largest single markets. What does this mean for entrepreneurs? Retrieved from May 2, 2019, https://www.weforum.org/agenda/2019/05/AfCFTA-africa-continental-free-trade-area-entrepreneur/

Chapter 2

Entrepreneurship Realities in the Light of COVID-19 in Ghana

Atsu Nkukpornu and Etse Nkukpornu

Contents

What Is Entrepreneurship?

Entrepreneurship is the oil that lubricates the engine that accelerates the socio-economic growth of countries. It improves the distribution of income, creates employment and forms the basis for the redesign of economic structures that have become dependent on large organisations (Hooi et al., 2016; Savlovschi & Robu, 2011). As a conduit for socio-economic development in both developed and developing economies, entrepreneurship cannot be underestimated (Adom & Asare-Yeboah, 2016; Buame, Asempa & Acheampong, 2013; Quaye & Acheampong, 2013).

In the developed world such as Europe and the United States, policymakers believe that more entrepreneurship is required to attain higher economic growth levels and innovation (Oosterbeek, Van Praag & Ijsselstein, 2010). Adom and Asare-Yeboah (2016) postulate that in Sub-Saharan

DOI: 10.4324/9781003302339-2

Africa (SSA), where the dominant constituents of economies are either developing or underdeveloped, entrepreneurship catalyses economic growth development. Rasmussen, Mosey and Wright (2011) aver that entrepreneurship is a remedy for problems such as unemployment and economic growth stagnation.

The concept of entrepreneurship has been around for some centuries (Long, 1983). Notwithstanding entrepreneurship's phenomenal achievements, its meaning remains contentious as there is no universally accepted definition of this concept (Kobia & Sikalieh, 2010). The primary definition from the literature obligates the 'entrepreneur to be involved in some form of business activity' (Quaye, Nkukpornu & Acheampong, 2018, p. 2). Thus, the Schumpeterian school of thought describes an entrepreneur from the imposition of creativity on new production processes (Chiles, Bluedorn & Gupta, 2007). However, the Kirznerian school of thought believes entrepreneurship emerges from the alertness of new possibilities and believes that the entrepreneur seizes the imbalance and opportunities in the marketplace and exploits them for profit (Malerba & McKelvey, 2020; Kirzner, 2019; Roininen & Ylinenpaa, 2009).

Schumpeter regards entrepreneurship as "the finding and promoting of new combinations of productive factors" (Malerba & McKelvey, 2020: p. 12). In other words, Schumpeter's view of entrepreneurship is focused on the creation of new products, services, and business models. He views entrepreneurship as the process of innovating and introducing new products, services, and business models to the marketplace, as well as promoting and bringing them to market. Schumpeter's approach to entrepreneurship has been particularly visible in the African context, for example in the continued development of new products and services such as mobile payment systems that are revolutionizing how people pay for goods and services. In Kenya, the mobile payment platform M-Pesa has become a dominant force in the payments industry, enabling people to transfer money and pay for goods and services without the need for cash (Burns, 2018). This has had a powerful effect on driving economic inclusion and financial inclusion in the region. Kirzner, on the other hand, views entrepreneurship as the act of recognizing market arbitrage opportunities and taking advantage of them (Kirzner, 2019). He believes that entrepreneurs have a unique ability to see and take advantage of opportunities that others may overlook or be unable to exploit. He views the entrepreneurial process as discovery-driven rather than innovation-driven. This kind of entrepreneurial initiative is seen, for instance, when a trader seizes a midnight market opening. Before the rest of the market has a chance to react, they may be able to make a profit by buying cheap and selling high. Kirzner's approach to entrepreneurship has also been particularly evident in Africa. For example, the growth of online platforms in Africa has opened up new opportunities to identify arbitrage opportunities. The Schumpeterian school of thought on entrepreneurship in Ghana emphasizes the need for entrepreneurs to be innovative, risk-taking, and ambitious. This approach encourages entrepreneurs to identify and exploit new opportunities and to create innovative products and services that can add value to their businesses. The Kirznerian school of thought, on the other hand, focuses on the importance of alertness and the ability to spot and act on existing opportunities. It emphasizes the need for Ghanaian entrepreneurs to be vigilant and to quickly identify and exploit available opportunities. This approach is especially useful for entrepreneurs in Ghana, where the market is constantly changing and new opportunities are emerging all the time. Both approaches are important for entrepreneurs in Ghana as it will help them to stay ahead of the competition and stay relevant in the market.

For Borasi and Finnigan (2010), entrepreneurship converts knowledge into endeavours that provide value, whether financial, scholastic or communal. From the business research perspective, Shane (2012) defines entrepreneurship as the process of discovery or co-creation, evaluation and exploitation of opportunities to produce goods and services.

Ogbor (2009, p. 3) asserts that entrepreneurship is "about coming up with something valuable and new which is considered an innovation". For Coulter (2001, p. 56), entrepreneurship is "the process whereby an individual or a group of individuals use organised efforts and means to pursue opportunities to create value and grow by fulfilling wants and needs through innovation and uniqueness, no matter what resources are currently controlled". The definitions highlighted entrepreneurial opportunities. Long (1983) conducted a study on the meaning of entrepreneurship. The author found that the definition of entrepreneurship would be incomplete if it fails to acknowledge the following three themes: uncertainty and risk, complementary managerial competence, and creative opportunism (Long, 1983). This chapter focuses on the opportunity component inherent in the meaning of entrepreneurship.

However, these opportunities take various forms and come into existence in different ways. They imply that what may be understood as an entrepreneurial opportunity may vary from one entrepreneur to another. This brings the difference between opportunity-driven entrepreneurship and necessity-driven entrepreneurship. On the one hand, opportunity-driven entrepreneurship posits that opportunities exist in the form of business ideas, and individuals who can see such opportunities exploit them by creating new ventures to pursue these ideas or by seizing the initiative through innovative developments within existing organisations (Kobia & Sikalieh, 2010). On the other hand, necessity-driven entrepreneurship is predicated on self-realisation and independence and displacement circumstances that one finds themselves in, such as the lack of employment (Kobia & Sikalieh, 2010).

The COVID-19 Scourge and Entrepreneurship in Ghana

Extensive research has been conducted on entrepreneurial survival and the factors that constrain the progress of small firms. However, how an outbreak of disease could affect entrepreneurs' success trajectory took practitioners and scholars by surprise. Although all companies across varying sectors in the world have been affected by the pandemic, micro-entrepreneurs, particularly in Africa, were the major victims. (Shafi, Liu & Ren, 2020). Hence, micro-entrepreneurs are yet to recover from the pandemic.

In Ghana, even before the outbreak of COVID-19 pandemic, most entrepreneurs already encountered a lot of financial challenges, inadequate government support and growth stagnation.

The challenges posed by COVID-19, therefore, had dire consequences on the operation of entrepreneurs in Ghana. Battling with both the physical and cognitive trauma of entrepreneurs to search for an approach to minimise business risk in an era of the COVID-19 pandemic is the underlying issue that informs this chapter.

Policy directions to curb the spread and the packages to relieve the shock of COVID-19 on entrepreneurial ventures vary across nations. This chapter is scoped in Ghana, focusing on the effect of the COVID-19 pandemic on three entrepreneurial ventures namely,; sports entrepreneurship, micro-entrepreneurship and digital entrepreneurship, which were no exception to the shock of COVID-19.

The chapter begins with a discussion of entrepreneurship and the impact of COVID-19 on entrepreneurship in Ghana. We further discuss the nature of entrepreneurship in Ghana and the effect of COVID-19 on entrepreneurial ventures including sports entrepreneurship, micro-entrepreneurship and digital entrepreneurship. We then examine the impact of COVID-19 on entrepreneurial orientations and social entrepreneurs in Ghana. Based on the research findings, the study suggests policy directions that could lessen the burden of COVID-19 on some Ghanaian entrepreneurs and then concludes by discussing recommendations for policy and managerial practice.

Nature of Entrepreneurship in Ghana

Entrepreneurship has been acknowledged as a contour of employment, innovations, opportunities, economic development and social change (Acheampong, 2018; Adom, 2015 Chowdhury, Yeasmin & Ahmed, 2018; Goktan & Gupta, 2015). Entrepreneurship is a process (McMullen & Dimov, 2013) that entails actions to create or seize an opportunity and innovate or spur a new venture (McMullen & Shepherd, 2006). Shane (2012) explains that entrepreneurship does not necessarily take place in a strategic or orderly fashion but comprises sub-processes. The process of entrepreneurship rests on three pillars: planned activities, unplanned activities, and a consequence of experience (Hlady-Rispal & Servantie, 2018). However, the context in which it operates influences the nature of the entrepreneurial activity. Hence, context matters in the nature of entrepreneurship.

In Ghana, entrepreneurship encompasses male and female businesses and their economic development roles (Acheampong, 2018; Adom, 2015; Kuada, 2009). Scholars have argued that male entrepreneurial activities are in the formal sector as the primary source of family income, while women engage in informal entrepreneurial behaviour to complement family income (Adom & William, 2012; Dzisi, 2008). Women are also known to have the highest participation in the rate of entrepreneurial activities in Africa, for which the situation in Ghana is no exception – implying that the nature of entrepreneurship in Ghana is dominated by the informal sector. Acceding to this, scholars have argued that in the Sub-Saharan African context, entrepreneurship takes place outside of formally registered businesses (Gough, Langevang & Namatovu, 2014). Hence, the activities of entrepreneurs in the informal sector are unplanned. They are characterised by poor bookkeeping behaviour and usually operate in non-designated places. These situations inhibit entrepreneurs from accessing funding from the financial service sector due to the difficulties in tracking their business operations. Also, it restrains most of the entrepreneurs in the informal sector to scale their activities. The alternative source of resources available to these entrepreneurs is to use resources at their disposal as start-up capital to manage the entrepreneurial venture. Entrepreneurs in Ghana often operate at the micro-level with the motive of complementing the family income. Therefore, they are hindered from innovating from scratch; instead, they are propelled to copy each other.. Studies have found that most entrepreneurial ventures are unable to survive within 5 years of operations (Gyimah, Appiah & Lussier, 2020; Neshamba, 2006).

The recent unannounced arrival of COVID-19 exposed most Ghanaian entrepreneurs to the reality of uncertainty. The phenomenon made Ghanaian entrepreneurs "trend trackers and opportunity seekers" than shrewd entrepreneurs who relied on causal logic backed by rigid business plans. It is difficult for the entrepreneur to make predictions in an environment with high uncertainty. However, innovation becomes the panacea for entrepreneurial survival in such environments. For instance, innovative entrepreneurs responded swiftly to the protocols of the World Health Organization to combat COVID-19. In this regard, they turned their resources at hand to manufacture hand sanitisers, nose masks and face shields. Others took advantage of the social distancing protocol to venture into door-to-door dispatch services to deliver food items to households.

The narrative suggests that the nature of entrepreneurship is dynamic, not static. Hence, entrepreneurs vary and much as their focus. The subsequent sections examine the effects of COVID-19 on sports entrepreneurship, entertainment entrepreneurship, micro-entrepreneurship and digital entrepreneurship in Ghana.

Sports Entrepreneurship and COVID-19

According to Ratten and Ferreira (2017), sport-based entrepreneurship is a distinct form of entrepreneurship that enables people to view sports activity from creativity and a futuristic perspective. The sports industry represents one of the most entrepreneurial economic sectors of the global economy (Ratten, 2020). Sport is a dynamic and unique industry that is inherently entrepreneurial on numerous fronts. Ciletti (2012) argues that sports provide a lucrative and continually growing marketplace worthy of immense investment, delivering economic impact and entertainment for millions of people globally. The sports arena also serves as a force for gender equality; strengthens the social fabric; promotes communication; and fosters unity among people, communities and the entire nation (Charway & Houlihan, 2020). Therefore, there is a growing interest in the sports industry by entrepreneurs.

The sports industry in Ghana presents a broad scope of participants, beginning from schools and colleges to the professional level. The sporting activities include football, boxing, basketball athletics, table tennis, tennis, hockey, cricket, rugby, golf and badminton. Sports entrepreneurship in Ghana is contributing to the well-being of society and communities. For instance, professional football involves significant leagues, tournaments and events that attract masses of individuals. During the COVID-19 pandemic, some Ghanaian football fanatics subscribed to online channels to watch European football leagues. The question that will remain unanswered until COVID-19 is over is, "how would Ghanaian sports entrepreneurs pay their players, management team and other stakeholders"? By implication, sports entrepreneurs are not only affected by the COVID-19 instead, companies that use sports sponsorship as a competitive edge to win market share are also adversely affected.

Micro-entrepreneurship and COVID-19

Unequivocally, COVID-19 has brought much upheaval to the world. It has unleashed unprecedented shocks across all facets of societies, from strained healthcare systems to the closure of schools and economies, with a ripple effect on every aspect of human life (Akrofi & Antwi, 2020; Nicola et al., 2020). The pandemic has brought some of the worst economic impacts since World War II (Yan & Vadila, 2022). It has sparked fears of an impending financial crisis and recession. People were instructed to remain indoors or practice social distancing when going out to get essential items. Other directives included the closure of borders, international travel restrictions and quarantine of persons suspected of carrying the virus. These directives had dire consequences on micro-entrepreneurs and their operations because day-to-day activities were halted.

In Ghana, the micro-businesses worst affected by the COVID-19 pandemic were small shop owners, household businesses, street vendors, event planners who work daily for wages to meet their needs. With the devastating effect of the pandemic on entrepreneurs, it is imperative to understand how it affected them and its implications for the future.

Prior to the COVID-19 pandemic, most micro-entrepreneurs in Ghana had challenges with access to financial support (Abor & Quartey, 2010). By their nature, micro-businesses are unable to provide the required collateral that large firms often use in obtaining loans from the banking sector (Quartey et al., 2017; Abor & Quartey, 2010). COVID-19 restrictions in the early days, such as total or partial lockdown, rendered entrepreneurs' operations at the micro-level inactive. For instance, Accra, Ghana's capital city, most of the micro-entrepreneurs that sale merchandise on the streets and pavements depend on daily sales to cater for themselves and their families. A massive proportion of the population is engaged in informal sector activities for their livelihood (Akrofi & Antwi, 2020). Therefore, the micro-entrepreneurs' little retained earnings would be used to take care of families and dependants. The situation eroded most businesses' working capital, especially micro-entrepreneurs, yet limiting COVID-19-related damage demanded a significant amount of money to enable micro-entrepreneurs to get back on track.

Digital Entrepreneurship and COVID-19 in Ghana

The present world is changing drastically in all fields, especially in information and communication technology (ICT). People worldwide rely on the Internet for daily use in various ways, from downloading information, staying connected with family and friends, and doing business. The internet is a global network system that publicly links millions of people (Almarabeh, Majdalawi & Mohammad, 2016). The exponential growth that has recently characterised the diffusion of electronic commerce (EC) applications could make companies of any size plan to invest in the digital space. The internet and a range of other ICTs are transforming how businesses are locally and globally conducted.

However, the unannounced arrival of COVID-19 sent a signal that brick-and-mortar businesses need to adjust to new realities by adopting ICT if they were to survive the restrictions of face-to-face interactions. Therefore, companies in Ghana needed to figure out how, when, if and where to use EC techniques to reap these gains. Digital entrepreneurs, with their new ways of doing business, benefited enormously during the COVID-19. (Elia, Margherita & Passiante, 2020; Ghezzi & Cavallo, 2020; Kraus et al., 2018). Technology giants like Google, Facebook, Microsoft and Appeal adapted quickly to the changing trends in the business environment posed by COVID-19 (Kraus et al., 2018).

As the digitisation phenomenon causes various implications through rapid and transformative change, it is relevant for entrepreneurs to be aware of its related outcomes and connections and identify emerging business opportunities. Digital entrepreneurship refers to entrepreneurial activities that transfer an asset, service or significant part of a business into digital formats (Kraus et al., 2018). In simple terms, Le Dinh, Vu and Ayayi (2018) defined digital entrepreneurship as the reconciliation of traditional entrepreneurship with the new way of creating and doing business in the digital era. Digital entrepreneurship, as a concept, has attracted multiple definitions (Le Dinh, Vu & Ayayi, 2018; Hull et al., 2007, p. 4). Also, Hull et al. (2007, p. 4) state that "digital entrepreneurship is a subcategory of entrepreneurship in which some or all of what would be physical in a traditional organisation has been digitised". The digital era has propelled companies to step into an online business by transforming or extending their existing businesses into the market space/ digital world.

Entrepreneurs in developing countries, particularly Ghana, need to take advantage of the digital space to project their businesses to the international market. The situation where young entrepreneurs pay huge sums of money to occupy physical structures (stores) will become a thing of the past if entrepreneurs in Ghana and beyond embrace the digital market.

Digital entrepreneurs have advantages in the market space such as the ease of internationalising their operations and reduction in operational cost even though they must not lose sight of the fact that human beings are involved. They need to deliver excellent customer service. The following need to be considered by digital entrepreneurs as crucial success factors.

First, digital entrepreneurs need to position themselves well on the platform where the digital business is built. There is the view that digital platforms of some businesses cannot be trusted by customers; hence, positioning becomes imperative. Therefore, if a platform does not enjoy a considerably high reputation and good positioning, emerging small business on such a platform is limited (Srinivasan & Venkatraman, 2018). For Kraus et al. (2018), relationship capital is vital for digital entrepreneurship. Srinivasan and Venkatraman (2018) outlined personal relationships, stable business networks, interactions with users and participants on platforms including assembling resources as increasingly essential factors for digital entrepreneurs to build legitimacy for their businesses and conduct business their activities. Hair et al. (2012) argue that customer-centric culture is paramount in digital entrepreneurs' success trajectory. The digital era has propelled companies to step into online markets by transforming or extending their existing businesses into the market space or digital world.

Entrepreneurial Orientation and COVID-19 in Ghana

Entrepreneurial orientation (EO) has been operationalised in several ways in the entrepreneurship literature. At the organisation level, EO is seen as the strategy-making process that provides organisations with a basis for entrepreneurial decisions and actions (Rauch et al., 2009). For Lumpkin and Dess (1996), EO is a process, practice and decision-making activity that leads to a new venture. Hooi et al. (2016) posit that EO is essential to the success of entrepreneurs. Creating successful sustainable entrepreneurship requires the entrepreneur to be innovative, proactive, a risk-taker (Hooi et al., 2016) and understand sustainability issues (Kuckertz & Wagner, 2010). The characteristics mentioned by scholars (Hooi et al., 2016; Kuckertz & Wagner, 2010) are termed entrepreneurial orientation (Miller, 2011). Miller (2011) conceptualised the dimensions of EO as risk-taking, innovation and proactiveness. Lumpkin and Dess (1996) operationalised EO as proactiveness, risk-taking, innovativeness, competitiveness and aggressiveness. Kuckertz and Wagner (2010) identified the understanding of sustainable issues as an important element of EO. According to Miller (2011), the orientation of the entrepreneur influences the achievement of the economic and non-economic gains of their businesses. Lumpkin, Cogliser and Schneider (2009) postulate that EO catalyses how entrepreneurs or organisations recognise opportunities and start new ventures.

The COVID-19 pandemic influences an individual's lifestyle, culture, and social interactions (Ratten, 2020). This will have a ripple effect on the EO of the individual. Anecdotally, Ghanaian entrepreneurs are innovative because they are creating new businesses or changing their business practices in the face of the COVID-19 pandemic. For instance, most entrepreneurs in the food and beverage businesses resort to online order-taking and delivery services. However, they have reduced their risk-taking behaviours due to the business environment's uncertainty. The assertion about the EO of Ghanaian entrepreneurs in the era of COVID-19 needs to be empirically validated by scholars. Though prior studies have been conducted in this area, little is known about EO in an era of COVID-19.

Social Entrepreneurs and COVID-19 in Ghana

In Ghana and other parts of the world, prominent commercial entrepreneurs took advantage of the COVID-19 pandemic to manufacture products such as hand sanitisers, nose and face masks, veronica buckets (handwashing basin) and other preventive equipment. The manufacturers charged exorbitant prices which the poor and vulnerable in societies could not afford. The nose masks were sold at an average price of GH₵5 ($0.87149), GH₵10 ($1.74297) and GH₵20 ($3.48594). Hand sanitisers were sold at prices of GH₵10 ($1.74297) and above. Though the price of the nose masks in Ghana has been reduced, it is still expensive for the average Ghanaian to buy a nose mask at GH₵1 ($0.17430), which is supposed to be used for only eight hours a day. This situation makes it difficult for the average Ghanaian to comply with the government of Ghana's regulation on wearing a nose mask and the frequent use of hand sanitisers.

Commercial entrepreneurs' selfish profit-making motives have been exposed in the era of COVID-19 in Ghana. Due to the relatively recent nature of the COVID-19 pandemic, there is still much uncertainty as to how entrepreneurship has developed due to social value (Ratten, 2020). Social entrepreneurs who blend two distinct and ostensible competing organisational objectives – creating social value and creating economic value (Austin, Stevenson & Wei, 2006) – are needed to seek the welfare of the vulnerable individuals in society and the underprivileged.

Social entrepreneurs seek to grow not only profits but also improve human well-being. They are often motivated by altruism, compassion, prosocial motivations and a philosophical aspiration to promote the growth of equity in civil societies as they develop effective, innovative and viable means to fulfil the needs and desires of the unfit, disadvantaged, disenfranchised and marginalised members of the community (Fayolle & Matlay, 2010). Social entrepreneurs are recognised as heroic, visionary, and change agents whose preoccupation is to provide solutions to social problems that bring about the social change desired and brush aside limitations of available resources (Dees, 2007; Mair & Marti, 2006; Najafizada & Cohen, 2017; Peredo & McLean, 2006).

The astounding achievements of social entrepreneurs make it challenging to pigeon-hole them. For example, Soronko Solutions, a social enterprise in Ghana, attempts to overcome the marginalisation of women in impoverished communities in Ghana. To do so, the social entrepreneur behind Soronko Solutions introduced the concept "TECH NEEDS GIRLS" – an academy for training girls in ICT. This academy trained girls to acquire IT skills, which uplift the hitherto marginalised girls into socio-economic independence.

Other social entrepreneurs use social innovation to produce hand sanitisers, face and nose masks to the marginalised in societies who hitherto could not afford to have access to them. The business practices in the era of COVID-19 should be hinged on social initiatives. This will trigger the effective use of entrepreneurial passion for alleviating the shock posed by COVID-19 in vulnerable communities in Ghana.

Mitigation Efforts on COVID-19

Governments worldwide are taking measures to support entrepreneurs to ease the devastating effect of the COVID-19 pandemic through the disbursement of stimulus packages that vary from country to country (Akrofi & Antwi, 2020).

In a developing country like Ghana, the government announced a disbursement of GH₵ 600 million (US$ 55402314.00) to over 200,000 micro-, small and medium-sized enterprises (MSMEs) hardest hit by COVID-19. This initiative forms part of the Coronavirus Alleviation Programme Business Support Scheme (CAP BuSS) (mofep.gov.gh). In Ghana, the MSMEs make up about 70% of businesses in the economy. Besides the CAP, the government of Ghana introduced other relief packages such as free utility bills within three months, a reduction of interest rates on loans from banks, an extension of loan repayment plans for businesses and an extension of tax filing dates (myjoyonline.com). To access the stimulus package, the Ghana Enterprise Agency

(GEA) developed hard copy application forms supported by an online portal to enable SMEs across the country to benefit from the stimulus package.

The GEA requires entrepreneurs to provide the following information: Tax Identification Number (TIN), voters identification card, business registration certificate, permanent business location address, business bank account number and records of past business activities. The fulfilment of these requirements formed the basis for the qualification of MSMEs to access the stimulus package.

Conclusion

Society has changed forever due to COVID-19 with a new normal lifestyle change that includes social distancing and working from home. Despite the COVID-19 pandemic's daunting experience, its effects on businesses differ from one entrepreneur to another. For instance, while digital entrepreneurs are envisaged to continue benefiting from … in the post pandemic era in Ghana, sports and micro-entrepreneurs will take time to recover as they were hardest hit.

This conceptual paper highlights important implications for practitioners. Here are some implications to practitioners of entrepreneurship in the era of Covid-19:

Virtual Solutions: Entrepreneurs must be able to think outside the box and provide virtual solutions to their customers. This means that entrepreneurs must be able to provide virtual services, virtual meetings, virtual conferences, and virtual marketplaces. Entrepreneurs must find innovative ways to use technology to stay connected and collaborate with customers and employees. This means entrepreneurs will have to increased investment in digital infrastructure, such as websites, e-commerce platforms, cloud-based software, and more.

Leveraging Technology: Entrepreneurs must also be able to utilize technology, such as automation and artificial intelligence, to expedite and enhance their processes. This will enable business owners to maintain competitiveness and maximize profits. Entrepreneurs should also focus on digital transformation in order to survive. This means that entrepreneurs must be able to transform their businesses to become more digital and use the latest technology to remain competitive.

New Products and Services: Entrepreneurs must also be able to identify new products and services that customers will find useful and profitable. This means creating new products and services that meet the changing needs of customers in the wake of the pandemic.

Re-evaluation of Business Strategies: Entrepreneurial ventures in Africa and Ghana in particular must rethink their strategies in order to stay afloat during this crisis. This includes re-evaluating their current business model, exploring new revenue sources, and finding cost-effective ways to deliver services.

Opportunities for Innovation: The pandemic has also resulted in new opportunities for entrepreneurs in Ghana to innovate and create new products and services. With the rise of remote working and online learning, businesses are finding new ways to use technology to deliver their services.

Most sporting clubs in Ghana rely on donations from team supporters and sponsorships for their operational activities, which is unsustainable during a crisis. To deal with the COVID-19 crisis, sports practitioners need to develop more entrepreneurial thinking in sports-related ventures.

The COVID-19 pandemic has significantly aggravated several societal issues that can be addressed through social enterprises. This conceptual paper will inspire social entrepreneurs to utilise a value co-creation approach to alleviate the difficulties COVID-19 has created to produce positive results. Micro-entrepreneurs need to develop adaptation skills and implement innovation strategies to thrive in an environment of uncertainty and increased social pressure.

References

Abor, J., & Quartey, P. (2010). Issues in SME development in Ghana and South Africa. *International Research Journal of Finance and Economics*, *39*(6), 215–228.

Acheampong, G. (2018). Microfinance, gender and entrepreneurial behaviour of families in Ghana. *Journal of Family Business Management*, *8*(1), 38–57.

Adom, K. (2015). Recognising the contribution of female entrepreneurs in economic development in sub-Saharan Africa: Some evidence from Ghana. *Journal of Developmental Entrepreneurship*, *20*(1), 1550003.

Adom, K., & Asare-Yeboa, I. T. (2016). An evaluation of human capital theory and female entrepreneurship in sub-Sahara Africa. *International Journal of Gender and Entrepreneurship*. *8*(4), 402–423.

Adom, K., & Williams, C. C. (2012). Evaluating the motives of informal entrepreneurs in Koforidua, Ghana. *Journal of Developmental Entrepreneurship*, *17*(1), 1250005.

Akrofi, M. M., & Antwi, S. H. (2020). COVID-19 energy sector responses in Africa: A review of preliminary government interventions. *Energy Research & Social Science*, *68*, 101681.

Almarabeh, T., Majdalawi, Y. K., & Mohammad, H. (2016). Internet usage, challenges, and attitudes among university students: A case study of the University of Jordan. *Journal of Software Engineering and Applications*, *9*(12), 577–587.

Austin, J., Stevenson, H., & Wei–Skillern, J. (2006). Social and commercial entrepreneurship: Same, different, or both?. *Entrepreneurship Theory and Practice*, *30*(1), 1–22.

Borasi, R., & Finnigan, K. (2010). Entrepreneurial attitudes and behaviors that can help prepare successful change-agents in education. *The New Educator*, *6*(1), 1–29.

Buame, S., Asempa, N., & Acheampong, G. (2013). Exploring the skills, knowledge and attitudes of successful female entrepreneurs in Ghana. *Management Science Letters*, *3*(2), 395–404.

Burns, S. (2018). M-Pesa and the 'market-led'approach to financial inclusion. *Economic Affairs*, *38*(3), 406–421.

Charway, D., & Houlihan, B. (2020). Country profile of Ghana: Sport, politics and nation-building. *International Journal of Sport Policy and Politics*, *12*(3), 497–512.

Chiles, T. H., Bluedorn, A. C., & Gupta, V. K. (2007). Beyond creative destruction and entrepreneurial discovery: A radical Austrian approach to entrepreneurship. *Organization Studies*, *28*(4), 467–493.

Chowdhury, T. Y., Yeasmin, A., & Ahmed, Z. (2018). Perception of women entrepreneurs to accessing bank credit. *Journal of Global Entrepreneurship Research*, *8*(1), 1–16.

Ciletti, D. (2012). Sports entrepreneurship: A theoretical approach. In S. Chadwick & D. Ciletti (Eds.), *Sport entrepreneurship, theory and practice* (pp. 1–14).

Coulter, M. (2001). *Entrepreneurship in action*. Printeci-Hall.

Dees, J. G. (2007). Taking social entrepreneurship seriously. *Society*, *44*(3), 24–31.

Dzisi, S. (2008). Entrepreneurial activities of indigenous African women: A case of Ghana. *Journal of Enterprising Communities: People and Places in the Global Economy*, *2*(3), 254–264.

Elia, G., Margherita, A., & Passiante, G. (2020). Digital entrepreneurship ecosystem: How digital technologies and collective intelligence are reshaping the entrepreneurial process. *Technological Forecasting and Social Change*, *150*, 119791.

Fayolle, A., & Matlay, H. (2010). Social entrepreneurship: A multicultural and multidimensional perspective. In A. Fayolle & H. Matlay (Eds.), *Handbook of research on social entrepreneurship* (1–14). City here: Edward Elgar Publishing.

Ghana Covid-19 Alleviation and Revitalisation of Enterprise Support. (2020). Ghana care "obaatanpa" programme. Retrieved from mofep.gov.gh, accessed on October 3, 2022.

Ghezzi, A., & Cavallo, A. (2020). Agile business model innovation in digital entrepreneurship: Lean startup approaches. *Journal of Business Research*, 110, 519–537.

Goktan, A. B., & Gupta, V. K. (2015). Sex, gender, and individual entrepreneurial orientation: Evidence from four countries. *International Entrepreneurship and Management Journal*, 11(1), 95–112.

Gough, K. V., Langevang, T., & Namatovu, R. (2014). Researching entrepreneurship in low-income settlements: The strengths and challenges of participatory methods. *Environment and Urbanisation*, 26(1), 297–311.

Gyimah, P., Appiah, K. O., & Lussier, R. N. (2020). Success versus failure prediction model for small businesses in Ghana. *Journal of African Business*, 21(2), 215–234.

Hair, N., Wetsch, L. R., Hull, C. E., Perotti, V., & Hung, Y. T. C. (2012). Market orientation in digital entrepreneurship: Advantages and challenges in a Web 2.0 networked world. *International Journal of Innovation and Technology Management*, 9(6), 1250045.

Hlady-Rispal, M., & Servantie, V. (2018). Deconstructing the way in which value is created in the context of social entrepreneurship. *International Journal of Management Reviews*, 20(1), 62–80.

Hooi, H. C., Ahmad, N. H., Amran, A., & Rahman, S. A. (2016). The functional role of entrepreneurial orientation and entrepreneurial bricolage in ensuring sustainable entrepreneurship. *Management Research Review*, 39(12), 1616–1638.

Hull, C. E. K., Hung, Y. T. C., Hair, N., Perotti, V., & DeMartino, R. (2007). Taking advantage of digital opportunities: A typology of digital entrepreneurship. *International Journal of Networking and Virtual Organisations*, 4(3), 290–303.

Kirzner, I. M. (2019). The ethics of pure entrepreneurship: An Austrian economics perspective. *The Review of Austrian Economics*, 32(2), 89–99.

Kobia, M., & Sikalieh, D. (2010). Towards a search for the meaning of entrepreneurship. *Journal of European Industrial Training*, 34(2), 110–127.

Kraus, S., Palmer, C., Kailer, N., Kallinger, F. L., & Spitzer, J. (2018). Digital entrepreneurship: A research agenda on new business models for the twenty-first century. *International Journal of Entrepreneurial Behavior & Research*, 25(2), 353–375.

Kuada, J. (2009). Gender, social networks, and entrepreneurship in Ghana. *Journal of African Business*, 10(1), 85–103.

Kuckertz, A., & Wagner, M. (2010). The influence of sustainability orientation on entrepreneurial intentions—Investigating the role of business experience. *Journal of Business Venturing*, 25(5), 524–539.

Le Dinh, T., Vu, M. C., & Ayayi, A. (2018). Towards a living lab for promoting the digital entrepreneurship process. *International Journal of Entrepreneurship*, 22(1), 1–17.

Long, W. (1983). The meaning of entrepreneurship. *American Journal of Small Business*, 8(2), 47–59.

Lumpkin, G. T., & Dess, G. G. (1996). Clarifying the entrepreneurial orientation construct and linking it to performance. *Academy of Management Review*, 21(1), 135–172.

Lumpkin, G. T., Cogliser, C. C., & Schneider, D. R. (2009). Understanding and measuring autonomy: An entrepreneurial orientation perspective. *Entrepreneurship Theory and Practice*, 33(1), 47–69.

Mair, J., & Marti, I. (2006). Social entrepreneurship research: A source of explanation, prediction, and delight. *Journal of World Business*, 41(1), 36–44.

Malerba, F., & McKelvey, M. (2020). Knowledge-intensive innovative entrepreneurship integrating Schumpeter, evolutionary economics, and innovation systems. *Small Business Economics*, 54(2), 503–522.

McMullen, J. S., & Dimov, D. (2013). Time and the entrepreneurial journey: The problems and promise of studying entrepreneurship as a process. *Journal of Management Studies*, 50(8), 1481–1512.

McMullen, J. S., & Shepherd, D. A. (2006). Entrepreneurial action and the role of uncertainty in the theory of the entrepreneur. *Academy of Management Review*, 31(1), 132–152.

Miller, D. (2011). Miller (1983) revisited: A reflection on EO research and some suggestions for the future. *Entrepreneurship Theory and Practice*, 35(5), 873–894.

Najafizada, S. A. M., & Cohen, M. J. (2017). Social entrepreneurship tackling poverty in Bamyan Province, Afghanistan. *World Development Perspectives*, 5, 24–26.

Neshamba, F. (2006). Why do some small businesses grow faster and become "successful" while others do not get beyond the 'foothills'? Some evidence from Kenya. *Journal of African Business, 7*(1–2), 9–30.

Nicola, M., Alsafi, Z., Sohrabi, C., Kerwan, A., Al-Jabir, A., Iosifidis, C.,... & Agha, R. (2020). The socio-economic implications of the coronavirus and COVID-19 pandemic: A review. *International Journal of Surgery, 78*, 185–193.

Ogbor, O. J. K. (2009). Entrepreneurship studies and development in Nigeria: A major mission. *Journal of Entrepreneurship and Technology, 1*(1), 21–24.

Oosterbeek, H., Van Praag, M., & Ijsselstein, A. (2010). The impact of entrepreneurship education on entrepreneurship skills and motivation. *European Economic Review, 54*(3), 442–454.

Peredo, A. M., & McLean, M. (2006). Social entrepreneurship: A critical review of the concept. *Journal of World Business, 41*(1), 56–65.

Quartey, P., Turkson, E., Abor, J. Y., & Iddrisu, A. M. (2017). Financing the growth of SMEs in Africa: What are the constraints to SME financing within ECOWAS?. *Review of Development Finance, 7*(1), 18–28.

Quaye, D. M., & Acheampong, G. (2013). Are SME owner-managers entrepreneurs? Evidence from Ghana. *European Journal of Business and Management, 5*(23), 37–47.

Quaye, D. M., Nkukpornu, A., & Acheampong, G. (2018). Brokering: Africa's unique brand of entrepreneurship. In L. P. Dana, V. Ratten, & B. Q. Honyenuga (Eds.), *African Entrepreneurship* (pp. 261–274). Palgrave Macmillan.

Rasmussen, E., Mosey, S., & Wright, M. (2011). The evolution of entrepreneurial competencies: A longitudinal study of university spin-off venture emergence. *Journal of Management Studies, 48*(6), 1314–1345.

Ratten, V. (2020). Coronavirus disease (COVID-19) and sport entrepreneurship. *International Journal of Entrepreneurial Behavior & Research, 26*(6), 1379–1388.

Ratten, V., & Ferreira, J. (2017). Entrepreneurship, innovation and sport policy: Implications for future research. *International Journal of Sport Policy and Politics, 9*(4), 575–577.

Rauch, A., Wiklund, J., Lumpkin, G. T., & Frese, M. (2009). Entrepreneurial orientation and business performance: An assessment of past research and suggestions for the future. *Entrepreneurship Theory and Practice, 33*(3), 761–787.

Roininen, S., & Ylinenpää, H. (2009). Schumpeterian versus Kirznerian entrepreneurship: A comparison of academic and non-academic new venturing. *Journal of Small Business and Enterprise Development, 16*(3), 504–520.

Savlovschi, L. I., & Robu, N. R. (2011). The role of SMEs in modern economy. *Economia, Seria Management, 14*(1), 277–281.

Shafi, M., Liu, J., & Ren, W. (2020). Impact of COVID-19 pandemic on micro, small, and medium-sized enterprises operating in Pakistan. *Research in Globalization, 2*, 100018.

Shane, S. (2012). Reflections on the 2010 AMR decade award: Delivering on the promise of entrepreneurship as a field of research. *Academy of Management Review, 37*(1), 10–20.

Srinivasan, A., & Venkatraman, N. (2018). Entrepreneurship in digital platforms: A network-centric view. *Strategic Entrepreneurship Journal, 12*(1), 54–71.

Yan, L., & Vadila, Y. (2022). *COVID-19: Impacts of Indonesia's Trade* (No. DP-2021-48). Economic Research Institute for ASEAN and East Asia (ERIA).

Chapter 3

Challenges and Prospects of Informal Entrepreneurs in Ghana: Lessons from Agbogbloshie Market

Gertrude Mensah

Contents

DOI: 10.4324/9781003302339-3

Introduction

Recent studies have revealed the informal sector's importance to economic growth and the opportunities it presents to its citizens (Llanes & Barbour, 2007; Williams, 2011). However, informal entrepreneurs still face some peculiar challenges that the literature has not paid attention to. This chapter discloses these challenges in the Ghanaian economy, how it affects contributions to the economy and the suggested solutions that can help curb the challenges.

Investigating the challenges faced by informal entrepreneurs in Ghana is still rare in literature. The literature for instance shows informal entrepreneurship in Ghana has devoted much attention to women's entrepreneurship (Chu, Benzing & McGee, 2007; Korantemaa, 2006; Adom, 2016; Boachie-Mensah & Marfo-Yiadom, 2005), assessment of the feasibility of upskilling informal workers (Debrah, 2007; Haan, 2006; Palmer, 2009), as well as problems with regard to financing informal businesses (Abor, 2007; Abor & Biekpe, 2009; Tagoe, Nyarko & Anuwa-Armah, 2005).

Other studies have been focused on the characteristics of informal entrepreneurs (Williams, 2006; Aidis, Welter, Smallbone & Isakova, 2006; Williams, Nadin & Rodgers, 2012; Mróz, 2012), motives for entrepreneurs operating informally (Chen, 2012; Williams, 2009; 2013; Williams & Lansky, 2013) as well as the possibility of formalising the informal sector (Dellot, 2012; Williams & Nadin, 2012, 2013, 2014; Barbour & Llanes, 2013; Williams, Nadin, Barbour & Llanes, 2013; Adom, 2017).

In particular, few studies have been conducted on challenges faced by women in the informal sector (Benzing, Chu & Kara, 2009; Halkias, Harkiolakis & Caracatsanis, 2011). Furthermore, the few available studies were conducted in Turkey and Nigeria, but not in Ghana.

It is, therefore, the reason Adom (2016) calls for immediate research to properly understand and address the specific problems of informal entrepreneurship in Ghana. This study thus explores the reasons informal entrepreneurs in Agbogbloshie in Ghana set their businesses in the informal sector, identify the challenges confronting informal entrepreneurs, explore the steps these informal entrepreneurs take to curb the challenges they face and identify the prospects of everyday entrepreneurs. The second section of this chapter reviews the literature on informal entrepreneurship and its challenges. The third section discusses the methodology used in the study; the fourth section presents the analysis; and the last and final section presents the conclusions and recommendations for further research.

Literature Review

Informal Entrepreneurship

Now, defining informal entrepreneurship has become difficult because there has not been any consensus regarding the informal economy/entrepreneurship literature. One reason for the lack of a specific term could be that informal economy means different things in different economic landscapes due to its multidisciplinary nature. For instance, Webb, Ireland and Ketchen (2014) define the informal sector as activities within the economy that are not within the institutional boundaries' confines, yet legal. On the contrary, LaPorta and Schleifer (2008) categorised activities within the informal sector as unofficial or unrecorded economic activities operated by registered firms or unregistered firms that avoid the payment of taxes. Also, International Labour Organisation (ILO) (2002) explains the informal sector comprises every activity by all workers and economic units in the economy that are in law or practice not covered or covered insufficiently by formal arrangement.

This article adopts the definition of informal sector enterprise adopted by the International Conference of Labour Statisticians (ICLS) in 1993 (ILO, 2012). The ILO describes informal the informal sector as "those individuals whose economic units and services are unregulated or covered or recorded insufficiently for taxes by formal arrangement". ILO's (2012) explanation of the informal sector is adopted because it gives a broader perspective of the informal sector. Therefore, informal entrepreneurship in this study is characterised as visible trading activities and services, which, despite its illegality in payment of "normal taxes" (based on income) and business registration, participate in producing and distributing authorised goods and services in the economy.

Literature Review

Institutional Theory and the Informal Economy

The term institutional theory is described by Scott (2007) and Rowan (1991) as activities that concern themselves with how various groups and firms secure legitimacy in a better manner by sticking to the norms and rules of the institutional context. There are two types of institutions: formal institutions (codified laws and regulations) and informal institutions (codes of conduct, values and norms). According to De Castro, Khavul and Bruton (2014), informal entrepreneurs are those that operate outside formal boundaries but within informal institutional boundaries. As per the views of Beck and Kunt (2006), there is a deficiency of development structures within the regulatory environment to support the growth of micro-businesses. Onwe (2013) added that the institutional environment's neglect contributes to the informal sector's growth in the Ghanaian economy. It, therefore, means that the propensity for entrepreneurs to operate in the informal sector is explained to result from the unevenness between informal and formal institutions in an economy.

Motivation Factor for Informal Sector Participation

Some of the motives for informal sector entrepreneurship include; 1) power, affiliation and achievement, 2) push and pull factors, 3) Necessity and opportunity entrepreneurs, 4) Economic factors and 5) Opportunity and Structural Factors.

One of the main reasons people are willing to be entrepreneurs is because they want to fulfil their need for achievement, power and affiliation. Empirical studies of Lee and Tsang (2001), Rahman (2011), Fuad and Bohari (2011), Indarti and Wulandaru (2003) have confirmed that the need for achievement, power and affiliation are dominant factors for self-employment in many sectors.

Also are the push and pull factors. The results of a study conducted by Williams, Rounds and Rodgers (2009) indicate that people who conduct their own businesses are motivated by either push or pull factors. According to William et al. (2009), some people start their businesses because of the opportunities they foresee or because it is a necessity. In this case, it becomes clear that differences exist between negative factors that push individuals' entry to entrepreneurship and the positive factors that pull people into starting their own business activity (Thurik, Hessels, Verheul & van der Zwan, 2010). Most of the time the pull factors embrace the drive theory. These include personal satisfaction and self-realisation (Van Gelderen & Jansen, 2006; Staniewski & Awruk, 2015), the desire to be independent or become autonomous in order for one to direct his/her actions or make decisions by him/herself. For instance, Verheul and Van Stel (2010) mention that the need for achievement of one's vision, one's knowledge about business, creativity, the acquisition of priceless experience and one's endeavour to manage activities are examples of the pull factors. Accumulation of wealth, the endeavour to achieve high earnings, opportunity to be aware of one's own potential and be content with one's work are also pull factors (Van Gelderen & Jansen, 2006; Bernat & Corso, 2008; Staniewski & Awruk, 2015). Sequentially, push factors may comprise motives such as family pressure, dissatisfaction with one's current situation, risk of unemployment (Verheul & Van Stel, 2010), bad situation in the labour market and lack of interesting offers and job positions (Earle, & Sakova, 2000; Bernat & Corso, 2008).

Again, Necessity and opportunity entrepreneurs present reasons for informal businesses. Necessity entrepreneurs are individuals who are involved in entrepreneurial effort because they have no other option of work. Furthermore, opportunity entrepreneurs are perceived to be individuals who pursue an entrepreneurial opportunity (Williams & Williams, 2014). This means that people who work in the informal sector, such as street hawking, are customarily perceived as 'pushed' because it is considered as a final option (Castells & Portes, 1989; Gallin, 2001; Sassen, 1997) and characterised as "forced", "reflexive", "survivalist" or "reluctant" (Hughes, 2006; Travers, 2002; Singh & De Noble, 2003). The necessity-opportunity drivers of entrepreneurial conduct appeared as a scientific structure against which third world countries began to measure how the activities of individual entrepreneur participants differ (Williams & Gurtoo, 2012). This analysis may make it too simple to understand the complicated motives of entrepreneurs. It is, therefore, put under the limelight to give recognition to entrepreneurs in developing countries who engage voluntarily in entrepreneurial activities out of choice and not as a survival strategy. Nevertheless, Gerxhani (2004), contends that most people desire to engage in the informal sector because they gain or achieve more freedom, flexibility and autonomy in the informal economy than they would in the formal economy.

In addition, economic factors that propel people into informal entrepreneurship are related to the rigid formal labour market; a decrease in the actual price of capital; the high cost of formal production; and unemployment. Economic reasons for informal entrepreneurship are related to a larger flexibility and substantial satisfaction at work and increased leisure time (Davis, 2003).

Moreover, other factors that push or pull individuals to participate in informal businesses, the opportunity and structural factors are one of the essential reasons people work in the informal sector. The opportunity elements comprise background such as education, skills, living situation; as well as non-individual factors such as cultural, traditional, environmental, geographical factors, values and standards (Renooy, 1990). The structural factors comprise socio-psychological pressure, institutional constraints and financial pressure. The researcher proposes that the elements of the opportunity factors describe the reasons for the existence of different kinds of informal economies. The person's free choice influences the decision to pay tax based on an integration of insufficient information and the absence of credence of how taxes are consumed. In a situation where the government does not have any confidence in the population and individuals do not feel support from the government, the economy declines and gives rise to informal businesses.

Challenges within the Informal Sector

Though informal entrepreneurs contribute about 60% of the global workforce, they lack social protection (ILO, 2018). They are among 71% of the worldwide population with little access to social security (ILO, 2017). The absence of social protection is a substantial source of vulnerability for both employers and employees within the informal sector. This is a considerable challenge that affects the enjoyment of human rights and individual welfare and affects countries' social and economic development (OECD & ILO, 2019). Energy is another factor. For instance, frequent power cut during working hours damages most informal business equipment since most do not have other energy sources (generators, solar, etc.) (Tonelli & Dalglish, 2012). Auyeung (2004) confirms technology to be one of the challenges that informal entrepreneurs face in Nigeria in a similar vein.

In Ghana, for instance, the relatively poor power supply in the country frustrates the activities of most people working in the country's informal sector (Chu et al., 2007).

Another challenge is the lack of getting access to finance. The informal sector is denied access to finance whereas the organised sector enjoys the benefits of the credit market. Spring and McDade (1998) mention that it is because informal entrepreneurs in developing countries cannot meet the collateral requirements for taking loans or because the interest rate from financial institutions is too high. This, therefore, makes the informal sector rely mainly on informal means of accessing credit or through unorganised credit market. For instance, Ozsoy, Oksoy and Kozan (2001), in a study in Turkey, report that business owners depend on family resources for financial solutions. The scholars mention that lack of access or inadequate access to finance limits the growth of firms in Turkey.

More so, the majority of informal entrepreneurs find it difficult to transport their goods from one location to another which is a huge challenge. This is partly because some transport systems do not have access to the dwelling place of informal traders, and in situations where they have access, it becomes difficult for informal entrepreneurs or traders to afford the service. Besides, informal entrepreneurs are sometimes restricted to the kind of goods to transport on a bus. When this happens, it influences informal traders to use the services of people as carriers to transport the goods (Rwigema, Urban & Venter, 2008). This causes delays of goods on the market and limits profitability.

Aside from the above mentioned, poor environmental conditions remain one of the challenges in the informal sector. This happens when people work from homes as well as from the public by usually spreading clothes on a table to sell and working under trees (Osei-Boateng & Ampratwum, 2011). Mitullah (2006) and Sidzatane and Maharaj (2013) confirm that individual entrepreneurs who work under harsh environmental conditions demoralise their health issues. This is because entrepreneurs in the informal sector do not have knowledge of hazardous practices. Some of these health issues include flu, malaria, cholera, just to mention a few. Kwankye, Anarfi, Tagoe and Castaldo (2007) argue that the challenge is not just about the environmental conditions of people in the informal sector but also how to minimise the challenges. In this regard, the subsequent section delves into such literature.

Prospects of Informal Entrepreneurship

The prospects of the informal sector cannot be discussed without mentioning its ability to provide employment opportunities. There is a piece of evidence that the informal economy in Africa is increasing in size. Jackson (2016) mentions that in the 1990s, about 93% of the new jobs created were in the informal economy. For instance, the share of employment as a percentage of domestic non-agricultural work climbed from 40% in 1985–1989 to 61% from the year 2000–2007. More so, other researchers (Duncan, 1992; Gutmann, 1977) contend that informal and formal work are a gross replacement for each other; that is, when individuals lose jobs or are unable to find employment in the formal sector, they turn to the informal sector to seek jobs. Researchers emphasise that the informal sector has prospects in terms of potential for growth (Adom & Williams, 2014; Adom, 2014); economic development (McArthur & Sachs, 2001) and creation of a safety net or employment opportunities (Haltiwanger, Jarmin & Miranda, 2010).

Regarding the potential for growth, the informal sector is a major element in most parts of the countries within Sub-Saharan Africa. It has had a hand in providing a percentage between 25 and 65 of Gross Domestic Product (GDP) and accounts for between 30 percent and 90 percent of the entire non-agricultural based employment. The United Nations Conference on Trade and Development (UNCTAD) Africa Report for 2013 indicated that a feature that is common to countries in Africa is its large informal sector. These large informal sectors account for some 38% of GDP as compared to East Asia and the Pacific with 18%, Middle East and East Africa accounting for 27%, South Asia with 25% and the Latin America and the Caribbean accounting for about 35%. The majority of the businesses in Sub-Saharan countries are overshadowed by either self-employment businesses or microenterprises businesses. These businesses are conducted in apparel or clothing businesses, traditional medicine, retail shops, hairdressing, metalwork, tailoring services, as well as building and construction. These types of businesses employ less than ten people and mainly do not register or license their businesses, consequently there is an evasion of the payment of taxes (Pretes, 2002). Again, IMF Blog (2017) contends that there is a notable difference in the magnitude of informal sectors. This difference varies from a meagre 20 percent to 25 percent of GDP in Namibia, South Africa and Mauritius to as high as 50 percent to 65 percent GDP in Nigeria and Tanzania. The ILO (2003) provides an average estimation of GDP as 41% in Sub-Saharan Africa. This varies from below 30% in South Africa to 60% in Tanzania, Zimbabwe and Nigeria.

When it comes to Ghana, the informal sector represents the 'conventional' economy with about 80% of every single job of the national sector in this economy (Adom & Williams, 2014; Adom, 2014; Debrah, 2007). One thread of research foresees informal activities as a perpetual circumstance, emphasising strongly on the contributions of the informal economy to social and economic development and employment, irrespective of whether or not informal business firms are registered or legal.

Consequently, scholars' debate that the informal sector could be a breeding ground for more considerable businesses as time goes on. Informal entrepreneurship could be perceived as the foundation throughout serving to accumulate starting capital and testing the market niche, as well as the life cycle of a business (Williams, Round & Rodgers, 2007; Bennett & Estrin, 2007; Guariglia & Kim, 2006; Slonimski, Slonimskaya, Linchevskaya & Pobol, 2009). With the situation of underdeveloped economies, Bennett and Estrin (2007) exhibit the way activities of informal businesses allow entrepreneurs to investigate the profits derived from their business ideas, thereby enabling them to cheaply evaluate in an uncertain environment.

Another prospect is economic development. Economic development requires various indicators of development in sustainable growth, political and institutional changes, social, economic and then the right allocation of scarce resources (Todaro & Smith, 2009). All these indicators are considered to bring about the development of the lives of the poor in developing economies. A study by Porter, Sachs and McArthur (2002) propose that the meaning of economic development is the evolvement from a resource-based economy to a knowledge-based economy. There are three phases of development that can be differentiated here. They include the factor-driven phase, the investment-driven phase and the innovation-driven phase. The factor-driven phase, which is also known as the initial-driven phase, is established on primary factors of production such as primary commodities, unskilled labour and availability of land. The next stage is the investment-driven stage. With this, there is the rise of industrialisation and the country has a middle-income reputation (Ocampo, 2003). In order to progress from the initial stage to the second stage, the third phase becomes necessary for the accumulation of capital, which enables the economy to attain an increase in growth. The very high level of economic development is innovation. With the spread of globalisation and capitalism, entrepreneurship has received much attention than previously and there is a sign of a remarkable relationship between levelling of entrepreneurial activity and its economic growth (Global Entrepreneurship Monitor [GEM], 2002; Carree & Thurik, 2003). Moreover, one-third of the variation in national economic development may be as a result of the level of entrepreneurial activity (GEM, 2002). Empirically, research studies finalised that there is a better way to give a vast foundation for the swift growth of the economy rather than to substantially grow the number of active entrepreneurs in the economy (Mehta, 2009). It is moreover debated that economic growth, entrepreneurial processes, industrial dynamics, job creation and technological innovation are foundational impulses of various countries (Freeman, 2013; Acs & Audretsch, 2003). It is further debated that entrepreneurship is the driver for the growth of the economy as well as an instrument of social transformation in many developing countries and in capitalist societies (Valliere & Peterson, 2009). In addition to the above mentioned, the stunning growth of the economy in the West is indebted to the role of entrepreneurship and these economies are changed from managed to entrepreneurial economies. In these entrepreneurial economies, entrepreneurship makes a special contribution to the growth of the economy by pervading commercialising ideas and filtering knowledge (Acs & Armington, 2004).

In addition is the prospect for the creation of a safety net or employment opportunities. Some perceive the informal economy as dynamic with the possibilities of creating employment and functionally imparting to the growth of the economy. On the other hand, some others degrade informal activities to survivalist for poor households, low productivity employment and a cliché, in the situation of Zimbabwe. The informal economy plays a passive role in the development of economies and provides a social protection in the absence of formal-sector-led growth process. Thereby, Basu (2010) postulates that the informal sector in the urban site has turned out to be an essential part of the landscape of the economy throughout the developing countries within Africa. Also, Blunch, Canagarajah and Raju (2001) contend that the informal economy may take part in the contribution of the development and growth of the economy. Contrary to the views provided above, Klapper and Love (2010) mention that the relationship between the economic growth and the informal sector is mixed. The informal sector is linked integrally to the formal economy, in a way that it widens so extensively when the other declines, a perspective highlighted by a sociologist (Portes et al., 1989). Consequently, Arvin-Rad, Basu and Willumsen (2010) ascribe the existence, emergence and the broadening of the informal sector to the effect of regulatory systems influencing the formal economies. Broadenly, Carree and Thurik (2010) mention a deficiency of theoretical frameworks connecting entrepreneurship to mainstream measured economic growth, in spite of the many claims connecting them. They propose that a framework linking entrepreneurial activity to economic growth must recognise the micro-economic basis of growth, highlight the role played by knowledge externalities in the growth procedure and recognise intermediate connections from entrepreneurial activity to the progress of the country.

Research Methodology

The qualitative research approach is used to capture expressive information not conveyed in quantitative research about beliefs, values, feelings and motivations that underline behaviours. The study's objectives are to understand the reasons for informal entrepreneurs' participation, challenges, ways of curbing the challenges they face and the prospects of informal entrepreneurs.

The suitability of using a qualitative research approach was based on the fact that it helps researchers understand people and the socio-cultural environment. Many scholars have conceived informal entrepreneurship as people who are driven to the sector out of economic necessity (McElwee, 2009) or volution (Williams, 2006; Williams & Round, 2007). Hence, the qualitative research methodology's suitability helped the researcher to understand why informal entrepreneurs set up their businesses in the informal sector through the subjective responses that were provided.

The population for this study was both men and women within the "Agbogbloshie" market. The study used a population of both men and women informal entrepreneurs because mostly, women are perceived as those who face such challenges in the informal sector (Halkias et al., 2011). Using both men and women informal entrepreneurs provided a universal view of the challenges faced by informal entrepreneurs in their entrepreneurial activities. The population includes barbers, food processors, artisans, craft workers, agro-based workers, aluminium workers, hairdressers, nail cutters, fish processors, head porters, affairs (middlemen in the informal sector), cooked food sellers, informal health sanitation workers and garages (auto mechanics, television repairers, etc.).

The researcher used the "Agbogbloshie" market as the case study because the Agbogbloshie market has a diverse group of individuals from all the regions of the country engaging in trade. It helped to obtain unique information from the traders. Agbogbloshie is one of the informal business districts in Accra, the nation's capital. It is located along the Korle Lagoon of the Odaw River, not far from the city centre of Accra. It is one of Accra's market areas where almost every food item is traded. Except for Sundays when there are few business activities, the area is notoriously known for heavy vehicular and human traffic.

Given the study's qualitative nature, it became more suitable to use homogeneous purposive sampling for selecting the participants under study. It is a sampling technique that focuses on a sample with similar characteristics in terms of age, gender, background, occupation, among others. It concerns itself with discovering and choosing groups of individuals or individuals experienced with a phenomenon of interest or exceptionally knowledgeable about a phenomenon (Cresswell & Plano Clark, 2011). This technique was suitable for this study because it provided the researcher with greater freedom and flexibility in selecting the sample. Moreover, this sampling technique ensured that the informants possessed the relevant information and required knowledge needed for the study.

Also, the study used 23 informal entrepreneurs, made up of men and women who were within the age range of 24 to 61. This number of respondents was sufficient to obtain answers to the research study's questions (Marshall, 1996). This is because qualitative research focuses more on the sample's adequacy other than the sample size (Bowen, 2008). The data collection instrument used for this study was a semi-structured interview guide. Utilising this instrument was grounded because it gave much flexibility where the researcher could probe further where necessary (Malhotra & Birks, 2007). Therefore, using this instrument gave the participants a chance to willingly give other salient information not initially captured in the interview guide. The interviews were conducted in the Agbogbloshie market. All respondents took part in a face-to-face interview that lasted an average of 35 minutes for each participant. The interview sessions were audio-recorded with permission from the participants involved in the study. The audio-recorded interviews were transferred to an email to serve as a backup. The recorded audios accurately helped the transcription and analysis of the data with no critical discussions left out. The participants were identified as "Agbogbloshie 1" to "Agbogbloshie 23" (AG 1–AG 23) for the purpose of anonymity. Besides, all the respondents communicated in "Akan" (a central Ghanaian dialect) and paved the way for transcription through translation.

The data were analysed using thematic analysis. Data analysis commenced after conducting the first interview. The data from the respondents were transcribed, coded, analysed, interpreted and verified. The data analysis aimed not only to explain the data but also to understand, analyse and explain the research phenomenon's meanings.

Results and Discussion

The outcome of the face-to-face interviews in Accra uncovers some specific problems in their informal business activities around the Agbogbloshie market.

Findings

Reasons for Informal Participation

Notably, though literature proposes that people work informally to avoid: paying taxes, costs in registering businesses, burdensome procedures, among others, it has come to light that aside from these reasons, there are dominant reasons people operate in the informal sector. These include the menial nature of their job, the temporary nature of their career and low self-esteem. These reasons can add more knowledge to the literature.

Menial Nature of the Job

First, informal entrepreneurs' menial nature has prompted them to settle in the informal sector. To them, the lowly nature of their job does not call for any registration of their businesses. Respondents mentioned that the nature of their jobs includes selling yam, plantain (street vending) and other trading activities such as fish processing, food processing, head pottering, craft making, among others. When asked how these business activities became the reasons for settling in the informal sector, they claim that in Ghana, no registration form is required. The respondents mention that the nature of their jobs/businesses is "hand to mouth", which is solely for the purpose of caring for the entire nuclear family. Again, the participants reported that their jobs' menial nature disqualifies them from formally registering their business activities. This misconception emanates from the lack of formal education and knowledge about businesses' formalisation among most informal entrepreneurs. From the responses gathered, AG 3 mentions that

> To me, currently looking at the nature of my job here, do you think I should go all the way to register formally? Selling yam, as you see here, is not a matter of registration. It is for this reason, I am working here, in the informal sector.

> (AG 3)

> [...] Oh, the nature of this job does not call for registration at all, and I am working in this sector because I have come to realize people with this nature of jobs are always in this sector and nowhere else.

> (AG 5)

In addition to the above responses, AG 9 also mentions:

> I am working in the informal sector because I wanted to start a business that does not call for registering a business, thereby dealing in this type of business. Those who register their businesses are the big companies, not us. Who would go and register "momone" (salted fish) or plantain or anything you find here? It is not possible in Ghana because this is how we also operate.
>
> **(AG 9)**

This implies that since two-thirds of the respondents lack or have inadequate formal education, they do not know the significance of formalising businesses. It is the underlying reason why their business activities' menial nature impedes their businesses' registration to become formal.

Temporary Nature of the Business

Furthermore, informal entrepreneurs are of the perspective that the nature of their business activities is temporal. Consequently, they believe it is irrelevant to formalise their business. The temporal nature of their business is, thus, another factor they operate as informal entrepreneurs. Testing for the viability of profit-making in other companies makes their trading activities temporal. According to them, they do multiple activities, and the registration is for one business at a time. They claim that they keep changing jobs from season to season, so registering it will mean choosing a different name for every business type. It is the main reason they choose to work in the informal sector. For instance, the comments below reflect the preceding argument:

> I come to work here every four months when the working condition in the Northern region is slow, so I am not stable with working with one particular job. Do you see why I cannot formally register my business? I do not know what to use as my business name. All those people who have the same work, do the same. We all go back to the Northern region when our season is over and then come here at the due time to work.
>
> **(AG 2, AG 6)**

AG 6 also asserts that

> I am the kind of person who tests other business activities to see if I will make more profit. When I realize there is much profit-making in other businesses, I pause a particular business or even stop and venture into the other profit-making business. That is the reason I want to settle here in the informal sector.
>
> **(AG 6)**

From the argument put forward, informal entrepreneurs are risk-takers and engage in almost every kind of business. It means they try to venture into other businesses once they foresee an opportunity in that business by taking the risk. It does not matter whether they will make a loss or not; they love to pursue other profit-making ventures. It also means that informal entrepreneurs are not in a position to work because of the temporal nature of their job.

Low Self-Esteem

One crucial factor that stands out from the reasons they work in the informal sector is low self-esteem. They explain that due to their lack of formal education, they feel repudiated and not recognised by society. As such, they do not want to have anything in common with formal processes. Because of their lack of recognition and acceptance, they regard all aspects of business registration, formalisation and "paperwork" as belonging to an elite to which they do not belong.

The respondents mention that since they feel repudiated by society because most are illiterate, they try to fend for themselves by doing business in the informal sector. They perceive the informal sector as a place that does not require any form of documentation or recognition. It signifies that people who engage in the informal sector feel marginalised and have no desire to be absorbed in the formal sector for employment. Hence, the only surviving option is the informal sector. Reportedly are comments from sample respondents:

AG 17 states,

> I am not valued in any situation in this country because I have not been to school. As a man, you cannot stay in the house idle because you need to survive. You need to do something to survive, and because I cannot get a salaried job or work in the formal sector, I decided to learn this shoe business just to fit into the economy, hence, the informal sector.
>
> (AG 17)

AG 3 also stresses that

> [...] Who cares, the government or who? Those of us who have not been to school are at a disadvantage. We do not get any help from the government or anyone. People think we are nobody, but without us, they cannot survive. I have not received any form of formal education before. Thus, I do not have the skills and knowledge to either work in the formal sector or formally operationalize my business, so I decided to settle in this sector.
>
> (AG 3)

The preceding discussion shows that lack of recognition makes informal entrepreneurs feel repudiated by society because two-thirds of them are illiterates. They believe that in order to survive, they must work in the informal sector, which is the only one that does not require any documentation.

Challenges Faced by Informal Entrepreneurs in Accra

Constant Harassment from City Authorities

"Aaba ee" (the indigenous dialect of the people of Accra, which means they are coming) has remained an issue of concern to informal entrepreneurs. Respondents mentioned that the harassment by city authorities comes in the form of beatings and seizing goods, among others. These acts of harassment are meted out to informal entrepreneurs who sell at unapproved places (i.e., on pavements, roadsides and under small huts). Some of the women are also compelled to trade sex in return for their seizured goods. According to the respondents, some city authorities refuse to take money for sex once they recognise that the confiscated goods belong to a woman. For instance, AG 22 complains that

> [...] I am even shy saying this but, the truth is that the Accra Metropolitan Assembly (AMA) task force ("Aaba ee") guys seize our goods and it takes time and effort before releasing the goods to us. I cannot say anything because I need my goods back to sell to fend for myself, so I have to comply, and there is nobody to complain or report to.
>
> **(AG 22)**

Some of these challenges cause some informal entrepreneurs to lose their self-worth, rights and freedom. Responses from some of the respondents indicate that they believe that they are not regarded in society. So, even if they complain about the matter, their voice would not be heard as they are considered marginalised in society.

It is recognised that some informal entrepreneurs lose their lives in the course of struggling with the city authorities (AMA), which becomes devastating and life-threatening. For instance, AG 19 stresses that

> [...] AMA guys come and fight with the sellers just to vacate selling from here to the extent that some of us die. I have seen people die during the struggle with these people. It happens here all the time. Just because we want to survive, the government also sends these people to seize our goods and spoil our business and even kill us.
>
> **(AG 19)**

Doing business in the informal sector is very unsafe and risky since there is constant harassment from city authorities all the time.

Invasion of Counterfeit Goods

In addition to the discussions put forward, participants complain that their business activities have slowed down due to the invasion of cheap and counterfeit goods by competitors from foreign countries such as China, Nigeria, Togo and other emerging economies.

According to the respondents, foreigners invade the market with cheap products and makes locally manufactured goods less competitive. By implication, they assert that customers patronise foreign products and disregard homemade quality goods. This makes informal entrepreneurs experience slumping sales. According to them, because they have no formal education and no other employment form, they learn a trade and produce affordable but quality products to serve the economy to make ends meet. Conversely, their efforts in coming out with quality and affordable products are often raided by the invasion of counterfeits from foreign competitors, the results of which significantly affect their operations and existence. By this, AG 13 and AG 23 stress that

> [...] As I said, the Chinese people and others from other countries like Togo bring fake and cheap products. We, therefore, lose customers. Since customers do not locate us because we do not have an appropriate location, they buy different Chinese products. This has been our headache.
>
> **(AG 13)**

The above propositions suggest that easy entry into the Ghanaian market in the informal sector has called for foreigners to take advantage of everyday business activities. Since these informal entrepreneurs are not well established, and most do not have shops, they become disadvantaged and are left at the mercy of these foreign competitors. Like the informal entrepreneurs, these invaders do not also operate formally but in the same informal manner, in the same informal sector. The informality of business affects different sectors, age groups and genders differently.

Informal Institutions – A Challenge?

The study uncovers the contribution of institutions such as "Konkonba baayere amanmre" ("Konkonba" yam traditional rites), "Nana hemaa / hene edwemu mmra" (Queen or king's market rule) and Ghana Customs Service on the business operations of informal entrepreneurs. In this study, queen mothers or king fathers are the chief traders in the market. They are usually older adults who started trading in the market. The "konkonba" yam traditional rites are institutions that perform some traditional rites annually, usually in the last month of every year. It is expected that goods are sold after the performance of these rites. Also, with the "Nana hemaa / hene edwemu mmra", they collect some goods from the informal entrepreneurs. This is a rule for every first-time trader to help continue the informal entrepreneurs' informal sector. Again, the Ghana Customs Service is an institution in Ghana that helps prevent contraband goods from entering the country.

According to the respondents, they have a market queen and a market king, who set rules governing market activities. These leaders also set rules regarding customer service such as a trader who speaks anyhow to any customer and is caught is made to pay a fee of one cedi (Gh¢1). Although this fee is not punitive, it serves as a deterrent to anyone who goes contrary to the behaviour code. According to the respondents, the punishment meted out to them has paved the way for discipline on their part and has helped them build unique relationships with their customers. Below are sample responses from AG 2 and AG 12:

> [...] we have a rule which is not from the government and is such that all of us here need to speak well to our customers and make them feel cherished. But if we do not do that, our Queen and King punish us by taking some amount from us, and because of that, we are cautious. It has even helped us to build a cordial relationship with our customers.
>
> (AG 2)

> [...] I'm very proud of the rules we have here. At first, you will always see customers complaining or a customer and a trader exchanging insults because of some misunderstanding. The present situation is different since our leaders came out with this rule. We all know how to talk to our customers well and make them feel good anytime they come to purchase from us.
>
> (AG 12)

The introduction of the code of behaviour promotes consistent and extraordinary customer service, which is even more than financial profitability.

In the limelight of informal institutions, however, is the frequent decrease in trader sales patterns. Some institutional practices also come in traditional rites that are performed annually before goods are sold. In the yam market for instance, there is a practice known as the "konkonba baayere amanmre" (Konkonba yam traditional rites). It is believed that performing such rituals helps to increase sales throughout the year. Until the rituals are performed, informal retailers cannot purchase anything for reselling or are allowed to go to the wholesaler's arena to sell. The rite takes typically up to two days before anyone can make a purchase or market to customers. This belief makes informal entrepreneurs not to trade for a day or two, which decreases sales. It reduces the sale of informal entrepreneurs, hence affecting profitability. This is what AG 22 says to bolster the assertion:

> We have some rites that need to be performed to ensure that the year goes well for all of us. Though we all want the year to be good for all of us, it affects us because we do not have the chance to purchase to resell. We wait until the rites are performed, which takes about a day or two before starting our individual business. Imagine, I am the breadwinner of my family; what will happen that particular day I don't sell? My family will starve.

> **(AG 22)**

More so, "Nana hemaa/ hene edwemu mmra" (Queen or king's market rule) are institutions that, however, affect business expansion and profitability. This is due to a situation where informal entrepreneurs need to offer about half of the goods, they sell to their queen mothers for free. For instance, if the informal entrepreneur brings goods to market, the queen or king needs to make his/her selection by picking the items of her choice before the remaining is given to the informal entrepreneur to sell. Aside from this rule, a commission of 10% is also given to the queen/king on every sale made. This is to ensure their continuity of stay in the informal sector.

The respondents mention that it is a challenge to them and affect business expansion. They cannot expand their business to a specific limit due to the nature of their informal rules. Sample expressions from the respondents are revealed below:

Similarly, AG 4 and AG 13 confirm that:

> [...] though the rules assist us in many ways, the problem is that we cannot even notice we make profits. This is because our queen/king takes close to half of the goods we are even selling and demands commission besides, so we work for their pockets.

> **(AG 4 and AG 13)**

The respondents feel that it is exploitation because they are not regulated, which tends to exploit their colleagues' informal operators.

Moreover, the informal sector in Ghana is facing much competition from counterfeit products. This results from the failure of the Ghana Customs Service to ensure that contraband goods do not enter the country. The respondents mention that the invasion of counterfeit goods has resulted in slumping sales and decreased revenue, and sometimes make losses. This is because they need to lower their prices to increase sales because customers are not buying from them as expected. This, as a result, makes AG 21 lament that:

> [...] In fact, it is a pity in Ghana that foreigners can enter the country and start a business with no one questioning them. It will not be my problem at all if they bring in the right goods. Mostly, the goods brought into the country are not original, and we all know that. When this happens, we, the traders who are citizens, face much

competition because customers tend to purchase from them more. This is due to the low prices of the goods. The goods are, in fact, very cheap but do not last long. For example, you buy cloth, and in the next week or month, the cloth gets torn. This same thing goes for shoes, bags, and towels, among others. In other developed countries, I do not think this is going to be possible. I do not blame anyone; I blame the government; I mean those in charge to make sure goods do not just enter into the country anyhow.

(AG 21)

Curbing the Challenges

The chapter identifies some ways to address the challenges faced by informal entrepreneurs in Ghana. First, the respondents believe branding their products will help curb the competition they face due to the invasion of counterfeit products. According to them, competition is keen, and the needed action needs to be taken to stay in the sector. It is of such motive that the branding of their products takes place. Two-thirds of them do not know what they can personally do to help address the constant harassment they face. They feel that they are marginalised and do not have what it takes to do anything. However, a few adopt branding to help address some of the challenges they face. The comments below attest to the arguments above.

AG 13 comments that

With regards to the Chinese people, when customers come to me, I tell them to be vigilant when shopping because some products are fake. I tell them Ghanaian goods are of good quality and that if they do not buy from us, how would they want us to survive in the economy? I also decided to put a label on my sandals, and it read "shine your eyes" (look at the products well before buying), so my friends have nicknamed me that. This helps customers locate my workplace easily.

(AG 13)

To bolster this, AG 23 makes the expression that

Again, with the issue of "Aaba ee" (to wit, they are coming), we cannot go and report because we do not have that authority. Also, if you do not have anyone or know anyone, nobody takes your matter seriously. Even if you have a good story, it becomes nonsense because you do not have cash; money! Everything is about bribery in this country, so we have not been able to take any step to address the problem of constant harassment because of these reasons.

(AG 23)

Another way to help curb the challenge in the informal sector is the provision of support structures and programs for informal entrepreneurship. A study conducted by O'Neill and Viljoen (2001) on support programmes concluded that there must be well-developed programmes to facilitate the growth and curb the challenges of those in the informal sector. Also, training and skills should be enhanced to improve the quality of activities in the informal sector. As specified by De Faoite, Henry, Johnston and Van der Sijde (2003), a predominant subject matter that has come into view of entrepreneurship literature on training programmes is the negligence of most initiatives and programmes to bring to light the educational backgrounds, specific needs, social and cultural backgrounds of the individual entrepreneurs in improving support systems and training. The scholars concur that a precondition for coaching individuals is to comprehend their historical experiences, cultural values, and mindset. De Faoite et al. (2003), emphasise that some training and support programmes sometimes do not work to help those in need, so there should be a variety in emphasis according to the different needs of individuals in the sector.

Also, business assistantships and support programmes are other solutions to curb the challenges in the informal sector. Entrepreneurial training and education are essential tools for individual entrepreneurs to successfully manage a business as they give updates to entrepreneurs on future and present business direction (Iwu & Nxopo, 2015; Chinomona & Maziriri, 2015). Also, Shane and Venkataraman (2000) note that, to ensure business growth, resources are much needed, and this could be acquired through business assistantship from authorities. This is confirmed by Kor, Mahoney, and Michael (2007) who opine that at the heart of entrepreneurship are the skills, resources, and knowledge and these can be acquired when business assistantships are given to entrepreneurs. Consequently, this is supported by Woldesenbet, Ram and Jones (2012), Teece (2012) and Klein, Mahoney, McGahan and Pitelis (2013) in that, for entrepreneurs to take action in their work activities, there should be the presence of capability of management. Therefore, skills, experience, and education in the particular firm where an individual entrepreneur begins a business activity impacts on its possibility of succeeding (Lose & Tengeh, 2015).

Moreover, access to financial institutions is an important asset that helps people in the informal sector to get the required capital to support their business activities. Anthony (2005) and Mayoux (2005) mention that access to finance support structures become mechanisms that give self-assurance against any risks unanticipated. Okpara (2011) rightly says that lack of financial support to those working in the informal sector hinder their growth. Curtain (2001) likewise confirms that it is as a result of the very few microfinance support structures in existence that hinder the growth of informal entrepreneurs. Curtain (2001) further mentions that, even though there are a few of these structures, entrepreneurs find it difficult to access the structures because of the collateral requirements they are asked to bring, hence, there seems to be a limited design on appropriate financial support structures for these workers.

Prospects

The respondents mention that there are prospects for growth, prospects for social networking, skills development and product innovation.

The possibility of growth remains a prospect in the informal sector. The fact that their revenue sometimes decreases does not necessarily mean there is no hope for the future. According to them, the informal sector is expanding every day. They attribute this to the increased nature of migrants in the sector and some formal businesses' collapse, especially in the financial market. The informal economy becomes the destination for some of these retrenched workers, which swells up the numbers operating in the informal economy. Respondents mention that activities in the informal sector help them improve their living conditions. Even though presently, things have not remained the same, it does not mean there is no possibility for growth. The respondents added that there are prospects for new skills development from retrenched workers who joined the informal sector due to the recent pandemic COVID-19. They add that due to this, social networking has also become a massive prospect in the sector.

For instance, AG 19 indicates that

> I'm sure by next year, I will be able to wholesale plenty of yams as compared to this year, and in the next five years, I will be able to be a wholesaler where people can also come and retail from me.

(AG 19)

Again, AG 11 adds that

> My son started selling some of my products on WhatsApp and Instagram for me. The world is going global, and you would need to have your products on other social networking sites to sell more. I weave an extraordinary basket from what I was doing previously to stay in the competition.

AG 5 mentions that

> I see that more people would want to add more value to what they were previously selling because lots of people have joined the sector due to the pandemic. This means that one's products need to be unique. I also see that everyone would want to learn other skills to improve on existing skills.

Discussion

Harassment by City Authorities as a Challenge to Informal Entrepreneurs

The study reveals that constant harassment by city authorities locally known in the Ghanaian "Ga" as "Aaba ee" has remained an issue of concern to informal entrepreneurs and has become a challenge that limits their growth. Mitulla (2003) aptly noted that during a study in South Africa, it finds that harassment meted out to informal entrepreneurs makes them lose customers, decreases income and distracts their business activities because city authorities make the environment insecure for informal entrepreneurs. Moreover, the study discovered that the "Aaba ee" fuels corrupt practices by taking an unapproved sum of money in return for the goods seized. It has also come to notice that these city authorities have sexual intercourse with female informal entrepreneurs before their goods are returned, thereby placing the informal workers' health at risk.

Besides, the study finds that some informal entrepreneurs lose their lives and sometimes get serious injuries during a struggle with these "Aaba ee". The reason for the constant harassment is that informal entrepreneurs sell at undesignated places. Adom (2016) suggests that formalising the informal sector is not through harassment but through continuous education and sensitisation on the significance of paying social security and tax to make people accept the need to formalise their business operations.

Invasion of Counterfeit Goods as a Limitation to Informal Business Growth

Invasion of counterfeit goods by foreigners primarily affects informal entrepreneurs' businesses. Counterfeit goods come in the form of shoes, slippers, bags, clothes, among others. In the study area, these counterfeit goods are very cheap and attract customers to patronise them other than the locally made ones. This results from the failure of the Ghana Customs Service to ensure that contraband goods do not enter the country. The situation poses many challenges to informal entrepreneurs and stands out as a critical finding as it is a big challenge in the business operations of informal entrepreneurs. This challenge results in slumping sales which limits their profitability level.

Activities of Queens/Kings as a Constraint to Informal Entrepreneurs' Business Expansion

The study reveals that the activities of queen mothers limit the expansion of informal businesses. This poses a hindrance to the growth of informal businesses. In this study, the burden comes from presenting some quantities of wares and a 10% commission on goods sold to king/queen mothers. It is believed that king/queen mothers ensure the informal entrepreneurs' safety in the informal sector.

Low Self-Esteem as a Constraint for Curbing Informal Entrepreneurship Challenge

Low self-esteem is discovered as a hindrance to curbing the challenges informal entrepreneurs face in their business operations. From the study, it is recognised that authorities do not pay heed to informal entrepreneurs' woes, so there is no need to report to them the challenges faced in the sector. This sheds light on "Decent work" by ILO (2002), which indicates that informal entrepreneurs lack voice representation to make their work protected. This limitation excludes them from getting little or no access to public infrastructure and benefits.

Informal Entrepreneurship Serves as Employment Opportunities/Product Innovation

It is highly recognised that informal business helps create jobs and gives employment opportunities to many. This highlights Jackson (2016), who mentions about 93% of the informal sector jobs that are created in sub-Saharan regions since the 1990s. This sheds light on the study of Baptista and Preto (2011), who found that higher start-up rates lead to job creation in Portugal and the Netherlands. Accra, the capital city of Ghana, is swamped with the activities of informal entrepreneurs creating more jobs for people in the country. Highlighting Adom (2016), it has become clear that the informal sector employs approximately 80% of Ghanaians.

In resonation with Aghion, Harris, Howitt & Vickers (2001), informal entrepreneurship has prospects for product innovation regarding the competition in the sector. This makes the informal sector grow and expand because people venture into the sector all the time.

Conclusions

Despite the growth and vigorous activities of the informal sector across the globe, these informal entrepreneurs still face many challenges. This chapter, therefore, sought to explore the challenges and prospects of informal entrepreneurs and further sought to find out how these market women and men seek steps to circumvent the challenges faced. The main finding is that "Nana hemaa/ hene edwemu mmra" (Queen or King's market rule) are institutions that affect business expansion and profitability. This is due to a situation where informal entrepreneurs must provide approximately half of the goods that they sell to their queen mothers for free. For example, if the informal entrepreneur brings goods to sell, the queen must make her selection by selecting the items she prefers before the remainder is given to the informal entrepreneur. Aside from this rule, a commission of 10% is also given to the queen's mother on every sale made. This is to ensure their continuity of stay in the informal sector. The respondents mentioned that it is a challenge to them and affects business expansion. They cannot expand their business to a specific limit due to the nature of the informal rules.

Furthermore, the informal sector in Ghana is facing much competition from counterfeit products. This results from the failure of the Ghana Customs Service to ensure that contraband goods do not enter the country. The respondents mentioned that the invasion of counterfeit goods has resulted in slumping sales and decreased revenue, and sometimes made losses. Though informal entrepreneurs are faced with challenges within the informal sector, they also adopted branding as a strategy to help curb the challenges they face regarding the invasion of foreign products. This strategy came in the form of branding their products from foreign invaders.

Recommendations

First, the government should bring out clear policies at addressing the challenges of informal entrepreneurs in the informal sector. There should be a policy to address informal entrepreneurs' needs and not an approach that is geared toward harassing them. Again, there should be enforcement of existing regulations to prevent foreigners from operating in the informal economy. Furthermore, informal market leaders should not only focus on taking a commission on the wares of informal entrepreneurs but also focus on how they can improve other traders' businesses by collaborating with other institutions to organise basic business training for them. This would go a long way to help them understand the basic business concept and understand that they can adequately brand themselves. Also, there should be more educative programmes to educate individuals on their rights in Ghana. This will help to instil enough confidence in every Ghanaian to take the needed action when the need arises, thereby boosting their self-esteem. Finally, though most informal entrepreneurs have not received a formal education, there is a need to educate them by creating awareness on the importance of business formalisation. This will help to eradicate the mindset informal entrepreneurs hold on running a formal business.

Future Directions for Research

The study recommends that future research be directed at extending the study's scope to explore the challenges and prospects of informal entrepreneurs.

Again, other researchers could employ a quantitative approach as this study used a qualitative approach.

Finally, researchers could assess the relationship between formal and informal institutions on informal entrepreneurship in Accra.

References

Abor, J. (2007). Industry classification and the capital structure of Ghanaian SMEs. *Studies in Economics and Finance, 24*(3), 207–219.

Abor, J., & Biekpe, N. (2009). How do we explain the capital structure of SMEs in Sub-Saharan Africa: Evidence from Ghana? *Journal of Economic Studies, 36*(1), 83–97.

Adom, K. (2014). Beyond the marginalization thesis: An examination of the motivations of informal entrepreneurs in Sub-Saharan Africa: Insights from Ghana. *The International Journal of Entrepreneurship
and Innovation, 15*(2), 113–125.

Adom, K. (2016). Tackling informal entrepreneurship in Ghana: A critical analysis of the dualist/mod-
ernist policy approach, some evidence from Accra. *International Journal Entrepreneurship and Small
Business, 28*(3), 216–233.

Adom, K. (2017). Formalization of entrepreneurship in the informal economy in Sub-Saharan Africa and
the role of formal institutions: An analysis of Ghana's experience. In *The Informal Economy in Global
Perspective* (pp. 277–291). Palgrave Macmillan.

Adom, K., & Williams, C. C. (2014). Evaluating the explanations for the informal economy in third world
cities: Some evidence from Koforidua in the eastern region of Ghana. *International Entrepreneurship
and Management Journal, 10*(2), 427–445.

Aghion, P., Harris, C., Howitt, P., & Vickers, J. (2001). Competition, imitation and growth with step-by-
step innovation. *The Review of Economic Studies, 68*(3), 467–492.

Aidis, R., Welter, F., Smallbone, D., & Isakova, N. (2006). Female entrepreneurship in transition economies: The case of Lithuania and Ukraine. *Feminist Economics, 13*(1), 157–183.

Baptista, R., & Preto, M. T. (2011). New firm formation and employment growth: Regional and business
dynamics. *Small Business Economics, 36*(4), 419–442.

Barbour, A., & Llanes, M. (2013). *Supporting people to legitimize their informal businesses.* Joseph Rowntree
Foundation.

Beck, T., & Demirguc-Kunt, A. (2006). Small and medium-sized enterprises: Access to finance as a growth
constraint. *Journal of Banking & Finance, 30*(11), 2931–2943.

Benzing, C., Chu, H. M., & Kara, O. (2009). Entrepreneurs in Turkey: A factor analysis of motivations,
success factors, and problems. *Journal of Small Business Management, 47*(1), 58–91.

Boachie-Mensah, F. O., & Marfo-Yiadom, E. (2005). *Entrepreneurship and small business management.*
Ghana Universities Press.

Bowen, G. A. (2008). Naturalistic inquiry and the saturation concept: A research note. *Qualitative Research,
8*(1), 137–152.

Chen, M. A. (2012). *The informal economy: Definitions, theories and policies* (Vol. 1, No. 26, pp. 90141-4).
WIEGO Working Paper.

Chu, H. M., Benzing, C., & McGee, C. (2007). Ghanaian and Kenyan entrepreneurs: A comparative analysis of their motivations, success characteristics and problems. *Journal of Developmental
Entrepreneurship, 12*(3), 295–322.

Creswell, J. W. (2014). *A concise introduction to mixed methods research.* Sage Publications.

Cresswell, J. W., & Plano-Clark, V. L. (2011). *Designing and conducting mixed-method research.* Sage.

De Castro, J. O., Khavul, S., & Bruton, G. D. (2014). Shades of grey: How do informal firms navigate
between macro and meso institutional environments?. *Strategic Entrepreneurship Journal, 8*(1), 75–94.

Debrah, Y. A. (2007). Promoting the informal sector as a source of gainful employment in developing
countries: Insights from Ghana. *The International Journal of Human Resource Management, 18*(6),
1063–1084.

Dellot, B. (2012). *Untapped enterprise: Learning to live with the informal economy.* Royal Society of the Arts.

Duncan, C. M. (Ed.). (1992). *Rural poverty in America.* Greenwood Publishing Group.

Fuad, N., & Bohari, A. M. (2011). Malay women entrepreneurs in the small and medium-sized ICT-related business: A study on need for achievement. *International Journal of Business and Social Science, 2*(13), 44–57.

Gutmann, P. M. (1977). The subterranean economy. *Financial Analysts Journal, 33*(6), 26–27.

Haan, H. C. (2006). Informal micro-enterprises in Sub-Sahara Africa. In *Training for Work in the informal
micro-enterprise sector* (pp. 13–46). Springer.

Halkias, D., Harkiolakis, N., & Caracatsanis, S. M. (2011). Challenges facing women entrepreneurs in
Nigeria. *Management Research Review, 34*(2), 221–235.

Haltiwanger, J. C., Jarmin, R. S., & Miranda, J. (2010). *Who creates jobs? Small vs. large vs. young* (No.
w16300). National Bureau of Economic Research.

ILO. (2002). *Women and men in the informal economy: A statistical picture.* International Labour Office.

ILO. (2012). *Statistical update on employment in the informal economy.* International Labour Organisation

ILO. (2017). *Statistical update on employment in the informal economy.* International Labour Organisation

ILO. (2018). *Statistical update on employment in the informal economy.* International Labour Organisation

Indarti, N., & Wulandaru, D. R. (2003). Profil dan motivasi entrepreneur wanita di Yogyakarta. *Journal of Indonesian Economy and Business, 18*(4), 367–373.

Jackson, T. (2016). *Prosperity without growth: Foundations for the economy of tomorrow.* Routledge.

Korantemaa, G. (2006). Ghana's 2006 performance to shape destiny (March 3, 2006). *Ghanaian Chronicle,* Retrieved from www.allafrica.com

La Porta, R. L., & Shleifer, A. (2008). *The unofficial economy and economic development* (No. w14520). National Bureau of Economic Research.

Lee, D. Y., & Tsang, E. W. (2001). The effects of entrepreneurial personality, background and network activities on venture growth. *Journal of Management Studies, 38*(4), 583–602.

Llanes, M., & Barbour, A. (2007). *Self-employed and micro-entrepreneurs: Informal trading and the journey towards formalization.* Community Links.

Malhotra, N. K., & Birks, D. F. (2007). *Marketing research.* Pearson Education.

Mondello, M., & Maxcy, J. (2009). The impact of salary dispersion and performance bonuses in NFL organizations. *Management Decision, 47*(1), 110–123.

McArthur, J. W., & Sachs, J. D. (2001). *Institutions and geography: Comment on Acemoglu, Johnson and Robinson (2000)* (No. w8114). National Bureau of Economic Research.

McElwee, G. (2009). The ethics of exploring entrepreneurship beyond the boundaries. *Journal of Small Business and Entrepreneurship, 22*(1), III.

Mitullah, W. V. (2003). *Street vending in African cities: A synthesis of empirical finding from Kenya, Cote d'Ivoire, Ghana, Zimbabwe, Uganda and South Africa.*

Mróz, B. (2012). Entrepreneurship in the shadow: Faces and variations of Poland's informal economy. *International Journal of Economic Policy in Emerging Economies, 5*(3), 197–211.

Onwe, O. J. (2013). Role of the informal sector in the development of the Nigerian economy: Output and employment approach. *Journal of Economics and Development Studies, 1*(1), 60–74.

Palmer, R. (2009). Skills development, employment and sustained growth in Ghana: Sustainability challenges. *International Journal of Educational Development, 29*(2), 133–139.

Rahman, M. (2011). Does labour migration bring about economic advantage? A case of Bangladeshi Migrants in Saudi Arabia. ISAS Working Paper No. 135.

Raijman, R., & Tienda, M. (2000). Immigrants' pathways to business ownership: A comparative ethnic perspective. *International Migration Review, 34*(3), 682–706.

Rowan, B. (1991). The shape of professional communities in schools.

Scott, W. R. (2001). Institutional theory: Contributing to a theoretical research program. *Great Minds in Management: The Process of Theory Development, 37,* 460–484.

Tagoe, N., Nyarko, E., & Anuwa-Armah, E. (2005). Financial challenges facing urban SMEs under financial sector liberalization in Ghana. *Journal of Small Business Management, 43*(3) 331–343.

Tonelli, M., & Dalglish, C. L. (2012). The role of transport infrastructure in facilitating the survival and growth of micro-enterprises in developing economies.

Webb, J. W., Ireland, R. D., & Ketchen, D. J. (2014). Toward a greater understanding of entrepreneurship and strategy in the informal economy. *Strategic Entrepreneurship Journal, 8*(1), 1–15.

Williams, C. C. (2006). The nature of entrepreneurship in the informal sector: Evidence from England. *Journal of Developmental Entrepreneurship, 12*(2), 239–254.

Williams, C. C. (2009). Formal and informal employment in Europe: Beyond dualistic representations. *European Urban and Regional Studies, 16*(2), 147–159.

Williams, C. C. (2011). Entrepreneurship, the informal economy and rural communities. *Journal of Enterprising Communities: People and Places in the Global Economy, 5*(2), 145–157.

Williams, C. C. (2013). Entrepreneurship, the informal economy and rural communities. *Journal of Enterprising Communities: People and Places in the Global Economy, 5*(2), 145–157.

Williams, C. C., & Lansky, M. A. (2013). Informal employment in developed and developing economies: Perspectives and policy responses. *International Labour Review, 152*(3–4), 355–380.

Williams, C. C., & Nadin, S. J. (2012). Tackling entrepreneurship in the informal economy: Evaluating the policy options. *Journal of Entrepreneurship and Public Policy, 1*(2), 111–124.

Williams, C. C., & Nadin, S. J. (2014). Evaluating the participation of the unemployed in undeclared work: Evidence from a 27-nation European survey. *European Societies, 16*(1), 68–89.

Williams, C. C., & Renooy, P. (2009). *Measures to combat undeclared work in 27 European Union Member States and Norway.* European Foundation for the Improvement of Living and Working Conditions.

Williams, C. C., & Round, J. (2007). Entrepreneurship and the informal economy: A study of Ukraine's hidden enterprise culture. *Journal of Developmental Entrepreneurship, 12*(01), 119–136.

Williams, C. C., Nadin, S., & Rodgers, P. (2012). Evaluating competing theories of informal entrepreneurship: Some lessons from Ukraine. *International Journal of Entrepreneurial Behaviour and Research, 18* (5), 528–543.

Williams, C. C., Nadin, S., Barbour, A., & Llanes, M. (2013). *Enabling enterprise: Tackling the barriers to formalisation.* Community Links.

Chapter 4

Internationalisation of Rural Business Marketing

Kenny Odunukan

Contents

Based on the extant literature, this chapter developed structural models on the barriers of internationalisation of rural SMEs marketing in Nigeria. To validate these models, this chapter used quantitative approach with positivist philosophy as a research paradigm, questionnaire survey as a data collection method, cluster sampling as a sampling technique and partial least square-based structural equation modelling (PLS-SEM) as a data analysis technique. The findings of the chapter show that the barriers of internationalisation of rural business marketing in Nigeria are second-order hierarchical models. In addition, analysis of the findings appears to provide rural SMEs marketing own explanation that complicates and somehow even challenges some widely

DOI: 10.4324/9781003302339-4

held assumptions of the traditional theories on SMEs internationalisation. The structural models that lie at the heart of this chapter provide a new theoretical basis for understanding SME marketing and internationalisation in a rural African context. This challenges some of the assumptions implicit in existing internationalisation theories which underplay the significance and realities of the physical, geographical and socio-economic contexts experienced by rural SMEs in developing countries.

The contribution of the chapter can provide a better guidance to the marketing of internationalising SMEs operating in rural Nigeria, and presents opportunities for further research to examine rural SME internationalisation marketing in other developing countries. Methodologically, this chapter is one of the few endeavours to develop and validates hierarchical models using PLS based SEM to identify the key barriers of internationalisation in the context of rural SMEs. In addition, this chapter contributes to the advancement of PLS based SEM through methodological contribution. Practically, this chapter is very useful and significant to policymakers, owners and marketing managers of rural SMEs and international businesses.

Introduction

For over two decades now, internationalisation has been considered an important marketing strategy for businesses (Odunukan et al., 2022). Internationalisation defined by Welch and Luostarinen (1988) as the process of increasing involvement in international markets is considered a preferred and more effective strategy for small business growth. SME internationalisation is considered a viable strategy for rural businesses to grow their businesses for a long period, foster economic growth and expand their market territories and activities across national borders while leveraging several advantages like cheap workforce, abundant resources, economies of scales, market power effects and risk reduction, and others (Lee, 2008; Rahman et al., 2021).

Although research on SMEs internationalisation has increased over the years, empirical research and theories on SMEs and internationalisation as a marketing strategy for growth have mainly analysed and focused on developed countries, some parts of Asia and urban SMEs leaving a potential research gap for Africa and its rural SMEs. The theories and findings in these regions may not apply to African developing countries based on socio-economic, political and cultural differences (Rahmah et al., 2021). Therefore, generalising theories discovered in developed countries may be misleading (Rahmah et al., 2017). Few studies have addressed the challenges faced by rural SMEs and businesses as they attempt to internationalise and become competitive in the marketplace and leverage potential opportunities in expanding their market and business growth. It is within this context that this chapter identified and assessed the key barriers of internationalisation of rural business marketing in Nigeria.

This chapter focuses on Nigeria, a developing country where rural regions occupy 90% of the geographical landscape and two-thirds of its population live and work in rural areas. Studies show that 90% of enterprises in rural regions are micro, small enterprises (MSEs), family-driven businesses and SMEs (Etuk et al., 2014), which is like the share of small and micro-enterprises in rural regions of the UK and other western economies. However, a 2020 SMEs and MSEs report by the Central Bank of Nigeria claimed that out of about 200,000 businesses created between the years 2010 and 2020, less than 5,000 managed to survive and the remaining 195,000 businesses were forced out of business (Adisa et al., 2014). In part, this is explained by assertions that small businesses and entrepreneurs in developing countries operate in high-risk environments and are characterised by high failure rates (Rahmah et al., 2021). Therefore, this chapter is founded on the concern of how to improve the low market growth rate of SMEs in rural areas and possibly foster economic growth and development of developing countries' rural regions while focusing on internationalisation strategies.

This chapter is organised as follows: the first section of this chapter reviews the literature to identify the key barriers to internationalisation for rural SMEs marketing with a particular focus on Nigeria. Then a conceptual model is developed followed by a series of hypotheses. Furthermore, the chapter describes the research methodologies used for the empirical investigation of the model. The model specification is further presented, and it is followed by a model assessment. Finally, data analysis and findings are discussed in the last section of the chapter along with a concluding remark.

Review of Literature on Internationalisation of Rural Business Marketing

Research on SMEs and (Rural) International business marketing has experienced phenomenal growth over the last few decades (Rahman et al., 2019; Odunukan et al., 2022). Theories and literature on marketing of SMEs Internationalisation have been developed through conceptual and empirical approaches (Rahman et al., 2017; 2019; Rahman & Mendy, 2019; Ruzzier et al., 2006). The body of literature, which has investigated the barriers to small firms and rural business marketing internationalisation process includes (Odunukan et al., 2022), Bose, 2016, Rahman et al., 2014, Ibeh et al., 2012; North, 1990; and Ruzzier et al., 2006). A study revealed that the marketing process of small firms' internationalisation barriers can be classified into informational, operational, internal and external barriers (Morgan et al., 2004). Yip et al. (2000) summarised it as scale and resource-related barriers. Okpara (2011) pointed out financial and non-financial barriers. Leonidou (2000) found that lack of managerial, human and financial resources are key barriers to small firm internationalisation. Rutashobya and Jaensson (2004) identified financial resources, management and marketing skills, currency risk management for exporting, knowledge, lack of foreign language knowledge, cultural experience, poor knowledge of foreign market information, fear of foreign market risks and previous export experience as main internationalisation barriers. Scale and resource barriers include the obstacles faced by the firms due to their inability to compete internationally as they do not have sufficient working capital (Bose, 2016), funds (Amankwah-Amoah et al., 2018; Adebayo et al.2019), management resources or foreign currency (Kneller & Pisu, 2006; Leonidou, 2004). In addition to these financial and non-financial resources, firms require information related to the possible markets, buyers, sellers, products, prices and demand when seeking to internationalise (Amankwah-Amoah et al., 2018). Firms try to find information both from formal and informal networks to obtain real facts about potential opportunities (Crick et al., 2011). Therefore, firms having strong networks both in local and international markets may be in advantageous positions than firms having limited international or only domestic connections (Faloye, 2015; Ovadje, 2016). The information constraints faced by the firms towards international expansions and markets are lack of knowledge of foreign markets (Crick et al., 2011), limited information to locate/analyse markets, failure to recognize who to contact in the first instance (Kneller & Pisu, 2006), inability to identify the foreign buyers or sellers (Aspelund & Moen, 2005) or lack of skill to start the initial communication with the potential foreign partners (Kneller & Pisu, 2006). Besides, the firms may also face procedural barriers to starting international operations, such as dealing with legal, financial and tax regulations, and standards (Kneller & Pisu, 2006). This chapter classified the barriers to internationalisation for Nigeria's rural SMEs into 6 major categories following Rahman et al. (2019). These are (1) Governance and Political barriers, (2) Legal and regulatory barriers, (3) Physical and Geographical barriers, (4) Economic and Financial barriers, (5) Socio-cultural barriers and (6) Technological barriers.

Governance and Political Barriers

The concept of Governance is not new, it's probably as old as mankind. Studies show that the origin of the word 'Governance' emanated from the Greek word 'Kybernan' which often was interpreted "to steer or to pilot a ship". Apparently, the word was widely used during the Roman Empire via the Latin word "gubernare", which literary means to direct, rule and guide. As a result, the concept's meaning has evolved. Various definitions have however emerged on the concept, and these definitions are based on different perspectives, approaches and disciplines. From one perspective, governance is defined as how society or groups within it organise to make decisions (Flink & Ploder, 2009). It was also defined as the process by which societies or organisations make important decisions, determine who has a voice, who participates in the process and how accountability is maintained. (Graham et al., 2003). The World Bank on the other hand defines governance as the way power is exercised through a country's economic, political and social institutions (World Bank, 2017a). A modern-day view defines governance as the interaction between governments, business stakeholders and non-profit organisations by which policy decisions are undertaken (Ysa, 2007). It is clear from the last definition that governance involves multiple actors, not just the political government. Generally, governance determines who has power, who makes decisions, how other players make their voices heard and how accounts are rendered. Business is often considered part of the governing environment, thus the business actors are often influenced by the governing body.

The concept of politics or political institutions is equally not new. In fact, the famous Greek philosopher Aristotle once declared that "man is by nature a political animal".

The word "politics" is derived from the Greek word politika meaning affairs of the city-state. It was told then that the ancient Greek society was divided into a collection of independent city-states, each of which possessed its system of government. The largest and most influential of these city-states was Athens, often portrayed as the cradle of democratic government. In this light, politics can be understood to refer to the affairs of the polis – in effect, "what concerns the polis". The modern form of this definition is therefore "what concerns the state". Generally, politics (or political forces) has broadly been defined as the combination of efforts by the government, other institutions, fields and special interest groups to give future directions to the country considering the value and interest people hold in addition to carry on government and state affairs (Daunton, 2011).

There are several ways governance and political factors may possibly influence the business landscape. First, due to the decision-making process of the political environment, the government could enact or change laws, policies and regulations that may probably exacerbate or facilitate the ease of doing business in that environment. For example, the government may decide to raise taxes for business organisation. In the same vein, the government could also strengthen policies that protect labour law by ways of raising the minimum wage and, as a result, indirectly affect the cost of doing business. Apparently, the government is often saddled with the task of deciding the fiscal and monetary policies which in turn have a positive or negative effect on the ease of doing business. In addition, factors such as political instability and bad governance could adversely affect the ease of doing business (Rahman et al., 2018). In as much as governance and political factors are key elements in a nation's economy and its domestic market, they are even more important when considering foreign market operations. This is because each nation-state's interest differs from another. The political environment abroad might not necessarily be the same as at home (Adamoko, 2017). On one hand, governance and political factors like tax incentives for exporting firms may be favourable to firm internationalisation (Graham et al., 2003), on the other hand, governance and political barriers like political instability, corruption and bad governance could in fact constitute barriers to firm internationalisation (Rahman et al., 2017). For example, as a result of political instability and unrest, the possibilities of internationalisation have been grossly affected. Examples are 2011 Syrian civil war, the political upheaval in Venezuela and Indonesia civil unrest. These events have made businesses and investors stay away from these unsettled markets (Ademako, 2017). As a result, firms attempting to internationalise should consider the nature of the governance and political environment of the target markets (Johanson & Vahlne (2009; Johanson & Wiedersheim-Paul, 1975). Daniel (2014) argue that international firms must evaluate, monitor and forecast governance and political environments. They often study how government officials exercise authority, pass policies, regulate enterprises and punish wrongdoers. They monitor how politicians are elected and replaced. They assess whether the rule of law or the rule of man prevails. They gauge whether freedom is a practical ideal or a wishful abstraction and based on these insights, they forecast business scenarios. Thus, a better understanding of the governance and political factors of the foreign markets would help firms make more informed operational decisions.

Consequently, larger firms have adequate financial resources to carry out research and assessment of foreign market governance and political environments. SMEs and rural businesses however are financially constrained to administer primary market research and are most likely to use existing research findings to analyse the potential foreign market. In contrast to this higher importance, most of the research on barriers to internationalisation is focused on multinational firms and urban SMEs marketing (Ibeh et al., 2012; Rahman et al., 2013). Several researchers argued that marketing within rural SMEs is characteristically different from urban SMEs (Bosworth & Venhorst, 2018). As a result, they face unique and different barriers from urban SMEs. There are few studies that identify barriers to rural business internationalisation. For example, Bosworth and Venhorst (2018) revealed that rural businesses were more likely than urban firms to be vulnerable to sudden "external shocks", such as boom-and-bust cycles, trade conflicts and shifts in government and corporate policy, which means that diversification and adaptation are often reactive rather than anticipatory. "Forced adaptation" in the teeth of economic contraction makes it difficult to secure financing for the pursuit of new ventures, activities and clientele.

Almost all the research is based on developed countries and developing countries' urban SMEs. As a result, the findings may not necessarily be appropriate for rural SMEs in developing countries like Nigeria. Hence, it is very much important to conduct research with particular attention to governance and political barriers faced by international rural SMEs marketing in developing countries. Besides, it is very crucial to conduct empirical research based on firm-level data because most of the policies made by the government of developing countries do not emanate from firm-level data (Ibeh et al., 2012). Kolawole and Ajila (2015) disclosed reasons why some government of developing countries failed to reflect on policies that augment rural SMEs growth and marketing. First, rural regions and their businesses are often not part of central government policies and programmes. Second, Policymakers are often not aware of the barriers to internationalisation of rural firms marketing. In addition, rural SMEs do not develop constructive relationships with the existing government in order to defend their interest in the face of policymakers. Thus, it is very important to carry out empirical research on the governance and political barriers experienced by international SMEs, particularly from developing countries' views. From extant literature review, few studies have addressed the challenges faced by rural SMEs and entrepreneurs as they attempt to internationalise and become competitive in the marketplace and leverage potential opportunities in expanding their market and business growth (Etuk et al., 2014). Most of these studies might have only identified governance and political barriers as part of the overall barriers facing rural SMEs marketing, and barriers are conducted with a focus on a single commodity product like cocoa or exclusively focused on a sector of the economy. Therefore, the key barriers to internationalisation of Rural Business Marketing are still under debate. While articulating all the governance and political barriers from extant literature, this chapter developed four major factors– Political instability, Corruption, Capability of local politicians, Support from government and coordination of rural institutions – as key governance and political barriers to Internationalisation of rural business marketing.

Legal and Regulatory Barriers

The concept of law is old as mankind. Law exists in every cell of life. It affects almost everyone all of the time. It governs everything in life, including our afterlife. It applies to everything from embryo to exhumation. It regulates the air we breathe, the food and drink we consume, our travels, sexualities, family relationships and properties. It is defined as a system of rules that are created and enforced through social or governmental institutions to regulate individual and collective behaviour (Bosworth & Venhorst, 2018). The legal system determines the rules that regulate individual and firms' behaviour. The legal system provides laws and norms – that is, prescribes what is assumed to be a proper mode of behaviour. As a matter of fact, it does not only prescribe a certain pattern of behaviour, but it also requires that the prescribed behaviour be followed (Daniel, 2014). Law often includes a process approved by society for applying coercive sanctions against those who do not obey or transgress the rules (Bosworth & Venhorst, 2018).

There are several ways legal and regulatory factors may possibly influence the business environment. First, a coherent set of laws enables businesses and investors to plan where to invest and administer operations in order to comply with regulations. Second, how a country develops, interprets and enforces its laws is a key aspect of the business environment (Bosworth & Venhorst, 2018; Daniel, 2014). Lastly, businesses depend on the safety and assurance offered by the law to guarantee business certainty and prediction (Collinson & Houlden, 2005).

The modern-day legal system is designed to establish a comprehensive set of rules that support business formation, regulate transactions and stabilise relationships (Bosworth & Venhorst, 2018). Studies revealed that there are three components of modern legal system. First, constitutional law that preserves an open and just political order. Second, criminal law that safeguards the social order, and lastly civil and commercial laws that promote fairness and efficiency in business transaction (Daniel, 2014). All types of modern legal systems are made to ensure that an aspect of each component influences firms' actions in a host country. For example, the concept of due diligence requires that the statements in a firm's security registration forms be true and omit no material facts. Firms internationalising rely on due diligence to manage the risk of cross-border acquisition (Collinson & Houlden, 2005; Daniel, 2014).

However, just as political and governance ideologies differ from one country to another so does the legal and regulatory framework differ (Collinson & Houlden, 2005). Consequently, how a country develops, interprets and enforces its law is a key aspect of the business environment. If it is done legitimately, consumers and businesses can make lawful decisions that facilitate peace and prosperity. However, if it is done arbitrarily, all stakeholders will suffer and there would be a huge mistrust of the judiciary. Firms internationalising must recognise the existence of fundamental differences across countries particularly legal and regulatory differences. Firms must investigate what type of legal system exists in the foreign market. Is it the rule of law or the rule of man? Is it common law? Civil Law, Theocratic law, customary law? Or a mixed system? (Collinson & Houlden, 2005; Daniel, 2014).

When internationalising, firms are often concerned about how the legal system helps administer the operation of their business. For example, how do legal regulations impact day-to-day business and marketing? How does it enhance the registration and commencement of a new business? What is the position of laws and regulations as regards hiring and firing? What is the position of law as regards entering and enforcing contacts? What is the stand of laws and regulations in relation to export and import? What is the position of law as regards ending a business (Collinson & Houlden, 2005; Ibeh et al., 2012)? In addition, businesses are also concerned with the stands of laws and regulations as regards strategic issues within the business environment. They are often concerned with how the legal regulations affect the firm's short- and long-term competitiveness. They are concerned with issues like product safety and liability, marketplace behaviour and practices, product origin, legal jurisdictions and arbitration. More importantly, they are more concerned with the enforcement and protection of intellectual property rights (Daniel, 2014). Thus, firms' internationalisation decisions should be based on a clear understanding and analysis of the legal and regulatory landscape of the foreign market. While big firms and urban SMEs have strong financial resources and support to undertake research on the legal and regulatory environment, rural SMEs, on the other hand, often do not have the financial strength to carry out such primary research and, as a result, depend on existing secondary research. Thus, rural SMEs' inability to get funding for market research necessitates the need to carry out research that is relevant to the internationalisation of Rural Business Marketing.

While articulating all the legal and regulatory barriers from extant literature, this chapter developed four major factors- foreign market regulations, home market regulations, bureaucracy in home and foreign markets, and discriminatory policies and practices as key legal and regulatory barriers to internationalisation of rural business marketing.

Economic and Financial Barriers

The economic activities of a particular country influence the national economy of that country. Due to the nature of diversity based on size, geography, population and natural climate, the economic activity of one country differs from another (Danso & Adamako, 2014; Adomako, 2017). Studies show that some key economic factors have major influence on the overall business environment of the country, such as economic growth, interest rates, exchange Barkerates and the inflation rate, cost of living, income distribution, unemployment, debt, labour cost, productivity and balance of payment (Daniel, 2014; Mendy and Rahman, 2018). These economic factors may influence the business in many ways. For example, the cost of capital of the firm is influenced by the bank rate. Similarly, economic system influences the formation of business and nature of ownership. Again, economic policies may make the business environment for any industry favourable, unfavourable or usual. In the case of internationalisation, the effects of the economic environment are even higher as international firms are affected by the economies of both the home country and the host country. For example, the exchange rate influences the cost of international trade both at home and abroad. Similarly, international monetary system always influences the firms' willingness to trade across border. In addition to these usual influences, the current economic recession has a serious impact on the overall business environment. Therefore, the current economic and financial barriers influencing the business may differ from the post-recession findings and need updating. Although economic and financial barriers affect both large and small firms,

SMEs are more vulnerable due to their resource limitations. Limited resources restrict small and medium enterprises from the flexibility to changes, the product mix, to carry on repackaging, maintaining stricter inventory or to increase local procurement (Abdullateef et al., 2017; Adeleye & Boso, 2016). In addition to inadequate resources, SME marketing faces some other economic and financial constraints on their way to internationalisation. For example, lack of finance has been identified as the key obstacle to growth for SMEs (Adisa et al., 2014; Adeleye et al., 2015). This is also true for the international growth of SMEs (Adeleye & Esposito, 2014; Adomako et al., 2018; BarneIbeh et al. (2012). In contrast, Ajao (2015) did not include financing as one of the four major barriers to internationalisation for SMEs. Similarly, Ibeh et al. (2012) reported a lack of information as a more influential barrier to internationalisation than financing problems.

From existing literature reviews, this chapter reveals that there is no study to determine the influence of economic and financial barriers on the Internationalisation of Rural Business Marketing where the economic scenario is different from many other developing countries. Although some generic studies on the overall barriers to Nigeria's rural SMEs identified financial constraints as one of the major barriers to the growth of rural small firms in Nigeria (Ibeh et al., 2012; Kolawole & Ajila, 2015), the result could be dissimilar for the international SMEs. Due to the serious lack of research and based on the findings from previous studies, this chapter identifies lack of finance, competition, custom duty and foreign exchange risk as the key economic and financial barriers to internationalisation of rural business marketing.

Social and Cultural Barriers

Social and cultural factors comprise the beliefs, attitudes, tastes, behaviours, lifestyles and relationships among the people of a particular society in their day-to-day life (Daniel, 2014). In theory, business involves people, every business employs, sells to, buys from and is owned and regulated by people. Business transactions and activities are designed to meet the demand and needs of the people, whereas the needs and demands of the people are often based on social and cultural aspects. Business activities are often influenced and shaped by the culture and norms of its operating society. Thus, all business activities are subject to cultural differences.

When it comes to operating beyond borders, it involves people from different countries and that means people from diverse socio-cultural backgrounds. Thus, socio-cultural factors are important in international business activities. By crossing the national borders through internationalisation process, firms involve with a different culture and society. Although most of the theories of internationalisation raised these cultural issues as a dominant factor for internationalisation, the Uppsala internationalisation model shed light on the term "psychic distance". According to Johanson and Vahlne (1977; p. 24), psychic distance is "the sum of factors preventing the flow of information from and to the market". In further explanation of the psychic distance, they have given examples, such as language, education, culture, political factors, business practices and industrial development-related distances. Admitting the impacts of psychic distance or psychological distance, some other studies highlighted the importance of cultural factors and promotes the term "cultural distance" (Tikhonova, 2012). This raises the confusion between the terms psychic and cultural distances. This was also echoed by Sousa and Bradley (2005) where they have assumed that psychic distance should be assessed at the individual level whereas cultural distance should be considered at the national level. In contrast to this study, Beckerman (1956) clarifies and examines economic distance and psychic distance from the country's point of view without having any individual perceptions. Again, Evans and Mavondo (2002; p. 517) define psychic difference as "the distance between the home market and a foreign market, resulting from the perception of both cultural and business differences". In fact, according to the Uppsala model of internationalisation, culture is part of psychic distance. Another popular term in this context is national culture as stated by Hofstede (1980, p. 21Rahman), "the collective programming of the mind distinguishing the members of one human group from another". Although the extant literature confirms the popularity of Hofstede's (1980) definition of culture, some of the studies identify several problems. For example, Baskerville (2003) criticises Hofstede's theoretical framework for equating a nation with culture as a single nation may have a number of different cultural traits. Similarly, Williamson (2002) criticises the cultural definition by Hofstede for fusing two or more cultures. Accepting the usefulness of Hofstede's cultural framework, Orr and Hauser (2008) suggest re-examining the factor structure from a 21st-century context due to dramatic changes in cultural attitudes and behaviours. Considering the new dimensions (such as Global culture, multicultural), this study recognises the important contribution of Hofstede's cultural framework but suggests a review of the new cultural dimensions. The importance of the specific factor is also influenced by the context of the country. For example, the multicultural dimension is important while assessing the impact of social and cultural factors in UK-based business, whereas in Nigeria multicultural dimensions may not be important at all. Previous studies identify several social and cultural factors working as barriers of internationalisation to the firms including different socio-cultural traits, verbal and nonverbal language differences, different habits and attitudes of foreign customers and clients (OECD, 2006). Again, Barkema & Vermeulen (1997) reported cultural distance as one of the most influential barriers of internationalisation. Similarly, Rothaermel et al. (2006) identified strong connections between cultural dimension and internationalisation.

Mayrhofer (2004) also recognised the influence of cultural distance on the internationalisation of firms. In contrast, Descotes et al. (2007) found little to no relevance of cultural distance with internationalisation. Similarly, Ojala and Tyrväinen (2007) did not get support that cultural distance is the prevailing factor for internationalisation. Therefore, the significance of social and cultural barriers to the internationalisation of firms is contradictory and this chapter decided to carry on an empirical investigation from Nigeria's rural SMEs' point of view. Unfortunately, there is no study, so far, on the effect of social and cultural barriers on the internationalisation of rural business marketing. This chapter will fill this gap of knowledge. On the basis of extant literature review, this study has identified four factors: Different languages, different social approaches, high rate of illiteracy and expertise/skill shortage as the key social and cultural barriers to internationalisation of rural business marketing.

Technological Barriers

Technology is the use of methodological applications (such as tools, machines, crafts, instruments) to achieve results. The process of using technology starts with a need, followed by skill and ends up with the outcomes. In the current competitive environment, technological capacity and innovation are considered as one of the key driving forces for both the country and business (Ojala, 2009). Technology can influence almost every aspect of business including selling, buying, marketing, communicating, producing, distributing or even financing. In the case of international business, technological level of the country and the organisation have a more important role. For example, better communication systems or developed machines to maintain international standards. Based on the technological level, advanced technology may work as the driver of internationalisation for SMEs, or a lack of technological advantages may act as a barrier (Hessels and Parker, 2013). It has also been claimed that some business organisations choose internationalisation to use the developed technology and R&D facilities of their foreign partners (Zahra, 2005; Zahra and George,

2002). Therefore, it is very much important to identify the effects of the technological level from any specific country's point of view.

Ojala (2009) found strong connections between technological advancements and survival in the international market. Further, the positive effects of technological innovations towards internationalisation are identified in some studies, such as Yiu et al. (2007) and Zahra and George (2002). Some other studies found positive relations between technological advancements and the rate of internationalisation, such as Zhou et al. (2007) and Yamakama et al. (2008). Again, Wright and Etemad (2001) found positive impacts of technological innovations on the international performance of SMEs. Similarly, Worthington and Patton (2005) stated technological innovations as the key drivers of internationalisation. Again, advanced information and communication technology is a driver for SMEs in developed countries, and underdeveloped ICT might be the barrier for developing countries.

Conceptual Model and Hypothesis Development

Based on the extant literature on the barriers of internationalisation of rural business marketing in Nigeria, this chapter suggests that there are six types of barriers to internationalisation of rural business marketing in Nigeria. These are Governance and Political; Legal and Regulatory; Physical and Geographical; Economic and Financial; Social and Cultural; Technological barriers. It is clear from the review of literature in this chapter that governance and political barriers comprise political instability, corruption, the capability of local politicians and support from the government and coordination of rural institutions. Second, legal and regulatory barriers consist of custom regulations and standards, legal and compliance procedures, protectionist policies and inadequate legal support. Third, physical and geographical barriers include quality of rural infrastructure, geographical isolation, remoteness, not being familiar with the use of the internet and e-commerce, and a high rate of poverty. Fourth, economic and financial barriers consist of lack of finance, fierce competition, on-preferential custom duty and foreign exchange risk. Fifth, social and cultural encompasses different languages, different social approaches, high rate of illiteracy and expertise/skill shortage. Lastly, technological barriers include technological and digital facilities, electricity and power supply, mobile signal, and underdeveloped ICT and warehouse facilities.

Six hypotheses are formed based on the factors identified in the literature of internationalisation of SMEs and rural business. Barriers of internationalisation of rural business marketing in Nigeria are classified into 6 major categories. Out of the 6 hypothesis, 4 factors are related to the governance and political barriers and sub-categorised as (H1a, H1b, H1c and H1d), four factors are related to the legal and regulatory barriers and sub-categorised as (H2a, H2b, H3c and H4d), 4 factors are related to the physical and geographical barriers and sub-categorised as (H3a, H3b, H3c and H3d), 4 factors are related to the economic and financial barriers and sub-categorised as (H4a, H4b, H4c and H4d), four factors are related to the social and cultural barriers and categorised as (H5a, H5b, H5c, and H5d), and finally, four factors are related to the technological barriers and sub-categorised as (H6a, H6b, H6c and H6d). The subsequent section of the chapter is designed to highlight these hypotheses.

H1a: As a Governance and Political barrier, political instability will be positively related to Internationalisation of Rural Business Marketing
H1b: As a Governance and Political barrier, corruption will be positively related to Internationalisation of Rural Business Marketing

Table 4.1 Hypothesis on the internationalisation of rural business marketing

No	Hypothesis
H1a	As a Governance and Political barrier, political instability will be positively related to Internationalisation of Rural Business Marketing
H1b	As a Governance and Political barrier, corruption will be positively related to Internationalisation of Rural Business Marketing
H1c	As a Governance and Political barrier, ineffective capability of local politicians and support from government will be positively related to Internationalisation of Rural Business Marketing
H1d	As a Governance and Political barrier, ineffective coordination of rural institutions will be positively related to Internationalisation of Rural Business Marketing
H2a	As a Legal and Regulatory barrier, harsh custom regulations and standards will be positively related to Internationalisation of Rural Business Marketing.
H2b	As a Legal and Regulatory barrier, strict legal and compliance procedures will be positively related to Internationalisation of Rural Business Marketing.
H2c	As a Legal and Regulatory barrier, protectionist regulations will be positively related to Internationalisation of Rural Business Marketing.
H2d	As a Legal and Regulatory barrier, inadequate legal support will be positively related to Internationalisation of Rural Business Marketing.
H3a	As Physical and Geographical barrier, lack of rural infrastructure will be positively related to Internationalisation of Rural Business Marketing.
H3b	As Physical and Geographical barrier, geographical isolation and remoteness will be positively related to Internationalisation of Rural Business Marketing
H3c	As Physical and Geographical barrier, lack of internet and e-commerce will be positively related to Internationalisation of Rural Business Marketing
H3d	As Physical and Geographical barrier, rural poverty will be positively related to Internationalisation of Rural Business Marketing
H4a	As Economic and Financial barrier, lack of finance will be positively related to Internationalisation of Rural Business Marketing
H4b	As Economic and Financial barrier, fierce competition will be positively related to Internationalisation of Rural Business Marketing
H4c	As Economic and Financial barrier, non-preferential custom duty will be positively related to Internationalisation of Rural Business Marketing
H4d	As Economic and Financial barrier, foreign exchange risk will be positively related to Internationalisation of Rural Business Marketing
H5a	As Social and Cultural barrier, language differences will be positively related to Internationalisation of Rural Business Marketing

(Continued)

Table 4.1 (Continued) **Hypothesis on the internationalisation of rural business marketing**

No	Hypothesis
H5b	As Social and Cultural barrier, different social approaches will be positively related to Internationalisation of Rural Business Marketing
H5c	As Social and Cultural barrier, shortage of skilled labour will be positively related to Internationalisation of Rural Business Marketing
H5d	As Social and Cultural barrier, illiteracy will be positively related to Internationalisation of Rural Business Marketing
H6a	As Technological and Environmental barrier, underdeveloped ICT will be positively related to Internationalisation of Rural Business Marketing
H6b	As Technological and Environmental barrier, lack of electricity will be positively related to Internationalisation of Rural Business Marketing
H6c	As Technological and Environmental barrier, infrequent phone signal and coverage will be positively related to Internationalisation of Rural Business Marketing
H6d	As Technological and Environmental barrier, poor warehouse facilities will be positively related to Internationalisation of Rural Business Marketing

H1c: As a Governance and Political barrier, ineffective capability of local politicians and support from government will be positively related to Internationalisation of Rural Business Marketing

H1d: As a Governance and Political barrier, ineffective coordination of rural institutions will be positively related to Internationalisation of Rural Business Marketing

H2a: As a Legal and Regulatory barrier, harsh custom regulations and standards will be positively related to Internationalisation of Rural Business Marketing.

H2b: As a Legal and Regulatory barrier, strict legal and compliance procedures will be positively related to Internationalisation of Rural Business Marketing

H2c: As a Legal and Regulatory barrier, protectionist regulations will be positively related to Internationalisation of Rural Business Marketing

H2d: As a Legal and Regulatory barrier, inadequate legal support will be positively related to Internationalisation of Rural Business Marketing

H3a: As Physical and Geographical barrier, lack of rural infrastructure will be positively related to Internationalisation of Rural Business Marketing

H3b: As Physical and Geographical barrier, geographical isolation and remoteness will be positively related to Internationalisation of Rural Business Marketing

H3c: As Physical and Geographical barrier, lack of internet and e-commerce will be positively related to Internationalisation of Rural Business Marketing

H3d: As Physical and Geographical barrier, rural poverty will be positively related to Internationalisation of Rural Business Marketing

H4a: As Economic and Financial barrier, lack of finance will be positively related to Internationalisation of Rural Business Marketing

H4b: As Economic and Financial barrier, fierce competition will be positively related to Internationalisation of Rural Business Marketing

H4c: As Economic and Financial barrier, non-preferential custom duty will be positively related to Internationalisation of Rural Business Marketing

H4d: As Economic and Financial barrier, foreign exchange risk will be positively related to Internationalisation of Rural Business Marketing

H5a: As Social and Cultural barrier, language differences will be positively related to Internationalisation of Rural Business Marketing

H5b: As Social and Cultural barrier, different social approaches will be positively related to Internationalisation of Rural Business Marketing

H5c: As Social and Cultural barrier, shortage of skilled labour will be positively related to Internationalisation of Rural Business Marketing

H5d: As Social and Cultural barrier, illiteracy will be positively related to Internationalisation of Rural Business Marketing

H6a: As Technological and Environmental barrier, underdeveloped ICT will be positively related to Internationalisation of Rural Business Marketing

H6b: As Technological and Environmental barrier, lack of electricity will be positively related to Internationalisation of Rural Business Marketing

H6c: As Technological and Environmental barrier, infrequent phone signal and coverage will be positively related to Internationalisation of Rural Business Marketing

H6d: As Technological and Environmental barrier, poor warehouse facilities will be positively related to Internationalisation of Rural Business Marketing

Research Methodology

This chapter made use of primary data gathered during the research process from 6 geo-political zones of Nigeria – southwest, south-south, south-east, north-west, north-central and north-east of Nigeria from January 2018 to August 2018. As regards the data gathering, 300 questionnaires were distributed in each geo-political region following the cluster sampling technique. From each geo-political region, states were selected, and from each state, local governments were selected and from each local government council, international rural SMEs were selected from villages and remote villages. To ensure equal opportunity to be selected, a systematic random sampling technique was employed. The population respondents for the survey were defined as rural SMEs doing international business. Out of the 1800 questionnaires, 313 were responded to and returned. Among the 313 returned questionnaires, 9 were unstable as a result of excessive missing data in them. Consequently, 304 questionnaires were imputed and analysed. The data were collected from a diverse cross-sectional population. Out of 304 respondents, 65.5% are male and 35.5% were female. From the business sector point of view, 19.5% are from the agricultural and agro-foods sector, 25.5% are from manufacturing, 01.5% are from solid minerals, 09.5% from wood and furniture, 15% from wholesale and retail, 10% from tourism, 4.5% are from textile and garments and 14.5% from professional, business and financial services. With regard to geo-political zones, 34.5% from south-west, 15.5% from south, 15.5% from south-east, 14.5% from north-east, 10% from north-west and 10% from north-central. From the business type point of view, 30.50% sole trader, 14.50% partnership, 20.80% family business and 34.20% are co-operatives.

Items of the questionnaires were identified from systematic reviews and interview questions from rural SMEs owners and managers in the six geo-political zones in Nigeria. All these items of the questionnaires were measured using a 5-point Likert scale. Before the final data collected, a pre-test was carried out among 20 samples and 5 academics to ensure the appropriateness of wording, contents, scales, sequence and format. Very minor amendments were made based on pre-test. To achieve the research objectives, PLS-based structural models are developed and validated on the barriers, drivers and the performance of internationalisation from Nigeria's rural SMEs' viewpoint.

Findings and Results

Result findings from the research study related to the barriers of Internationalisation of Rural Business Marketing of rural SMEs are presented in three stages – evaluation of the model measurements, evaluation of the model and finally the relationship in the model tested. These three steps of presenting the results ensure the validity and reliability of the latent variables prior to drawing the conclusion on hypothesised relationships (Hulland, 1999; Bollen and Lennox, 1991; Fornell & Larcker, 1981).

Evaluation of the Measurement Model

This research study has employed PLS Graph 3.0 (Chin, 2010) to investigate the barriers of Internationalisation of Rural Business Marketing for Nigeria's rural SMEs by employing the hierarchical model with PLS path modelling with a path weighting scheme for the inside approximation (Akter et al., 2010; Wetzels et al., 2009; Chin, 2010). Following the path weighting scheme, this study used nonparametric bootstrapping (Akter et al., 2010; Wetzels et al., 2009; Chin, 2010) where the standard error of the estimates is obtained by using 500 replications. Following the suggestion made by Akter et al. (2010); Barney (1991); Barney (2001); Bollen & Lennox (1991); Clark & Pugh (2001); Chetty & Blankenburg Holm (2000); Chetty & Campbell-Hunt (2003); Chin & Gopal (1995); Crick et al. (2011) danieland Word (1985), this study has used the approach of repeated indicators to estimate the higher-order latent variables. Therefore, the second-order factor (Barriers of Internationalisation of Nigeria's Rural Business Marketing) is directly measured by the indicators (manifest variables) of the first-order factors (Governance, Legal, Physical-geographical, economic, social and technological).

Following models and theories postulated by Bollen & Lennox (1991), Akter et al. (2010), Chin (2010) and Wetzels et al. (2009), a confirmatory factor analysis (CFA) is conducted to test the model and analyse the reliability and validity. The result shows that the individual item loading is higher than 0.70, which is also significant at 0.01. Further, the reliability of the scale is assessed through the Composite Reliability (CR) and Average Variance Extracted (AVE) as recommended by Chin (2010) and Fornell and Larcker (1981). The result finds that CR for governance and political, legal and regulatory, physical and geography, economic and financial, social and cultural, and technological barriers are all well above the threshold point of 0.70 (Hulland, 1999), pato which indicates the scale consistency for each item. On the other hand, AVE for governance and political, legal and regulatory, physical and geography, economic and financial, social and cultural, and technological barriers in the result is also higher than the modest threshold of 0.50 (Fornell & Larcker, 1981). Again, this indicates that each construct captures adequate variance from its items and all the constructs are conceptually distinct. Therefore, the convergent validity of all the scales is ensured. Finally, the result of the square root of AVE ensures discriminant validity. The square root value of AVE confirms that they are higher than the corresponding correlation coefficients in the correlation matrix (Chin, 2010; Hessels & Parker (2013); Fornell and Bookstein, 1982; Hulland, 1999). Therefore, it can be concluded that all the empirical results related to the analysis of the measurement model are satisfactory concerning adequate reliability, convergent validity and discriminant validity.

Assessment of Higher-Order Model

A hierarchical construct model is developed to show the barriers of internationalisation for Internationalisation of Rural Business Marketing in Nigeria. The second-order constructs (overall barriers) are reflected in the first-order constructs and the degree of explained variances are Economic and Financial (86%), Technological (84%), Governance and Political (81%), Physical and Geographical (78%), Legal and Regulatory (78%), Social and Cultural (77%). The result shows that the path coefficients from overall barriers of internationalisation to second order (Governance-political, Economic, Social-cultural, Physical and Geographical, Legal and Regulatory, and Technological) are significant at $P < 0.01$. Further, the validity of the higher-order reflective model is confirmed by the CR and AVE values. CR and AVE for the first-order constructs (Political, economic, Legal, Physical-geographical social, and technological) are higher than threshold values of 0.70 and 0.50, respectively.

Analysis of Structural Model and Results of Hypotheses Testing

This chapter has estimated the relationship between the overall barriers and their sub-dimensions, for example, governance/political, economic, legal-regulatory, social and technological barriers with an objective to measure the structural validity of the model. The respective standardised beta finds for Gov-political, legal-regulatory, physical and geography, economic, social, technological barriers are 0.808, 0.776, 0.778, 0.863, 0.767, 0.839, respectively each; this result refers to a strong association between those variables. Further, all these path coefficients are significant at $P < 0.01$. Therefore, overall findings support the hypotheses.

Discussion

The major contribution of this chapter is to extend the existing knowledge by explaining the Barriers of Internationalisation of Nigeria's Rural Business Marketing through a hierarchical reflective model and investigating its impact on rural small and medium enterprises. Using the reflective hierarchical model and empirical results, this study proposed that 6 types of barriers, such as governance and political, legal and regulatory, physical and geographical, economic and financial, social and cultural, and technological and infrastructural affect the Internationalisation of Rural Business Marketing in Nigeria. In effect, each of these components reflects a unique principle, while together they offer a strong and dynamic fundamental for the hierarchical model of barriers to the internationalisation of rural SMEs in Nigeria. Although each of these categories (Governance and political, Legal and Regulation, Physical and Geographical, Economic and Cultural, Social and Cultural and Technological) has strong significance towards the overall barriers of internationalisation for rural business marketing, economic and financial barriers appear to be most influential with the degree of explained variances of 86%. There are four factors under the economic and financial dimensions. These are lack of finance, fierce competition, non-preferential custom and foreign exchange risk. The association between these items and the economic and financial barriers of Internationalisation of Rural Business Marketing in Nigeria are discussed later.

The associations between lack of finance and economic and financial barriers ($\beta = 0.816$) were significant at $P < 0.001$. Thus, lack of finance was confirmed as a significant factor in the context of the economic and financial barriers of internationalisation for the rural SMEs in Nigeria. By the empirical support, this study, therefore, extends the views of Dubois (2016), Ibeh et al. (2012) and Rahman et al. (2017). Similarly, the association between fierce competition and economic (and financial) barriers (β = 0.853) was significant at $P < 0.001$. Thus, fierce competition complexity was confirmed as a significant factor in the context of the economic and financial barriers of internationalisation for the rural SMEs in Nigeria. With the empirical support, this study then extends the views of Adeleye and Esposito (2018), Amankwah-Amoah (2018), Ngwu et al. (2015), Ibeh et al. (2012), Dubois (2016) and Kolawole and Ajila (2015). Again, the association between non-preferential custom duties and economic (and financial) barriers (β = 0.779) was significant at $P < 0.001$. Thus, non-preferential custom duty was confirmed as a significant factor in the context of the economic and financial barriers of internationalisation for rural SMEs in Nigeria. Using empirical support, this study thus extends the observations of Boso et al. (2017); Ibeh et al. (2012),Gaur & Kumar (2010); Ramamurti (2008); Schmidt & Hansen (2017); Shin et al. (2008); Hulten and Bonnedahl (2005). Again, the association between foreign exchange risk and economic (and financial) barriers (β = 0.792) was significant at $P < 0.001$. Thus, foreign exchange risk was confirmed as a significant factor in the context of the economic and financial barriers of internationalisation for the rural SMEs in Nigeria. By the empirical support, this study, hence, extends the interpretations of Rahman et al. (2017), Cavusgil and Knight (2009).

The empirical finding confirmed the role of technology and environmental barriers as a significant dimension of overall barriers faced by SMEs with a degree of explained variances of 84%. Like the economic and financial barriers, technology and environmental barriers are also based on four factors, these are underdeveloped ICT, lack of electricity, infrequent phone signal and coverage, and lack of warehouse facilities. The relationship between these items and the technological (and environmental) barriers of internationalisation for rural SMEs in Nigeria are discussed below. The association between underdeveloped ICT and technological (and infrastructural) barriers (β = 0. 860) was significant at $P < 0.001$. Thus, underdeveloped ICT was confirmed as a significant factor in the context of the technological and infrastructural barriers of internationalisation for the rural SMEs in Nigeria. By the empirical support, this study, therefore, extends the views of Rutihinda (2008), Seyoum (2007), and Rahman et al. (2013). Similarly, the association between lack of electricity and technological (and infrastructural) barriers (β = 0.898). Thus, lack of electricity was confirmed as a significant factor in the context of the technology and environmental barriers of internationalisation for the rural SMEs in Nigeria. With empirical support, this study then extends the opinions of the views of Vissak (2003), Wright and Etemad (2001). Also, the association between infrequent phone signal and technology (and environmental) barriers (β = 0.787) was significant at $P < 0.001$. Thus, infrequent phone signal and coverage were confirmed as significant factors in the context of the technology and environmental barriers of internationalisation for the rural SMEs in Nigeria. Through the empirical support, this chapter, therefore, extends the opinions of Audretsch (2007) and Glückler (2006). In this vein, the association between poor warehouse facilities and technological (and infrastructural) barriers (β = 0.941) was significant at $P < 0.001$. Thus, poor warehouse facility was confirmed as a significant factor in the context of the technological and infrastructural barriers of internationalisation for the rural SMEs in Nigeria. With empirical support, this study then extends the opinions of Udin et al. (2019) and Van (2003).

The empirical findings of the study confirm the role of governance and political barriers as a dimension of overall barriers faced by rural SMEs with a degree of explained variance of 81%. Like technological and (environmental) barriers, they are also based on four factors: political instability, corruption, capability of local politicians and coordination of rural institutions. The relationship between political instability and governance (and political) barriers (β = 0.960) was significant at $P < 0.001$. Thus, political instability was confirmed as a significant factor in the context of the governance and political barriers of internationalisation for the rural SMEs in Nigeria. By the empirical support, this study, therefore, extends the views of, Dubois (2016) ysaand Chin (2010). Also, the relationship between corruption and governance (and political) barriers (β = 0.969) was significant at $P < 0.001$. Thus, corruption was confirmed as a significant factor in the context of the governance and political barriers of internationalisation for the rural SMEs in Nigeria. By the empirical support, this study hence extends the interpretations of Okpara and Kabongo (2010); Rahman et al. (2018). In addition, the association between the capability of local politicians and governance (and political) barriers (β = 0.896) was significant at $P < 0.001$. Thus, the capability of local politicians was confirmed as a significant factor in the context of the governance and political barriers of internationalisation of rural business marketing in Nigeria. By the empirical support, this study hence extends the interpretations of Okpara and Kabongo (2010), Hulten and Bonnedahl (2005), Barker and Barkema & Vermeulen (1997) Rahman. Also, the association between the coordination of rural institutions and governance and political barriers (β = 0.886) was significant at $P < 0.001$. Thus, coordination of rural institutions was confirmed as a significant factor in the context of the governance and political barriers of internationalisation of rural business marketing in Nigeria. By the empirical support, this study hence extends the interpretations of Okpara and Kabongo (2010), Sarder and Hossain (2000), Barlett (2001), Sarder (2000), Yaprak (1985), Barkema & Vermeulen (1997), Bohata and Mladek (1999) and Rahman et al. (1979). Similarly, there are equally four factors under the physical and geographical dimensions. These are the quality of rural infrastructure, geographical isolation and remoteness, low use of the internet and e-commerce, and high rate of poverty. There is an association between these items and the physical and geographical barriers of internationalisation of rural business marketing.

Summary of Findings

One of the key objectives of this chapter is to identify the potential barriers to the internationalisation of rural business marketing. To fulfil this objective, this chapter has developed and validated a barriers model that is able to explain the major barriers faced by Nigeria's rural SMEs marketing to penetrate the international market. This chapter also contributes to extending our knowledge of the barriers to rural SMEs from Nigeria's perspective by categorising the barriers into six dimensions (governance, legal, physical-geography, economic, social, and technological) with 24 indicators. It has effectively enclosed barriers of internationalisation for rural SMEs in a second-order reflective model where all six dimensions reflect overall barriers of internationalisation of rural SMEs. Hence, it contributes to the theoretical findings by Dubious (2016), Söderbom & Teal (2003); Sousa Carlos & Bradley (2005); Studer et al. (2006); Teal (1999); Tesfom & Lutz (2008); Uddin & Boateng (2014); Wengel & Rodiriguez (2006); Wold (1985); Wold (1966); World Bank (2017a); World Bank (2017b); Ysa (2007) Young (2010), Pangarka (2008), Sokfa and Zimmermann (2008), Odunukan et al. (2016); Odunukan et al. (2018) and OECD (2006). In fact, this study extends all these conceptualisations as the model of this study is also competent to provide the ranking of these barriers. In general, economic and financial barriers seem to be the most influential barriers for the internationalisation of Nigeria's rural SMEs as it explains 86% of the overall variance. It is followed by technological barriers (84%), Governance and Political barriers (81%), Physical and geographical barriers (78%), Legal and regulatory barriers (78%), and social and cultural barriers (77%), respectively. Though the ranking has been done based on the explanation power of individual constructs, the magnitude of the difference is relatively very small. Therefore, it can be recommended that all these constructs should be given equal attention.

Another objective of this study was to demonstrate the complex relationship among the barriers of internationalisation for rural SMEs empirically through PLS path modelling. To support this objective, a second-order reflective hierarchical model is developed using the data collected from rural SMEs in Nigeria. This model should be better to explain the complex relationship as suggested by Chin (2010); Ohlin (1933); Okpara & Koumbiadis (2011); Fornell and Bookstein (1982). Following the suggestion made by Wold (1965), this study used repeated indicators from the first-order model to the second-order model. All results confirmed the validity of the measurement model and structural model. Therefore, it has successfully shifted individual barriers of internationalisation to overall barriers of internationalisation as stated by Wold (1985, p. 589), "PLS comes to the fore in larger models, when the importance shifts from individual variables and parameters to packages of variables and aggregate parameters".

The main objective of this chapter was to identify the key barriers to internationalisation of rural business marketing in Nigeria. To address this objective, a model on the barriers to internationalisation has been developed and validated. This has surely extended our knowledge, particularly from Nigeria's rural SMEs and their barriers to internationalisation context. However, it is believed that the findings of this study will assist policymakers and owners of rural SMEs to know their priority to back the internationalisation of rural SMEs. Through the PLS path model, this study clearly rated the barriers faced by rural SMEs to enter the international market. It shows that Economic/Financial, Technology barriers and Governance/Political barriers are more dominating over Physical/Geography, Legal/Regulatory and Socio-cultural barriers in developing countries' rural areas. Therefore, support services given by the government and non-government organisations in developing countries to assist the growth of rural SMEs should prioritise the economic and financial issues followed by technology, politics and governance. Subsequent priorities should be given to physical-geographical issues, followed by legal and regulatory issues, and lastly social and economic-related issues.

Limitations and Future Research Directions

This chapter has some limitations that may be considered for future research. First, the model developed in this study is based on rural SMEs, which may not be generalised to general SMEs. Also, the model was developed in a specific context (developing country) which may not be generalised in the other context (developed country). Thirdly, this study used cross-sectional data which may have some common method variance (Straub et al., 2004). By using longitudinal analysis, future research can get better measurement reliability. Finally, the comparative analysis between the hierarchical models of component-based PLS and co-variance-based SEM could be done under different research circumstances, as stated by Akter et al. (2010, p. 14), "number of manifest variables, sample size per latent variables, distributional properties of the manifest variables". These variations may be able to develop a model comparing both formative and reflective approaches of SEM.

Chapter Summary

This chapter has identified the key barriers to Internationalisation of Rural Business Marketing faced by Nigeria's rural SMEs. It has successfully framed the barriers to internationalisation for Nigeria's rural SMEs as a second-order hierarchical model, indicating all six dimensions of barriers significantly reflect on the overall barriers. All six hypotheses are supported. There is no study, so far, on the barriers to internationalisation of rural business marketing faced by rural SMEs from Nigeria's perspective. The research findings of this chapter will contribute to filling up this gap. Another key contribution of this chapter is the development of a hierarchical reflective model using PLS to assess the barriers to internationalisation faced by Nigeria's rural SMEs.

References

Abdullateef, R., Abubakar, Y., Danjuma, M. M., Abdul-Rasheed, S., & Adeyemi, R. A. (2017). Rural areas: The real home of the Nigerian economy. *International Journal of Social Sciences and Educational Studies, 4*(2), 251–263.

Adebayo, T. S., Alheety, S. N. Y., & Yusoff, W. S. W. (2019). Factors affecting SMEs' internationalization process in the Southwest Nigeria. *International Journal of Entrepreneurship and Management Practices, 2*(5), 44–62.

Adeleye, I., & Boso, N. (2016). Africa-to-Africa internationalization: Future trends and research avenues. In I. Adeleye, L. White, & N. Boso (Eds.), *Africa-to-Africa internationalization: Key issues and outcomes* (pp. 35–65). Basingstoke and New York: Palgrave Macmillan.

Adeleye, I., & Esposito, M. (2018). *Africa's competitiveness in the global economy*. Basingstoke and New York: Palgrave Macmillan.

Adeleye, I., White, L., Ibeh, K., & Kinoti, A. (2015). The changing dynamics of international business in Africa: Emerging trends and key issues. In I. Adeleye, K. Ibeh, A. Kinoti, & L. White (Eds.), *The changing dynamics of international business in Africa* (pp. 1–16). Basingstoke and New York: Palgrave Macmillan.

Adisa, T. A., Abdulraheem, I., & Mordi, C. (2014). The characteristics and challenges of small businesses in Africa: An exploratory study of Nigerian small business owners. *Economic Insights – Trends and Challenges, 66*(4), 1–14.

Adomako, S. (2017). CEOs' regulatory foci and firm-level innovativeness in competitive environments. *Journal of Business and Industrial Marketing, 32*(4), 235–244.

Adomako, S., Danso, A., Boso, N., & Narteh, B. (2018). Entrepreneurial alertness and new venture performance: Facilitating roles of networking capability. *International Small Business Journal, 36* (5).453-472.

Akter, M. S., Rajasekera, J., & Rahman, M. M. (2010). Serving the poor by marketing information: Developing a village phone model for Bangladesh. *International Journal of Economics and Business Research, 2*(3/4), 288–309.

Amankwah-Amoah, J. (2018). Why are so many African companies uncompetitive on the global stage? Insights from the global airline industry. In I. Adeleye & M. Esposito (Eds.), *Africa's competitiveness in the global economy* (pp. 195–216). Basingstoke and New York: Palgrave Macmillan.

Amankwah-Amoah, J., Danso, A., & Adomako, S. (2018). Entrepreneurial orientation, environmental sustainability and new venture performance: Does stakeholder integration matter? *Business Strategy and the Environment, 49*(20), 79–87.

Aspelund, A., & Moen, O. (2005). Small international firms: Typology, performance and implications. *Management International Review, 5*(2), 37–57.

Barkema, H. G., & Vermeulen, F. (1997). What differences in the cultural backgrounds of partners are detrimental for international joint ventures? *Journal of International Business Studies, 28,* (4), 845–864.

Barnelbeh, K., Wilson, J., & Chizema, A. (2012). The internationalization of African firms 1995–2011: Review and implications. *Thunderbird International Business Review, 54*(4), 411–427.

Barney, J. (1991). Firm resources and sustained competitive advantage. *Journal of Management, 17*(1), 99–120.

Barney, J. (2001). Resource-based theories of competitive advantage: A ten-year retrospective on the resource-based view. *Journal of Management, 27*(6), 643–650.

Baskerville, R. F. (2003, February 1). Hofstede never studied culture. *Accounting, Organizations and Society, 28*(1), 1–14.

Beckerman, W. (1956). Distance and the pattern of inter-European trade. *Review of Economics and Statistics, 38*(1), 31–40.

Bollen, K., & Lennox, R. (1991). Conventional wisdom on measurement: A structural equation perspective. *Psychological Bulletin, 110*(2), 305–314.

Bose, T. K. (2016). Critical success factors of SME internationalization. *Journal of Small Business Strategy, 26*(2), 87–109.

Boso, N., Danso, A., Leonidou, C., Uddin, M., Adeola, O., & Hultman, M. (2017). Does financial resource slack drive sustainability expenditure in developing economy small and medium-sized enterprises? *Journal of Business Research, 80*, 247–256.

Bosworth, G., & Venhorst, V. (2018). Economic linkages between urban and rural regions: What's in it for the rural? *Regional Studies, 52(8), 1075-2085*

Cavusgil, S. T., & Knight, G. (2009). *Born global firms.* New York: Business Expert Press.

Clark, T., & Pugh, D. S. (2001). Foreign country priorities in the internationalization process: A measure and an exploratory test on British firms. *International Business Review, 10*(3), 285–303.

Chetty, S., & Blankenburg Holm, D. (2000). Internationalisation of small to medium-sized manufacturing firms: A network approach. *International Business Review, 9*(1), 77–93.

Chetty, S., & Campbell-Hunt, C. (2003). Paths to internationalisation among small-to medium-sized firms: A global versus regional approach. *European Journal of Marketing, 37*(5/6), 796–820.

Chin, W. W. (2010). How to write up and report PLS analyses. In V. Esposito Vinzi, W. W. Chin, J. Henseler, & H. Wang (Eds.), *Handbook of partial least squares: Concepts, methods and application* (pp. 645–689). Germany: Springer.

Chin, W. W., & Gopal, A. (1995). Adoption intention in GSS: Importance of beliefs. *Data Base for Advances in Information Systems, 26*(2/3), 42–64.

Collinson, S., & Houlden, J. (2005). Decision-making and market orientation in the internationalization process of small and medium-sized enterprises. *Management International Review, 20*(1), 413–436.

Crick, D., Kaganda, G. E., & Matlay, H. (2011). A study into the international competitiveness of low and high intensity Tanzanian exporting SMEs. *Journal of Small Business and Enterprise Development, 18*(3), 594–607.

Daniel, W. D. (2014). The system worked: Global economic governance during the great recession. *World Politics, 1*, 123–164.

Danso, A., & Adomako, S. (2014). The financing behaviour of firms and financial crisis. *Managerial Finance, 40*(12), 1159–1174.

Daunton, M. (2011). The British industrial revolution in global perspective. *Victorian Studies, 53*(4), 773–775.

Descotes, R. M., Walliser, B., & Guo, X. (2007). Capturing the relevant institutional profile for exporting SMEs: Empirical evidence from France and Romania, International. *Management Review, 3*(3), 16–26.

Hulland, J. (1999). Use of partial least squares (PLS) in strategic management research: A review of four recent studies. *Strategic Management Journal, 20*(2), 195–204.

Dubois, A. (2016). Transnationalising entrepreneurship in a peripheral region – The translocal embeddedness paradigm. *Journal of Rural Studies, 100*(46), 1–11.

Etuk, R. U., Etuk, G. R., & Michael, B. (2014). Small and medium scale enterprises (SMEs) and Nigeria's economic development. *Mediterranean Journal of Social Sciences, 5*(7), 656–662.

Evans, J., & Mavondo, F. T. (2002). Psychic distance and organizational performance: An empirical examination of international retailing operations. *Journal of International Business Studies, 35*(3), 515–532.

Faloye, O. D. (2015). The key determinants of innovation in small and medium scale enterprises in Southwestern Nigeria. *European Scientific Journal, 11*(13), 12–25.

Fink, K., & Ploder, C. (2009). Balanced system for knowledge process management in SMEs. *Journal of Enterprise Information Management, 22*(1/2), 36–50.

Fornell, C., & Bookstein, F. L. (1982). Two structural equations models: LISREL and PLS applied to consumer exit-voice theory. *Journal of Marketing Research, 19*(4), 440–452.

Gaur, A., & Kumar, V. (2010). *The past, present and future of international business & management.* Bingley-UK, Emerald Group Publishing Limited

Glückler, J. (2006). A relational assessment of international market entry in management consulting. *Journal of Economic Geography, 6*(3), 369–393.

Goffee, R., & Scase, R. (1995). *Corporate realities.* London: Routledge.

Graham, J., Amos, B., & Plumptre, T. (2003). *Governance principles for protected areas in the 21st century: A discussion paper.* Ottawa: Institute of Governance/Parks Canada/Canadian International Development Agency. South Africa.

Hessels, J., & Parker, S. C. (2013). Constraints, internationalization and growth: A cross country analysis of European SMEs. *Journal of World Business, 48*(1), 137–148.

Hofstede, G. (1980). *Culture's consequences: International differences in work-related values.* Beverly Hills, CA: Sage.

Hulten, S., & Bonnedahl, K. J. (2005). Barriers to internationalisation in the Swedish grocery trade. *Paper to be presented at the 7th Annual SNEE European integration conference,* Grand Hôtel, Mölle, Sweden, May 24–27, 2005.

Ibeh, K. I. N., Wilson, J., & Chizema, A. (2012). The internationalization of African firms 1995–2011: Review and implications. *Thunderbird International Business Review, 54*(4), 411–427.

JohaAjai, O. (2015). Failure of Africa-to-Africa internationalization: Key factors and lessons. In I. Adeleye, K. Ibeh, A. Kinoti, & L. White (Eds.), *The changing dynamics of international business in Africa* (pp. 148–168). Basingstoke and New York: Palgrave Macmillan.

Johanson, J., & Vahlne, J. (1977). The internationalization process of the firm: A model of knowledge development and increasing foreign market commitments. *Journal of International Business Studies, 8*(1), 23–32.

Johanson, J., & Vahlne, J.-E. (2009). The Uppsala internationalization process model revisited: From liability of foreignness to liability of outsidership. *Journal of International Business Studies, 40*(9), 1411–1431.

Johanson, J., & Wiedersheim-Paul, F. (1975). The internationalization of the firm—Four Swedish cases 1. *Journal of Management Studies, 12*(3), 305–323.

Kneller, R., & Pisu, M. (2006). The role of experience in export market entry: Evidence for UK firms (2006). University of Nottingham Research Paper No. 2006/48, Available at SSRN. Retrieved from https://ssrn.com/abstract=951982 or http://dx.doi.org/10.2139/ssrn.951982

Kolawole, O. D., & Ajila, K. (2015). Driving local community transformation through participatory rural entrepreneurship development. *World Journal of Entrepreneurship, Management and Sustainable Development, 11*(2), 131–139.

kunduYamakawa, Y., Peng, M. W., & deeds, D. L. (2008). What drives new ventures to internationalize from emerging to developed economies? *Entrepreneurship Theory and Practice, 32*(1), 59–82.

Lee, S. Y. (2008). Drivers for the participation of small and medium-sized suppliers in green supply chain initiatives. *Supply Chain Management: An International Journal, 13*(3), 185–198.

Leonidou, L. C. (2000). Barriers to export management: An organizational and internationalization analysis. *Journal of International Management, 6*(2), 1–28.

Leonidou, L. C. (2004). An analysis of the barriers hindering small business export development. *Journal of Small Business Management, 42*(3), 279–302.

Mayrhofer, U. (2004). The influence of national origin and uncertainty on the choice between cooperation and merger–acquisition: An analysis of French and German firms. *International Business Review, 13*(1), 83–99.

Mendy, J., & Rahman, M. (2018). People and technology-oriented barriers to SME internationalisation: Application of the configuration model from a developing country context. In *International Conference on Technology and Humanities (IcoTECH 2018),* November 17th–18th, 2018, Penang, Malaysia.

Morgan, N. A., Kaleka, A., & Katsikeas, C. S. (2004). Antecedents of export venture performance: A theoretical model and empirical assessment. *Journal of Marketing, 68*(1), 90–108.

Ngwu, F., Adeleye, I., & Ogbechie, C. (2015). Africa-to-Africa internationalization: Rhetoric, reality and risks of intra-African regional expansion. In E. Nwankwo & K. Ibeh (Eds.), *The Routledge companion to business in Africa* (pp. 9–31). London and New York: Routledge, Taylor and Francis Ltd.

North, D. C. (1990). *Institutions, institutional change and economic performance.* Cambridge: Cambridge University Press.

Odunukan, K., Akter, M., Hack-Polay, D., Rahman, M., & Igwe, P. (2022). Internationalisation of rural small-and-medium enterprises from Nigeria: Examining social and organisational impact. *Business Strategy & Development*, 5(1), 80–93.

Odunukan, K., Bosworth, G., & Rahman, M. (2016). Developing structural models to study the internationalization of Nigeria's rural entrepreneurs. In *Academy of international business sub-Saharan Africa conference*, August 17–19, 2016, Lagos Business School, Lagos, Nigeria.

Odunukan, K., Rahman, M., Akter, M., & Haque, S. (2018). Examining economic and technology related barriers of internationalisation for SMEs: A hierarchical reflective model on an emerging economy context. In *BAM 2018*, September, 4–6, 2018, Bristol Business School, Bristol.

OECD. (2004). Accelerating pro-poor growth through support for private sector development- an analytical framework, *DAC network on poverty reduction*. OECD Publications, 2, rue André- Pascal, 75775 Paris Cedex 16. France.

OECD. (2006). Removing barriers to SME access to international markets, *Final background report of the OECD-APEC joint project*, November, 6–8. Athens, Greece.

OECD. (2008). Enhancing the role of SMEs in global value chains, *Organisation for economic cooperation and development*. OECD Publishing, Paris.

OECD. (2009). Top barriers and drivers to SME internationalisation, *Report by OECD working party on SMEs and Entrepreneurship*.

Ohlen, O. (2002). *Internationalizing in the digital economy: A pan-European study of business-to-business electronic marketplaces, FIM*. St. Gallen: University of St. Gallen.

Ohlin, B. (1933) *Interregional and international trade* (chap. 2). Cambridge: Harvard University Press.

Ojala, A. (2009). Internationalization of knowledge-intensive SMEs: The role of network relationships in the entry to a psychically distant market. *International Business Review*, 18(1), 50–59.

Ojala, A., & Tyrväinen, P. (2007). Market entry and priority of small and medium-sized enterprises in the software industry: An empirical analysis of cultural distance, geographical distance, and market size. *Journal of International Marketing*, 15(3), 123–149.

Okpara, J., & Kabongo, J. (2010). Export barriers and internationalization: Evidence from SMEs in emergent barleAfrican economy. *International Journal of Business and Globalization*, 5(2), 169–187.

Okpara, J. O., & Koumbiadis, N. J. (2011). Strategic export-orientation and internationalisation barriers: Evidence from SMEs in a developing country. *Journal of International Business and Cultural Studies*, 4, 1–10.

Okpara, O. J. (2011). Corporate governance in a developing economy: Barriers, issues, and implications for firms. *Journal of Corporate Governance*, 11(2), 184–199.

Orr, L. M., & Hauser, W. J. (2008). A re-inquiry of Hofstede's cultural dimensions: A call for the 21st century. *Marketing Management Journal*, 18(2), 1–19.

Ovadje, F. (2016). The internationalization of African firms: Effects of cultural differences on the management of Subsidiaries. *Africa Journal of Management*, 2(2), 117–137.

Pangarka, N. (2008). Internationalization and performance of small- and medium-sized enterprises. *Journal of World Business*, 43(4), 475–485.

Rahman, M., Uddin, M., & Chowdhury, A., & Shafique, S. (2017). Drivers for internationalisation of SMEs: Evidence from an emerging country. In *BAM 2017*, September 5–7, 2017, Warwick Business School, University of Warwick.

Rahman, M., Akter, M., Odunukan, K., & Haque, S. (2019). Examining economic and technology-related barriers of small- and medium-sized enterprises internationalisation: An emerging economy context. *Business Strategy and Development*

Rahman, M., Hack-Polay, D., Shafique, S., & Igwe, P. A. (2021). Dynamic capability of the firm: Analysis of the impact of internationalisation on SME performance in an emerging economy. *International Journal of Emerging Markets*, 2(1), 71–97.

Rahman, M., Lodorfos, G., & Uddin, M. (2013). The barriers of internationalization for SMEs in Bangladesh. *International Journal of Accounting and Business Management*, 1(1), 92–115.

Rahman, M., & Mendy, J. (2019). Evaluating people-related resilience and non-resilience barriers of SMEs' internationalisation: A developing country perspective. *International Journal of Organizational Analysis*, 27(2), 225–240.

Rahman, M., Uddin, M., & Lodorfos, G. (2014). Internationalisation of SMEs and firm performance: Evidences from Bangladesh. In *BAM 2014*, September, 9–11, 2014, Belfast Waferfront, Northern Ireland.

Rahman, M., Uddin, M., & Lodorfos, G. (2017). Barriers to enter in foreign markets: Evidence from SMEs in emerging market. *International Marketing Review, 34*(1), 68–86.

Rahman, M. B., Morsaline, M., & Hack-Polay, D. (2019). What is hindering change? Anticipating the barriers to the adoption of enzyme-based textile processing in a developing country. *Business Strategy and Development, 2(2), 137-147*

Ramamurti, R. (2008). What have we learned about emerging—Market MNEs? *Emerging Multinationals in Emerging Markets,* 2 (4), 399-426.

Rothaermel, F. T., Kotha, S., & Steensma, H. K. (2006). International market entry by US internet firms: an empirical analysis of country risk, national culture, and market size. *Journal of Management, 32*(1), 56–82.

Rutashobya, L., & Jaensson, J.-E. (2004). Small firms' internationalization for development in Tanzania: Exploring the network phenomenon. *International Journal of Social Economics, 31*(1/2), 159–172.

Rutihinda, C. (2008). Factors influencing the internationalization of small and medium size enterprises. *International Business & Economics Research Journal, 7*(1), 1–12.

Ruzzier, M., Hisrich, R. D., & Antoncic, B. (2006). SME internationalization research: Past present and future. *Journal of Small Business and Enterprise Development, 13*(4), 476–497.

Schmidt, A., & Hansen, M. W. (2017). Internationalization strategies of African firms. In *Internationalisation and economic growth strategies in Ghana*; A Survey of 210 Food Processing Firms from Tanzania, Kenya and Zambia. Copenhagen Business School, CBS. CBDS Working Paper No. 1, 2017.

Seyoum, B. (2007). Export performance of developing countries under the Africa growth and opportunity act: Experience from US trade with sub-Saharan Africa. *Journal of Economic Studies, 34*(6), 515–533.

Shin, D., Curtis, M., Huisingh, D., & Zwetsloot, G. I. (2008). Development of a sustainability policy model for promoting cleaner production: A knowledge integration approach. *Journal of Cleaner Production, 16*(17, November), 1823–1837.

Söderbom, M., & Teal, F. (2003). Are manufacturing exports the key to economic success in Africa? *Journal of African Economics, 12*(1), 1–29.

Sokfa, W., & Zimmermann, J. (2008). Regional economic stress as moderator of liability of foreignness. *Journal of International Management, 14*(2), 155–172.

Sousa Carlos, M. P., & Bradley, F. (2005). Global markets: Does psychic distance matter? *Journal of Strategic Marketing, 13*(1), 43–59.

Straub, D., Boudreau, M. C., & Galen, D. (2004). Validation guidelines for IS positivist research. *Communications of the Association for Information Systems, 3*(24), 380–427.

Studer, S., Welford, R., & Hills, P. (2006). Engaging Hong Kong businesses in environmental change: Drivers and barriers. *Business Strategy and the Environment, 15*(6), 416–431.

Teal, F. (1999). Why can Mauritius export manufactures and Ghana not? *World Economy, 22*(7), 981–993.

Tesfom, G., & Lutz, C. (2008). Evaluating the effectiveness of export support services in developing countries: A customer (user) perspective. *International Journal of Emerging Markets, 3*(4), 364–377.

Tikhonova, N. (2012). *Socio-cultural modernization in Russia; norms and values system shift- culture matters in Russia- and everywhere* (pp. 451–465). Lexington Books.

Uddin, M., & Boateng, A. (2014). *Cross-border mergers and acquisitions: UK dimensions. New York: Routledge.*

Uddin, M., Boateng, A., & Naraidoo, R. (2011). An analysis of the inward cross-border mergers and acquisitions in the UK: A macroeconomic perspective. *Journal of International Financial Management and Accounting, 22*(2), 91-113.

Uddin, M., Chowdhury, A., Zafar, S., Shafique, S., & Liu, J. (2019). Institutional determinants of inward FDI: Evidence from Pakistan. *International Business Review, 28*(2), 344–358.

Vissak, T. (2003). *The internationalization of foreign-owned enterprises in Estonia: An extended network perspective. (Doctoral dissertation, University of Tartu, Tartu).*

Welch, L. S., & Luostarinen, R. (1988). Internationalization: Evolution of a concept. *Journal of General Management, 14*(2), 34–57.

Wengel, Jt., & Rodiriguez, E. (2006). Export performance in Indonesia after the crisis. *Small Business Economics*, *26*(1), 25–37.

Wetzels, M., Schroder, G. O., & Oppen, V. C. (2009). Using PLS path modeling for assessing hierarchical construct models: Guidelines and empirical illustration. *MIS Quarterly*, *1*(33), 177–195.

Williamson, D. (2002). Forward from a critique of hofstede's model of national culture. *Human Relations*, *55*(11), 1373–1395.

Wold, H. (1985). Partial least squares. In S. Kotz & N. L. Johnson (Eds.), *Encyclopedia of statistical sciences* (Vol. 6, No. 1, pp. 581–591). New York: Wiley.

Wold, H. (1966). Estimation of principal component and related models by iterative least squares. In P. R. Krishnaiah (Ed.), *Multivariate analysis* (pp. 391–420). New York: Academic Press.

World Bank. (2017a). Data. Retrieved from https://data.worldbank.org/indicator/NY.GDP.MKTP.KD.ZG?locations=ZG&name_desc=false

World Bank. (2017b). World Bank in Africa. Retrieved from http://www.worldbank.org/en/region/afr/overview

Worthington, I., & Patton, D. (2005). Strategic intent in the management of the green environment within SMEs: An analysis of the UK screen-printing sector. *Long Range Planning*, *38*(2), 197–212.

Wright, R. W., & Etemad, H. (2001). SMEs and the global economy. *Journal of International Management*, 151–154.

Yip, G. S., Biscarri, J. G., & Monti, J. A. (2000). The role of the internationalization process in the performance of newly internationalizing firms. *Journal of International Marketing*, *8*(3), 10–35.

Yiu, D. W., Lau, C., & Bruton, G. D. (2007). International venturing by emerging economy firms: The effects of firm capabilities, home country networks, and corporate entrepreneurship. *Journal of International Business Studies*, *38*(4), 519–540.

Young, N. (2010). Globalization from the edge: A framework for understanding how small and medium-sized firms in the periphery go global. *Environment and Planning*, *42*(4), 838–855.

Ysa, T. (2007). Governance forms in urban public-private partnerships. *International Public Management Journal*, *10*(1), 35–57.

Zahra, S. A. (2005). Entrepreneurial risk taking in family firms. *Family Business Review*, *18*(1), 23–40.

Zahra, S., & George, G. (2002). International entrepreneurship: The current status of the field and future research agenda. In M. Hitt, D. Ireland, D. Sexton, & M. Camp (Eds.), *Strategic entrepreneurship: Creating an integrated mindset* (pp. 255–288). Oxford: Blackwell.

Zhou, L., Wu, W. P., & Luo, X. (2007). Internationalization and the performance of born-global SMEs: The mediating role of social networks. *Journal of International Business Studies*, *38*(4), 673–690.

Chapter 5

Exploring Potentialities and Limits of Internationalisation of High-Technology Family-Owned Start-Ups in Africa: A PESTEL Perspective

Ratakane Maime and Patient Rambe

Contents

DOI: 10.4324/9781003302339-5

Introduction

Although the African continent is infamously known for its socio-economic ills like poverty, corruption and political instability, the positives such as cultural diversity, youthful population and the abundance of natural resources hold the promise of advancing economic development. In as much as the negative factors imply a continent that is not enabling local business growth, those with entrepreneurial insight envision that the potential of African economies require some entrepreneurial orientation. For example, the growing population of the Sub-Saharan region may exert more pressure on the economic well-being of this region. Yet some foresee that the same population growth, coupled with increasing income levels will trigger immense business opportunities (Acha, Chironga & Georges, 2018).

On a global landscape, high-technology firms are beginning to show indications of success. Africa in particular may soon realise its dream of becoming a high-tech innovation hub. This fact is also proven by the 46% funding increase for high-technology start-ups between 2015 and 2020. This is six times the normal global funding rate (Maher, Laabi, Ivers & Ngambeket, 2021). As of 2022, in spite of the global challenges, 633 African technology start-ups raised over $3 billion in funding – a 12.2% increase from the previous year (Disrupt Africa, 2022). At the same time, there are some challenges this potentially successful technology entrepreneurship presents such as the disjointed nature of the market, poor purchasing power, underdeveloped funding structures, uncoordinated regulatory framework, unsophisticated Information and Communication Technology (ICT) infrastructure, and the scarcity of digital skills. Regarding regulations, much still has to be done to enable start-ups to overcome the uncompetitive nature of the industries caused by large enterprises. Large enterprises normally raise the barriers to entry and growth of new ventures, which proves to be a double-edged sword for such firms. While they create difficult conditions for small businesses to thrive, large enterprises simultaneously rely on international technological innovations for solutions that can be developed indigenously at lesser cost (Maher *et al.*, 2021).

Irrespective of business size, there are many reasons for firms to consider targeting international markets. Sometimes, their local markets may not be lucrative enough to sustain their business operations and achieve greater success. Some organisational operations may also function better in other countries than locally. For example, instead of importing resources, an organisation may benefit from situating its design or manufacturing division in a foreign country for easy and affordable access to resources. An organisation may also decide to place its core business in a foreign country where the host market is larger than its home market. Furthermore, an organisation may consider global presence to take advantage of lower labour costs or a high concentration of needed expertise (Sousa & Oz, 2016). Regarding high-technology start-ups, globalisation and the digital revolution are making it almost inevitable to internationalise and compete with larger firms (Baofo, Owusu & Jourdain, 2022; Sousa & Oz, 2016). This chapter presents the environmental challenges and opportunities, unique to the continent, that affect the internationalisation of high-technology family-owned start-ups in Africa. The enablers and inhibitors to the internationalisation of these start-ups are discussed using the constructs of a **PESTEL** (Political, Economic, Social, Technological, Environmental and Legal) framework used in business strategy to understand the environmental factors which pose both threats and opportunities to strategic objectives.

High-Technology Start-Ups

According to Jackson (2020), it is difficult to define an African high-technology start-up mainly because most successful start-ups choose to be registered elsewhere in the world. For example, fast-growing high-technology start-ups like Flutterwave, Paga and Paystack choose transcontinental presence. However, the most defining characteristic of high-technology start-ups is their innovative aptitude, which is a determining factor of their success. They rise or fall depending on the ground-breaking nature of their innovations. For example, at its inception by Steve Jobs and Steve Wozniak, the Apple computer was the first of its kind in the personal computer industry. A definition by Law Insider (2022) comes close to what this chapter considers a high-technology start-up as – "a business unit that has been in operation for less than five years, employs fewer than 10 employees, and produces a high proportion of advanced technology products". High-technology start-ups differ from high-tech-enabled businesses in that they develop the technologies and platforms that the latter use to achieve efficient and effective processes. The requirement for continuous innovation places high-technology start-ups at high risk of failure in case their ideas are not as disruptive (Hughes, 2022).

Many high-technology start-ups in Africa operate in fintech. Fintech simply means financial technology. It refers to a range of new technologies that make financial services more accessible. Unlike the traditional banking systems that are limited by their legacy systems, fintech tools are flexible and small-scale, making financial transactions seamless and more efficient (CSL Stockbrokers, 2020; Joy, 2022). Fintech companies normally enter the market by identifying gaps in the industry and creating ingenious innovations. They leverage on these initial innovations to spread the scope of their offerings into other banking-related services (International Monetary Fund, 2019). In Africa, fintech is growing precisely because the banking system cannot accommodate all people, especially in the informal sectors and rural areas. Fintech reduces financial exclusion in Africa as it connects both the underbanked and unbanked citizens to financial services like loans, savings, digital payments and cash transfers without the bank as an intermediary (CSL Stockbrokers, 2020; Joy, 2022). Because of its economic challenges like financial exclusion, inflexible financial structures and regulations, the Sub-Sahara African region is leading the world in terms of up-take of fintech. Technologies like MPESA are well known for affordable, quick and safe trans-border cash transfers (International Monetary Fund, 2019).

Perhaps the most successful fintech industry in Africa is in Nigeria where more than 200 fintech companies have been incorporated (CSL Stockbrokers, 2020; Joy, 2022). Again, in Nigeria, fintech thrives because of the young people who make up 50% of the population (CSL Stockbrokers, 2020). Kenya is also reported among the countries whose fintech industry is budding (International Monetary Fund, 2019). It can be inferred that the demographics of African countries, like a fast-growing population of young people, and significant numbers of rural communities that are not connected to mainstream banking services are the main contributors to the high growth of fintech start-ups. Fintech is also enabled by the growing use of smartphones. Out of 100 people in Sub-Saharan Africa, about 73 have smartphones. In fact, people of Sub-Saharan Africa have more access to smartphones than they have to electricity (International Monetary Fund, 2019).

The popularity of smartphones in Africa has a very unique background. While the traditional European telecommunication infrastructure was designed to connect its people, that of Africa was designed by the European colonisers to connect their representatives in Africa to their home countries during colonial times and to make Africa governable. In fact, up to the year 2000, a phone call from Brazzaville (Republic of Congo) to Kinshasa (Democratic Republic of Congo) (the closest capital cities in the world (Douniama, 2018) that are separated only by the Congo River), connected through Paris (France) (Rivett, 2017). So, in the late 1990s to early 2000, many African countries were still transitioning from state-owned and inefficient telecommunication services. A landline was prohibitively expensive for the average citizen at the time. Consequently, the mobile phone industry became a catalytic alternative to traditional colonial-age infrastructure in Africa. Despite the benefits of fintech, challenges like poor electricity and internet access hinder technology penetration in the Sub-Saharan region. There are some fears that because fintech transactions are not as regulated as traditional financial institutions, they can be used to fund fraudulent transactions including terrorism activities. These fears are legitimate, especially in a world where the rate of innovations is outpacing the regulatory framework. Although there are some expectations that Fourth Industrial Revolution (4IR) technologies like blockchain can be used to facilitate secure and transparent transactions, it is not yet clear how (International Monetary Fund, 2019).

Family-Owned Start-Ups

Research by PricewaterhouseCoopers (PWC) (2015a) defined a family business as an enterprise in which:

> (1) The majority of votes are held by the person who established or acquired the business (or their spouses, parents, child, or child's direct heirs); (2) At least one representative of the family is involved in the management or administration of the business; and (3) In the case of a listed company, the person/s who established or acquired the business (or their families) possesses 25% of the right to vote through their share capital, and there is at least one family member on the board of the company.

Family-owned businesses are autonomous and rely mainly on family ties and generational succession for their governance structures. Even though they have been contributing greatly to economic development, family-owned businesses are relatively a new phenomenon compared with other business formations (KPMG, 2020).

Although they are considered to contribute significantly to the economic development of Africa, it is difficult to measure the actual impact of African family-owned businesses because of their informal nature and the associated difficulty of collating their data. One key contributor to their success is their resilient and innovative nature (KPMG, 2020). Even during times of economic recessions, abilities as quick decision-making, coupled with their long-term outlook, better entrepreneurial orientation, openness to new ideas and reliance on non-financial indicators of success render them highly resilient and innovative (PricewaterhouseCoopers (PwC), 2015a). So even during social disruptions that threaten business prospects, African family-owned enterprises were positive about the future because they rely mainly on long-term capital and other forms of return than short-term returns on investment of private shareholding (KPMG, 2020).

Internationalisation of Family-Owned Start-Ups

Internationalisation is considered as the spreading of business products and services beyond local boundaries to foreign markets (Cruz, Barreto & Pinto, 2015). The Uppsala Internationalisation Process (UIP) model considers internationalisation as an "ad-hoc" process than a function of a formal business strategy. According to the model, internationalisation typically begins with firms sporadically exporting their products to foreign markets. This is followed by the formalisation of their business activities through foreign intermediaries or agents. As a firm experiences some revenue growth, it then replaces intermediaries by establishing sales units in foreign countries.

Provided that revenue continues to grow, a firm may establish its manufacturing activities in foreign countries. This gradual progression eliminates the "liability of foreignness" which is a psychological effect of alienation in a foreign country. To reduce this psychological feeling, small businesses normally start by entering geographically closer markets. Although entering foreign markets involves trans-border activities, the model considers internationalisation to be an expansion of a business network than an individual business project. That is because a business in the current world is not so much of an isolated entity as much as it is part of a network. It is social networks that are a determining factor of success in foreign markets as they eliminate a sense of being an outsider. Furthermore, it is through networks that business opportunities in foreign markets become accessible and knowledge of industries is formed (Johanson & Vahlne, 2009).

A study by Baofo et al. (2022) confirmed that business networks play a major role in promoting the internationalisation of both informal and formal businesses. In Africa, informal businesses account for over 79% of all enterprises and contribute to about 36% of the GDP (International Labour Organisation, 2018). Although the initial UIP model had suggested the gradual internationalisation process of businesses, globalisation and the growth of business networks are increasing the speed of internationalisation in Africa and the world at large. The authors of the previous UIP model (Johanson & Vahlne, 2009) revised it upon the recognition of this fact. Among informal businesses, business networks are facilitated through family ties and friendships which lead to buyer referrals. For example, out of 14 Ghanaian informal businesses, half of them did business in almost seven foreign markets and over half started to transact abroad within their start-up period of existence (Baofo et al., 2022).

Reaching international markets is one of the growth strategies among family-owned businesses (KPMG, 2020). In 2015, research conducted by PricewaterhouseCoopers (PWC) (2015a) predicted that international sales by family-owned businesses will grow from 15% to 24% in the next five years. In particular, 70% of South African-based family-owned businesses were contemplating intensifying their international market penetration. However, some African companies were only considering strengthening their business only in countries where little language and cultural barriers exist (PricewaterhouseCoopers (PWC), 2015a). By the year 2019, up to 60% of African family-owned businesses had transacted throughout Africa and in prominent international markets. Furthermore, 31% of these family-owned businesses had increased their international trade (KPMG, 2020). Generally speaking, the phenomenon of internationalisation of small businesses in Africa matches the observations of Johanson and Vahlne (2009) in their UIP model. Internationalisation in Africa is not a formalised process that follows calculated costs. There is a perception that high-technology start-ups should not rush the process of spreading to global markets before they gain a —product–market fit (Jackson, 2020).

PESTEL Perspectives on Internationalisation of High-Technology Family-Owned Start-Ups

Changes within the macro-environment of a business may have a positive or negative impact. Organisations rise or fall depending on their responses to the changes in the external environment. These changes affect the legitimacy of a business, and they shift customer interests and profitability and create new opportunities and threads. The inability to discern these external dynamics or failure to respond appropriately may render a business, its products or services, or its approaches irrelevant. According to Johanson and Vahlne (2009), the dramatic changes within the economic and regulatory environment also influence the nature of internationalisation. Subsequently, the effects of the COVID-19 pandemic as a social and external factor require at least four levels of strategic evaluations (Oosthuizen, Du Preez & Alexander, 2021), and they have implications for high-technology start-ups that are family owned:

■ At the societal or enterprise level, organisations may have to redefine their role within the international community to maintain their legitimacy. As a result of megatrends like COVID-19, the expectations and needs of society may no longer be the same. For example, in South Africa, recent *Operation Dudula* ("force out") movements and COVID-19 lockdowns have led to the closure of many businesses. These factors have caused debates around the employment of undocumented foreigners by local firms. The challenges created by COVID-19 in particular are also expected to increase the opportunities for businesses to partner with governments and international partners to facilitate internationalisation.

   This state of affairs may open more opportunities for high-technology start-ups to create new solutions for organisations to be technologically enabled to maintain business continuity in times of social unrest. More technologies will be needed not only by businesses but by societies at large to maintain connectivity and access to both private and public sector services.

■ At the corporate level, an organisation might have to rethink the scope of its industrial focus – whether local, regional or global. The digital age is expected to blur national boundaries while accelerating the internationalisation of small firms' products. At the same time, the demand for international products is also increasing. In Africa, the African Continental Free Trade Agreement (AfCFTA) is expected to become an enabler of international trade as a response to the socio-economic challenges exacerbated by the pandemic. It can be expected that the AfCFTA will also stimulate the idea of internationalisation by lowering the structural barriers to trade in the region.

■ At the business level, the competitive advantages of organisations will also be affected. This will be caused by the change of priorities (and their needs) within the societies. Also, new ways of offering products and services are infiltrating the market. Rapid innovations will also make it difficult for companies to sustain a competitive advantage.

   It has been discussed that high-technology start-ups disrupt industries through rapid innovations. It can be expected that the pace at which high-technology firms operate will become highly competitive. Many will rise and fall as unprecedented changes occur in the macro-environment. However, the family aspect of these start-ups makes them highly resilient and adaptable. As globalisation and digitisation increase, the parameters of an international market will soon become indistinguishable from those of a local market.

■ At the functional level, businesses will be forced to reconsider how their support functions execute their responsibilities. Several possibilities exist. First, organisations might decide to outsource functions like human resource, marketing, transport and logistics, and others. Second, organisations might make remote working a permanent arrangement, especially for support functions. Third, some organisations may only downsize functions that are not considered to be critical to their business. Irrespective of the approach, technology is expected to become a platform that supports business functions.

These facts will undoubtedly create opportunities for high-technology start-ups to create new solutions for new work arrangements. But the competition will be very high. Meanwhile, 53% of family-owned businesses in South Africa and 58% globally regarded the issue of price competition as a major inhibitor to growth (PricewaterhouseCoopers (PWC), 2015a), the current study examines PESTEL factors in detail to determine their implications on family-owned high-technology start-ups and the internationalisation of their ideas.

Political Factors

The decisions that governments and other political organisations make may affect businesses positively or negatively. The level of political stability also shapes the economic and/or business landscape. Political instability in Africa is one of the major causes of uncertainty among African family-owned start-ups which normally abhor government interference (KPMG, 2020). In South Africa, 54% of family-owned businesses regard political instability as a major impediment to business growth (PricewaterhouseCoopers (PWC), 2015a). Some high-technology start-ups decide to be incorporated in overseas markets and not in Africa because of fear of political intrusion. However, for family-owned start-ups that are self-funded, political instabilities will have little effect on their well-being. Any dubious relationship between a firm and the local government may affect the status and survival of that firm in overseas markets whose laws are very meticulous on unprofessional business practices. For this reason, to maintain a good image, some firms avoid political risks associated with their African countries by incorporating them elsewhere (Jackson, 2020).

Economic Factors

Economic constructs like buying power, employment rate, interest rates, inflations and GDP have an impact on all forms of business including family-owned businesses on the global spectrum and in Africa. Out of 239 global respondents from family-owned businesses, those from South Africa (77%) believed that unfavourable economic conditions will become the major inhibitor to their success for the next five years. Sixty-three (63%) per cent of global respondents held the same opinion (PricewaterhouseCoopers (PWC), 2015a). According to Fjose, Grünfeld and Green (2010), there is a relationship between GDP and access to finance. When GDP improves, access to finance also improves. Owing to poor economic conditions in Sub-Saharan Africa, poor access to finance is among the major inhibitors of start-up market entry and growth. Furthermore, poor access to finance is also associated with high risks of failure of small start-ups as compared to larger enterprises. For a fintech start-up like Funzo, migration to UK and Singapore was motivated by lower corporate tax and other forms of government support that are not available in South Africa. Moreover, there is greater potential for improved share capital value should the company consider funding through shares (Maher et al., 2021). As a result of the pandemic, 20% of 122 family-owned businesses in Africa consider the future of their growth to be uncertain. Some of the major contributors to this uncertainty are the fact that most African governments do not have clear economic recovery plans and have increased their international debt. These, coupled with fluctuating currencies and a lack of access to finance, have created a considerable level of fear that African economies may not provide a conducive environment for business (KPMG, 2020).

At the same time, there are a significant number of African family-owned businesses (80%) that still have a positive outlook for the future. That is because family-owned businesses are held together by other non-financial variables like continued family ties, legacy and commitment. Even for financial capital, many family-owned businesses rely on these family ties. Unlike large corporates, family-owned businesses are not always bound by professional goals that are unrelated to the family's purpose (KPMG, 2020). Another factor that has positive implications for the African business environment is the AfCFTA. The free-trade zone, if implemented well, will become the biggest trade agreement in the world and may elicit a regional GDP of 3.4 trillion US dollars. A growing younger population and improving income levels of Africans are expected to enhance household spending capacity (Acha et al., 2018) and stimulate regional markets and economies (Njima, 2020).

Social Factors

Social factors like culture, religion, demographics and geography also have an impact on the success of businesses. As a cultural dynamic, differences in language may also inhibit smooth international operations. Although there are some technologies that translate languages, the fact that they sometimes fall short of capturing unique local ethos renders them inadequate. The internet itself is perceived as embodying the American culture also because that is where it originates. This is tantamount to cultural imperialism and it inhibits the acceptance of foreign businesses' corporate image by locals (Sousa & Oz, 2016).

Regarding high-technology start-ups, language barriers appear to influence the direction of business expansion. Some businesses prefer to expand to countries that have similar languages and cultures to their home countries. For example, Truzo's migration to London was motivated by similarities in language and time zones (Maher et al., 2021). There is also an ethical factor that affects the internationalisation of high-technology start-ups. For example, Nigerian-based technology start-ups may be viewed with a considerable level of scepticism because of how the country is sometimes viewed globally. In one interview on the reasons for African tech start-ups to "domicile" overseas, a Nigerian international revealed that a Nigerian company bears the stigma of fraudulency on global business platforms and within Africa, including in Nigeria. So, even if the business owner is Nigerian by origin, they trade easier when their companies have an American corporate identity (Jackson, 2020). So, the perceived level of societal ethics has an impact on the success of internationalisation of family-owned high-technology start-ups.

Social elements like networking and affiliations are considered by Johanson and Vahlne (2009) as foundational to the success of internationalisation endeavours. When businesses are not part of any network within a foreign market, it affects their confidence and chances of success. Internationalisation does not always start as a formal process. It normally follows autonomous approaches and may be enabled by relationships established even before the internationalisation process (Coviello, 2006). Education is another factor that affects internationalisation in Africa. The lower the level of education, the less likely the internationalisation endeavours will be successful. That is because factors like cross-border transactions require a better understanding of international trade, customs and duties, and the relevant legal framework (Baofo et al., 2022). The pandemic is pushing some social dynamics among family-owned businesses to the front. Some are considering transferring ownership or control to the younger generation because of the uncertain outlook of the future and the apparent need for new skills. There is also a rising need for family-owned businesses to revise their social identity and community responsibilities (KPMG, 2020).

The potential for Africa's high-tech industry lies in what may be considered a challenge. A social dynamic like a growing population may exert pressure on the economy. However, the same fact may promote the high-tech industry to develop technologies that connect societies to key services like health, finance, education and energy. As mentioned before, the African population growth is coinciding with increasing income levels, which means that the spending capacity will enable money circulation, which increase the consumption of high-tech goods, products and services. The fact that young people constitute the largest proportion of the population suggests greater innovation potential and utilisation of new digital technologies (Maher et al., 2021).

Technological Factors

The use of technology, which today permeates most if not all organisational structures, leads to several strategic advantages. Technological innovations are popping up every day and causing some businesses to be ahead of others. At the same time, the state of foreign and local ICT infrastructure can inhibit global business activities. For economic reasons, some countries offer low bandwidth compared to others. In countries like the United States, the use of credit cards as a method of payment is widespread. However, in Europe, there is more preference for debit cards. In developing nations, internet-based transfers are viewed with scepticism because of the associated security risks (Sousa & Oz, 2016). The slow progress of the fintech industry in Nigeria, as a result of the lack of interoperable financial systems, forced some high-tech start-ups whose clients relied on PayPal and Stripe to incorporate outside of Africa (Jackson, 2020).

The advancements in technology and globalisation are playing the role of enabling and fast-tracking the process of internationalisation. Advanced payment systems are also enabling international transactions and money transfers even without banks as intermediaries (Baofo et al., 2022). This means that we can expect to see more informal types of international transactions. Considering the instrumentality of social networks in advancing internationalisation, one may infer that social media technologies will play a huge role in advancing internationalisation as the world becomes increasingly connected (KPMG, 2020). In 2015, a study conducted by PricewaterhouseCoopers (PWC) (2015a) established that 79% of African family-owned businesses considered that technology will change their business approaches in the next five years. The new business environment is requiring rapid innovation and the use of technology. Yet a recent study conducted on 231 African family businesses indicates that only one in five family businesses has made some significant digital technology developments (PricewaterhouseCoopers (PWC), 2021b). Family-owned businesses are considering passing the active responsibility of governance to the younger generation that can cope with the rapid changes (KPMG, 2020).

Access to electricity is still one of the major inhibitors of digital and business growth. Currently, only 43% of the African population has access to electricity compared with 87% of global electricity access (Njima, 2020). Even those who have access to electricity do not always enjoy a reliable supply because of frequent load-shedding incidences in Africa's big economies like Nigeria and South Africa. Unreliable electricity supply is, therefore, a major inhibitor to high-technology entrepreneurship in Africa. Poor internet penetration is another challenge of high-technology businesses. On average, only 39.3% of Africans have access to the internet. There is also a considerable level of a digital divide. For example, on the other extreme, a country like Kenya has better access at 87%. Yet on the other extreme is a country like Chad that has only 6.3% access. A country like Nigeria has about 74% access to the internet through smartphones for affordable access and only 24% via personal computers (Njima, 2020). Therefore, when the ICT infrastructure that supports technological innovations is lacking, this will affect the rapid innovative capacity of high-tech firms. It makes no difference what innovations they bring, they cannot be accessed and utilised proficiently in the absence of reliable internet and electricity.

Environmental Factors

Today's business activities cannot be performed without a keen consideration of their impact on the environment. At the global and regional levels, several initiatives have been developed to drive the idea of environmental sustainability. Examples include the well-known United Nations Sustainable Development Goals, Africa's Agenda 2063 and South Africa's National Development Plan (NDP) 2030, which seek to prioritise sustainable development and environmental protection for the benefit of future generations. A study by PricewaterhouseCoopers (PWC) (2015a) revealed that resource scarcity together with negative climate impact contributes to global economic challenges. The study goes on to reveal that the energy demand will increase by 50%, and that of water by 40% through 2030. Based on the assertions that African populations are growing rapidly (Acha et al., 2018; Njima, 2020), environmental challenges will have a dire impact on Africa and younger generations if left unattended. The environmental changes create perilous weather patterns which threaten agriculture and food security while rendering the traditional forms of living extraneous (PricewaterhouseCoopers (PWC), 2015a).

Perhaps the idea of future generational well-being is intrinsically embedded within the structure and purpose of family-owned businesses, more so for high-technology start-ups. There is an understanding by 79% of 231 family-owned businesses that digital technologies will salvage climate change and save resources while democratising economic power (PWC, 2015a). We have already discussed generational succession as a factor which ascertains that family members maintain control of family assets and the fact that family-owned start-ups are motivated not only by short-term profits but by a long-term outlook. This means that family-owned start-ups hold the potential to advance sustainability goals because they uphold the idea of future generational well-being (PricewaterhouseCoopers (PWC), 2021b). Experts are predicting that concepts like green technology and green finance will affect the success of businesses. Regarding green finance, there is a prediction that accesses to finance, which is already a challenge in Africa, will depend on the ability of businesses to adhere to ESG (environmental, social and governance) goals. Regarding green technology, there is a growing understanding that technology will have to be used to reduce the negative impact of humans on the environment (Duke Corporate Education, 2021). However, while the global family businesses are prioritising environmental factors like the reduction of carbon emissions, a major focus by African family businesses is on social responsibilities within their communities (PricewaterhouseCoopers (PWC), 2021b).

Legal Factors

Local and regional laws and regulations govern how businesses are run and determine their level of success. The tax regime of another country may be more enabling for business than that of another. The laws governing information sharing and freedom of speech in one country may differ across countries. One country may have very clear regulations governing intellectual property. But if another country in which an entity intends to do business does not have clear intellectual property laws, it may stir fears of unwanted innovation spillovers. Employees of an international business may not be able to adhere to the laws of a foreign country. Some of the laws of a foreign country may not be clear. For example, eBay only discovered after establishing its online auction business in Italy and Germany that the laws of those European countries do not permit online auctions (Sousa & Oz, 2016). Although research and development can help businesses to avoid or eliminate some of these challenges, it is not always affordable to small businesses (Matejun, 2016) including family owned businesses.

The SMME growth in Sub-Saharan Africa is reported to be inhibited by stringent tax regimes and bureaucratic government styles which are fertile ground for corruption. Because of these challenges that exclusively affect formal business enterprises, some businesses prefer to remain informal in form (Fjose et al., 2010). Overregulation of industries is a major inhibitor to business growth worldwide. A similar view was held by about 88% of South African CEOs (PWC, 2015a). According to Njima (2020), bureaucracy, corruption and weak rule of law are major inhibitors to entrepreneurship development in Africa. However, some countries are working hard to restructure their regulatory framework to attract investors (Maher et al., 2021). For example, countries like Ghana, Kenya, Nigeria and South Africa are among those that are working hard to ease business and eliminate corruption through efficient digital platforms of business registration (Njima, 2020). Working together with the World Bank, the eight-nation West African Economic and Monetary Union is in the process of developing an all-inclusive legal and regulatory structure to support private shareholding and venture capital funding (Maher et al., 2021). Other significant transformations in the legal framework include Rwanda and Morocco which are number 38 and 53 on the World Bank's *ease of doing business* ranking. However, nine African countries are among the last ten whose legal framework is considered unfavourable to business (World Bank Group, 2020).

Countries with efficient and effective legal systems have attracted some high-tech companies from Africa. For example, 70% of high-technology start-ups that are registered in the United States opt for the state of Delaware because of low corporate tax, efficient and high-quality courts, and judges. The state of Delaware is also said to provide investment options that are low risk and relaxed. The entire country of the United States attracts foreign businesses because of the low cost of doing business and the legal framework that protects businesses and intellectual property. It was because of high restrictions associated with multiple currency transactions in South Africa, that Trunzo (also a fintech company) chose to incorporate in the United Kingdom and Singapore. However, in Africa, Mauritius is one of the few countries that is regarded as attractive for high-technology start-ups because of the lack of foreign exchange controls and the absence of withholding tax on dividends and interest. Moreover, the Mauritius government does not impose a tax on capital gains of residents and non-residents on shares sold to a Mauritius company (Jackson, 2020). Notably, Mauritius is number 13 in the world according to World Bank's *ease of doing business index* (World Bank Group, 2020).

Diffusion of Innovation Theory

Diffusion of Innovation (DoI) Theory holds that the successful adoption of an innovation depends on its level of acceptance by intended users. Adoption refers to the actual migration from one way of doing things to another. Because early adopters of an innovation are not the same as late adopters, promoters of innovation within a given society must study the contextual features that may hinder or advance take-up of technologies (Lamorte, 2019). There are five types of adopters of innovations (Lamorte, 2019; Van der Zande, Gorter & Wismeijer, 2013, p. 1):

Innovators: Innovators desire to be the first to adopt an innovation because they are by nature exploratory and keen to try new inventions. In other words, they are risk-takers and creators of novel ideas.

Early adopters: This group is made up of thought leaders with capacity and ability to embrace change. They are highly informed and have a clear understanding of changes that are needed.

For this group to buy into new ideas, it takes as little information on how to implement a technology.

Early majority: This group is composed of people who cannot adopt a new technology until they are convinced that it works. They are among the average group of adopters who rely on evidence and success stories of innovators and early adopters.

Late majority: The term sceptical is synonymous with the late majority because of their unwillingness to adopt an innovation until the majority has tried it. They also depend on the successful implementation of the early majority.

Laggards: Because they are conservative by nature, laggards remain as non-users of an innovation irrespective of its perceived benefits because they view new ideas with scepticism. Some of the strategies that may be used to convince them to adopt new technologies include statistics of users, "fear of reprisals for non-use" and pressure from other groups of adopters.

Information Technology Diffusion Theory

Among the limitations of a DoI, one that is relevant for the current context is that it ignores some other environmental factors like resources and social structures that may enable or inhibit the successful adoption of an innovation. Therefore, as a derivative of DoI, the Information Technology Diffusion Theory (ITDT) postulates that technology acceptance follows these dynamics:

■ There must be some inherent and creative aspects of innovation. The level of acceptance depends on how adopters perceive "relative advantage", "compatibility", "complexity", "trialability" and "observability" of the technology.

■ Education and culture also determine the level of acceptance and adoption of technology among the intended users.

■ Adoption depends on the level of personal knowledge which is a derivative of conviction about the technology.

■ Factors internal to an organisation involve the power vested in some individuals to influence institutional take-up. This is true especially when intended adopters consider themselves to have something in common with the influencers.

■ Early adopters represent a very low rate of adoption. Yet the process of adoption increases in momentum as a result of external influences like take-up among peers. But over time, the rate of adoption begins to slow down when an innovation has been widely used (Fichman, 1992).

Apart from the above considerations, which are mainly autonomous, there are other top-down internal factors like managerial influence which prompted Fichman (1992) to argue that individuals do not always have the freedom to adopt or not adopt innovations. Management, through incentives, reward systems and instruction habitually forces institutional adoption of innovations.

Theoretical Application to the Study

Based on a DoI, it can be established that the spread of high-technology start-ups in Africa is an indication that the continent has enough innovators. But the environment needs to be enabling. Based on the ITDT, we understand that the environment is characterised by several inhibitors and enablers. Given Fichman's (1992) assertion that adopters are not always at liberty to adopt or resist an innovation, it can be postulated that the factors that will drive the growth of family-owned high-technology start-ups can be located within and outside the boarders of an entity. Outside an entity, the PESTEL framework can be used to identify the elements that will drive diffusion of high-tech products and the success of the related start-ups. So, the growth of high-tech start-ups will depend on how they respond to changes within the macro-environment. Factors like globalisation, the digital revolution and unique demographics will accelerate adoption of innovations. Social challenges like COVID-19 will strengthen organisational managers to institute strategic plans that enable technology acceptance. The external environment, therefore, can either stimulate or frustrate the growth and vitality of products and services of family-owned high-technology start-ups. The African population is growing faster than anywhere in the world. It is expected to double by 2030 with youth constituting the majority, and their income levels are expected to grow rapidly (Njima, 2020). As populations grow, technology becomes a better way to connect societies to services. Therefore, it can be expected that a combination of these social and economic dynamics will increase demand for high-technology start-ups in Africa. Even if there are obvious reasons necessitating the adoption, the underdeveloped infrastructure and the backward legal framework, if not addressed, will stand in the way of wide acceptance of technology innovations.

Conclusions and Recommendations

To make recommendations in this chapter, we draw from the PESTEL framework, the DoI and ITDT. Within the economic continuum, technology can be used to advance the development of Africa. In their study on "Why smart meter adoption in Africa lacks cohesion?" Maime and Mosala (2021) found out that a major inhibitor to smart metering adoptions was individualist national adoption approaches. Therefore, African countries need to advance regional cooperation including the sharing of best practices. The inequalities in the continent cannot be overcome when the economies of the continent strive to develop in fragmented ways. Just like there are regional agreements like AfCFTA, African countries need to develop a regional plan that guides the continental strategy for digitalisation. That plan must be inclusive of strategies to create an enabling environment for all forms of businesses including family-owned high-technology start-ups. This would be an effective way for equipping African economies to compete on the global scale.

From a theoretical perspective, the suggested strategy will have to consider barriers and enablers from a PESTEL perspective. Within the political environment, Africa needs to harness its efforts to promote greater stability and eliminate corruption. Economically, the continent has to develop inclusive strategies for enhancing access to finance and relaxing the tax regime, especially in areas that hold so much potential to enrich the regional economy as family-owned high-technology start-ups. Regarding technology, there is a need for a collective regional approach to advancing digital skills within the communities and organisations that will adopt high-technology products to create a demand-pull. At the pace that technology is being developed, most innovations may be a waste of creativity if the environment is not strategically ready to absorb them. A strategy must be devised to tackle environmental challenges and to achieve the sustainability goals of the United Nations with specific intention to promoting green technologies. Lastly, within the legal framework, there must be a clear plan to tackle corruption, lower firms' barriers to entry while improving the ease of doing business. Without a strategy, the continent will continue to have upper extremes like Nigeria and South Africa, which have a high concentration of high-technology start-ups, and lower extremes such as Somalia, Mozambique and Lesotho, which are lagging behind. Instead of sustaining fair and equitable development, the digital revolution if left unregulated, may perpetuate economic inequalities and abject poverty. African countries need a legal framework that is proactive and enabling of the digital revolution instead of a reactive one. According to the Competition Commission of South Africa (2020), the current legal framework is not able to effectively regulate organisations and their practices within the ever-changing digital environment.

References

Acha, L., Chironga, M., & Georges, D. (2018). *Africa's Business Revolution: How to succeed in the world's next big growth market.* Boston, MA: Harvard Business Review Press.

Baofo, C., Owusu, R. A., & Jourdain, K. G. (2022). Understanding internationalisation of informal African firms through a network perspective. *International Small Business Journal, 40*(5), 618–649.

Competition Commission South Africa. (2020). Competition in the digital economy. For public comments. Available on: http://www.compcom.co.za/wp-content/uploads/2020/09/Competition-in-the-digital-economy_7-September-2020.pdf (Accessed 20 September 2021).

Coviello, N. E. (2006). The network dynamics of international new ventures. *Journal of International Business Studies, 37*(5), 713–731.

Cruz, E. P., Barreto, C. R., & Pinto, C. P. (2015). Internationalization of small business: An investigation about Brazilian Business in Orlando City. *Journal of Management Policy and Practice, 16*(3), 78–94.

CSL Stockbrokers. (2020). *Nigeria's fintech industry 2020: The growth frontier of the new decade.* Available on: https://nairametrics.com/2020/01/10/nigerias-fintech-industry-2020-the-growth-frontier-of-the-new-decade/ (Accessed 19 March 2022).

Disrupt Africa (2022). African tech startups buck global VC trends in 2022, DRC. Available on: https://disrupt-africa.com/wp-content/uploads/2023/02/The-African-Tech-Startups-Funding-Report-2022.pdf (Accessed 07 April 2023).

Douniama, V. (2018). How to travel from Brazzaville, Congo to Kinshasa, DRC. Available on: https://theculturetrip.com/africa/congo/articles/how-to-travel-from-brazzaville-congo-to-kinshasa-drc/ (Accessed 21 March 2022).

Duke Corporate Education. (2021). Reimagining the financial services for 2035. The time for reinvention is now. Available on: https://info.dukece.com/reimagining-financial-services? (Accessed 15 March 2022).

Sousa, K. J., & Oz, E.. (2016). *Management Information Systems* (7th ed.). United Kingdom: Cengage Learning.

Fichman, R. G. (1992). Information technology diffusion: A review of empirical research. *ICIS*, 195–206.

Fjose, S., Grünfeld, L. A., & Green, C. (2010 June). SMEs and growth in Sub-Saharan Africa. Identifying SME roles and obstacles to SME growth. *MENON Business Economics* 14/2010.

Hughes, K. (2022). High Tech vs. Tech-Enabled Start-ups. Available on: https://www.karllhughes.com/posts/high-tech-enabled (Accessed 16 March 2022).

International Labour Organisation. (2018) *Women and men in the informal economy: A statistical picture* (3rd ed.). Geneva, Switzerland: ILO.

International Monetary Fund. (2019). Fintech in Sab-Saharan African countries: Game changer. African Department. No 19/04.

Jackson, T. (2020). Why African tech startups are increasingly domiciling overseas. Available on: https://disrupt-africa.com/2020/03/10/why-african-tech-startups-are-increasingly-domiciling-overseas/ (Accessed 16 March 2022).

Johanson, J., & Vahlne, J. (2009). The internationalization process of the firm: A model of knowledge development and increasing foreign market commitments. Available on: https://www.researchgate.net/publication/247918268_The_internationalization_process_of_the_firm_A_model_of_knowledge_development_and_increasing_foreign_market_commitments (Accessed 13 March 2022).

Joy, E. (2022). Top tech fintech companies in Nigeria. Available on: https://clacified.com/business/16/top-10-fintech-companies-in-nigeria (Accessed March 2022).

KPMG. (2020). *KPMG. Embracing innovation for a new reality in Africa* (3rd ed.). KPMG Services Proprietary Limited.

Lamorte, W. W. (2019). Diffusion of innovation theory. Available on: https://sphweb.bumc.bu.edu/otlt/mph-modules/sb/behavioralchangetheories/behavioralchangetheories4.html (Accessed 21 March 2022).

Lawinsider. (2022). High-tech start-up definition. Available on: https://www.lawinsider.com/dictionary/high-tech-startup#:~:text=High%2Dtech%20startup%20means%20a,proportion%20of%20advanced%20technology%20products (Accessed 16 March 2022).

Maher, H., Laabi, A., Ivers, L., & Ngambeket, G. (2021). Overcoming Africa's tech startup obstacles. Available on: https://www.bcg.com/publications/2021/new-strategies-needed-to-help-tech-startups-in-africa (Accessed 16 November 2022).

Maime, R. B., & Mosala, T. (2021).Why smart meter lack cohesion in Africa. *Esi Africa Issue, 1*, 60–61.

Matejun, M. 2016. Role of technology entrepreneurship in the development of innovativeness of small and medium-sized enterprises. *Management, 20*(1), 167–183.

Njima, R. 2020. Challenges for Africa's entrepreneurial leaders in the digital era. Available on: https://www.su.org/blog/challenges-for-africas-entrepreneurial-leaders-in-the-digital-era (Accessed 16 March 2022).

Oosthuizen, M., Du Preez, K., & Alexander, K. (2021). Navigating the strategic environment in Africa post-Covid-19. White paper. Gordon Institute of Business Science.

PricewaterhouseCoopers (PWC). 2015a. Head over heart? Family Business Survey. Available on: www.pwc.co.za/family-business (Accessed 10 March 2022).

PricewaterhouseCoopers (PWC). 2021b. African Family Business Survey. From trust to impact. Available on: https://www.pwc.com/gx/en/services/family-business/family-business-survey-2018.html (Accessed 15 March 2022).

Rivett, S. (2017, March). History of African telecoms - And importance of mobile telecoms governance in the future. LinkedIn. https://www.linkedin.com/pulse/history-african-telecoms-importance-mobile-future-sean-rivett (Accessed 1 May 2021).

Van der Zande, M. M., Gorter, R. C., & Wismeijer, D. (2013). Dental practitioners and a digital future: An initial exploration of barriers and incentives to adopting digital technologies. *British Dental Journal, 215*, 1–5.

World Bank Group. (2020). *Comparing business regulation in 190 economies*. World Bank Publications.

Chapter 6

Marketing Strategies and Performance of Second-Hand Spare Parts Dealerships: The Role of Environmental Dynamism

Gloria K.Q. Agyapong, Francis O. Boachie-Mensah and Kojo Kakra Twum

Contents

DOI: 10.4324/9781003302339-6

Introduction

Small businesses are vital components of any country's economic growth. Therefore, how they compete in today's business environment is of significance and deserves greater attention from all stakeholders. These businesses operate in an entirely different manner from large organisations and cannot hope to perform at the same level of marketing due to limited resources, limited expertise and limited impact on their environment. In Ghana, small businesses face some challenges, including the marketing of their products and services, and this affects their performance. For these businesses to achieve their objectives and improve their performance, they must have effective marketing strategies that will lead to customer acquisition and retention. Marketing strategies, according to Taiwo (2010), play an important role in improving the performance of businesses. They form the game plan or blueprint by which firms compete in the dynamic business environment (Mohammed, Rashid & Tahir, 2014). Within the field of strategic marketing, decisions on how to market products have been a challenge; with the focus on placing the product at the best place with the best possible price. Thus, businesses have to proactively manage and apply some suitable selection of marketing strategies to succeed. The situation is not different for spare parts dealerships whose activities have increased in Ghana in the last two decades. They need to develop viable marketing strategies to help them achieve performance advantages.

Today's business environment is probably the most dynamic that any business has faced. Practically, anything that can happen to a business is happening to some firms or others, as most seek to minimise the fallout from price wars, continuous cost efficiency drives and, at the same time, maximise new market opportunities (Amit & Zott, 2001). Notwithstanding the lack of universally accepted definitions for small and medium enterprises (SMEs) success and excellent/poor performance, a web of success/failure factors has emerged from the existing studies. It has been observed that most of the identified success/failure factors are endogenous. That is, they are attributable to elements internal to the firm and include such factors as owner's/manager's personal qualities/shortcomings, and strengths/weaknesses inherent in the financial and operational management of the firm.

While recognising the role of such endogenous factors, some researchers believe that exogenous factors (i.e., those external to the firm) pose important constraints and contingencies and can impact on competitiveness and survival (Boyd & Fulk, 1996; Theng & Boon, 1996). Particularly noted in this context is that environmental uncertainty or the absence of sufficient reliable information about environmental events and the inability to predict external changes (Duncan, 1972) can hinder success or cause failure. As Laanti, McDougall and Baume (2009) observe, the present-day business environment that is characterised by increased competition, demanding customers and great technological advances has resulted in a complex market. In this complex market environment, the marketing strategy of the company could improve the performance of the organisation. Organisations are, therefore, evaluating their products and services to come up with more focused strategies that help them meet their unit and organisation-wide objectives (Cravens, Piercy & Baldauf, 2009). They are working towards developing coherent strategies on how to differentiate, add value to their customers and, eventually, improve their performance.

The small- and medium-sized enterprises sector in Ghana, like many other economies, is very visible and is the largest provider of essential services and goods to the general public. The sector is an important component in the country, and it is often used as the benchmark in terms of its development and the general growth of the national economies. By being a major employer, the sector has, thus, contributed in constructive ways and positively to the people and economy of Ghana. However, global competition confronts the majority of purely domestic SMEs, whose products and sales are extremely localised or segmented. Against this development and the critical role SMEs play, local SMEs need to come out with effective marketing strategies that will ensure that the SMEs achieve their performance objectives.

Uncertainty in the environment requires businesses to adopt emergent strategies that would facilitate their operations. The study of Chari et al. (2014) reveals that firms can obtain a competitive advantage from emergent marketing strategies through planning on each component of the marketing mix. Their study again reveals that environmental dynamism is an important context within which firms operate. Thus, uncertainties in the environment influence the choice of marketing strategies. Other studies undertaken on marketing strategies include Anyika's (2010) study on marketing strategies applied by the major motorcycle marketing firms in Kenya, which found that changing macro-environmental factors, indeed, pose various challenges to these motorcycle marketing firms in Kenya. Macharia (2013) undertook a study on the influence of marketing strategies on the performance of real estate business and established that strategic marketing practices were adopted to a small extent by the real estate companies sector in Kenya due to many challenges that included inadequate capital, high operational costs and inadequate training among real estate companies. The study of Green, Whitten and Inman (2012) again reveals that the adoption of marketing strategies within a supply chain positively affects the supply chain performance and subsequently enhances organisational performance.

This study is necessitated by the fact that numerous studies have focused on other sectors other than spare parts dealership performance. Second-hand spare parts dealerships in Ghana form a larger portion of the informal sector and contribute to about 66% of employment in Ghana (Aryeetey, 1998). However, a look at the activities of these dealerships has revealed that even though they might engage in some form of marketing, it is still not clear the extent to which marketing mix strategies are adopted in their operations. The purpose of this study is to find out if they adopt marketing strategies and also establish the extent to which these marketing strategies influence the performance of second-hand spare parts dealerships. This is because many spare parts dealerships that operate within the small business framework in Ghana do not use formal management approaches. As a result, many of them do not survive due to competition from other local and international companies. This study, therefore, was undertaken to determine the effect of marketing strategies on the business performance of spare parts dealerships as well as the moderating role of environmental dynamism. Specifically, the study sought to:

1. Examine the relationship between marketing strategies and business performance of second-hand spare parts dealerships in Ghana
2. Determine the effect of environmental dynamism on business performance of second-hand spare parts dealerships in Ghana
3. Determine the moderating role of environmental dynamism on the relationship between marketing strategies and business performance in second-hand spare parts dealerships in Ghana

Literature Review

Marketing Strategies

Marketing strategy has become an important tool globally for any organisation to remain in a competitive market environment. Many researchers have given different definitions to the concept. Aremu and Lawal (2012) defined marketing strategy as a pattern of resource allocation decisions made throughout an organisation. Marketing strategy begins with market research, where needs and attitudes and competitors' products are evaluated, and continues through into advertising; promotion; distribution; and, where applicable, customer servicing, packaging, sales and distribution. Lin (1993) segregated marketing strategy into four, namely dual-oriented, rational, emotional and low involvement. Using a total of 29 questions on a seven-point Likert scale, he measured different product types with different marketing strategies such that the manufacturer's marketing strategy was divided into five parts, namely choice of the target market, product strategy, pricing strategy, channel strategy and marketing strategy.

Product refers to tangible items that are provided in one way or another from one party to another. Products should be derived from the needs and desires of a customer and it is important that spare parts dealers identify quality products that meet customers: needs and work to introduce unique products which differ from those of their competitors in order to attract customers. Price is one of the important variables in the marketing mix of spare parts dealerships. The right price plays a pivotal role in generating sales and profits for these businesses. Since rational customers are highly sensitive to price, spare parts dealers should make vital and timely decisions to determine the price of their products. Distribution or place means the place where the spare parts dealerships provide their products to the customer. The distribution of a product is vital to satisfy the customer. Thus, it should be easy to access and free from all sorts of hassles (Dahmiri, Octavia & Fatricia, 2017).

For spare parts dealers in particular, it is important for distribution channels to be closer to customers through networks that are within and outside the jurisdictions. Promotion is an essential element in the marketing mix of spare parts dealerships. To attract customers, these businesses need to use various tools and techniques, such as personal selling, advertising, event marketing and more. The objective of promotion is to increase customer awareness (Kadhim, Abdullah & Abdullah, 2016). Therefore, spare parts dealers should strive to adopt right marketing communications tools to promote their products

According to Ruiz (2013), marketing strategies can be classified into two categories: traditional and non-traditional. Traditional marketing strategies include television, newspaper, magazine, cinemas and billboards. Non-traditional marketing strategies include the internet, digital media, social media, websites, emails, mobile technologies and video conferencing. It is crucial to note that none of the strategies surpasses the other. However, finding the right mix of both strategies can create the best marketing strategy for SMEs.

Oloko et al. (2014) examined the marketing strategies adopted by telecommunication companies and found that these strategies spur remarkable growth in terms of market share as well as unprecedented strong super profit within the telecommunication industry in both Kenya and the entire East Africa region. Also, Mutambuki and Orwa (2014) assessed the marketing strategies of commercial fish farming in Kitui County. Their study established that product branding, sales promotion, market positioning and core competencies' marketing strategies affect commercial fish farming. To create an effective marketing strategy, it is necessary to include a communication strategy to support the actions to be taken. This strategy should also include a schedule that contains both traditional and non-traditional media (Tapia Ruiz, 2013). Most SMEs deploy technology-based marketing strategies in reaching their customers.

Influence of Marketing Strategies on Business Performance

Performance is an important aspect of SMEs since continued existence and business activities are a crucial benefit to them. Arguments focusing on SME performance generally posit that SMEs are capable of providing quality products and services and thus possess a competitive advantage

(Pett & Wolf, 2011). Hence, a good marketing strategy supports sales and expansion and contributes significantly to the growth of market share in competitive markets (Marjanova & Stojanovski, 2012). Various studies have established that marketing strategies play an important role in enhancing the performance of SMEs (Owomoyela, Oyeniyi & Ola, 2013; Rose & Shoham, 2002; Theodosiou & Leonidou, 2003).

A study conducted by Dzisi and Ofosu (2014) on the relationship between marketing strategies and the performance of SMEs in Ghana showed that there was a positive relationship between marketing strategies and SMEs' performance. Taiwo (2010) also found out that strategic marketing practices have a significant impact on performance. Santos-Vijande et al. (2012) also established that marketing capabilities exert a significant and positive effect on clients' satisfaction and loyalty, which ultimately leads to better organisational performance in terms of sales, profit and market share.

Haghighinasab et al. (2013) investigated innovative marketing methods based on product, price, place and promotion-based strategies and found that the impact of marketing strategies on innovation is through entrepreneurial orientation, which affects firms' performance. Kiveu (2013) also established that marketing strategies are great contributors to growth as well as to profits. David et al. (2013) conclude that there is a strong correlation between marketing strategies of SMEs and performance in terms of growth in revenue and job opportunities, improved efficiency and a wider connection with customers. Hence, marketing strategies are very crucial to the success of every business organisation.

Environmental Dynamics as a Moderator between Marketing Strategies and Performance

Consumers do not make purchase decisions in isolation. Various internal and external environmental factors may influence their purchase decisions. There are two levels of the business environment: internal and external. The external environment is normally divided into two categories – general environment and task environment. The task environment more directly interacts with the business operation and covers the forces relevant to an individual organisation within an industry. An organisation's task environment is fundamental to management research from virtually all major perspectives. Complexity and interdependence of factors constituting to the modern business environment affect the emergence of new variables creation that alters the existing relations.

Facing a competitive business environment, organisations are required to develop innovative marketing strategies to sustain competitive advantage. SMEs' competitive advantage is not only affected by the environment but also depends on the competitive strategy involved (Ting, Wang & Wang, 2012). According to Kohli and Jaworski (1990), to succeed in today's competitive environment, companies need to know their customers and prospects as thoroughly as possible. By understanding consumers' characteristics and buying behaviour, their decision-making process and factors influencing their purchase decisions, marketers can use this market intelligence to make better-integrated marketing decisions. Moreover, as every other brand is as good as its competitor, there is no particular reason for the consumer to opt for a particular brand. That is why today's marketers aim at an all-around marketing strategy covering all the available modes aimed at brand royalty.

Environmental dynamism normally acts as a moderator of the relationship between innovation strategy and firm performance (Li & Atuahen-Gima, 2001), while environmental turbulence is an environment with a high degree of inter-period change that causes dynamism and uncertainty.

Environmental factors such as complexity, hostility, changing needs and preferences of customers, regulatory and changing economic variables have been found to have a significant effect on SME performance (Jiao et al., 2013; Ting, Wang & Wang, 2012). Consequently, when there is a high degree of turbulent environment, there would be higher risk and uncertainty, and reinforcing a high level of proactive approach would be needed in the strategic planning process (Lindelöf & Löfsten, 2006). Strategic marketing strategies were again found to be drivers of organisational positioning in a dynamic environment, which helps to enhance the development of new products/services for existing markets (Dzisi & Ofosu, 2014). This shows that the external environment plays a role in facilitating SMEs' performance through effective marketing strategy. From the ensuing discussion, it is hypothesised as follows:

H_1: There is a significant positive relationship between marketing strategies and the business performance of spare parts dealerships in Ghana

H_2: Environmental dynamism has a significant effect on the business performance of spare parts dealerships in Ghana

H_3: Environmental dynamism moderates the relationship between marketing strategies and business performance of spare parts dealerships in Ghana

Methodology

Research Design

The research adopted a quantitative approach to be able to test the formulated hypotheses. This approach was preferred because the objectives of the study required the estimation of the effect of the independent variable on the dependent variable (Williams, 2007; Allwood, 2012). An explanatory cross-sectional design was adopted, which researchers (Creswell et al., 2003; Williams, 2007; Allwood, 2012) have identified as the best method for examining the relationship between variables measured as constructs in the social sciences and over a specific period. The target population comprised spare parts dealerships in the Kumasi Metropolis in Ghana. This city was chosen because it is the hub of spare parts with a population of over 5,000 dealerships. Data were collected from 350 spare parts dealerships, using a structured questionnaire. However, 217 usable questionnaires were retrieved resulting in a 62% response rate. A pilot study was conducted using 50 spare parts dealerships in the Cape Coast Metropolis in the Central Region of Ghana. Cape Coast was chosen for the pilot study because spare parts dealerships in the Metropolis exhibit similar characteristics to those of their counterparts in the Kumasi Metropolis where the main study was conducted.

Data Collection

A structured questionnaire was used to collect data in this study. The questionnaire had five sections with the first section requesting information on the business. The second section focused on information on the independent variable – marketing strategies (product, price, place, promotion and Corporate Responsibility Management (CRM)) whilst the third section measured the moderating variable, which was environmental dynamism. The fourth section measured business performance and the last section sought information on the demographic characteristics of the owners/managers. As part of the data collection, informed consent forms were sent to the leaders of their association, which made up the accessible population. The leaders were used because they had a lot of influence on the willingness of the members to participate in this study. After obtaining approval from the association leaders, research assistants were hired to administer the questionnaires for two months. Those individuals who could not respond immediately requested that the research assistants returned the next day or two. Of the 300 questionnaires distributed, 217 participants completed and returned the questionnaire. Thus, the response rate was 62%.

Measures

Business performance was measured based on subjective measures such as customer satisfaction, creating value for customers, the successful launch of new products, sales revenue, creating employment, business profitability, lower operational cost and industry leadership. Research has shown that subjective measures of organisational performance are positively related to the objective measures and that they exhibit equivalent relationships with the independent variables (Laura, Shawnee & Cornelia, 1996; Wall et al., 2004; Simpson, Tuck & Bellamy, 2004, Nishii, Gotte & Raver, 2007).

Analytical Techniques

The study employed the SPSS version 21 to code, edit and process the data. Analysis was done using hierarchical regression modelling to examine the effects of the independent variables on business performance. This multi-stage hierarchical regression approach helps minimise the concerns of endogeneity due to the use of continuous scales on the three constructs (Hamilton & Nickerson, 2003). Hierarchical regression was performed to determine the impact of the marketing strategies variables and environmental dynamism on the business performance of spare parts dealerships. The confounding variables were made up of gender, age of business, owner, education, type of business, ownership status and the number of employees, whilst the main variables, marketing strategies, environmental dynamism and performance were added to the model later. The next section discusses the results.

Results

This section of the study presents and analyses data obtained from the field survey in an attempt to address the research objectives of the study. It focuses on the descriptive analysis of the key variables of interest, which provides a clear and concise numerical summary of the data obtained to facilitate the performance of inferential statistics, correlational analysis and, finally, presents and discusses the ordinary least square regression.

Socio-demographic Characteristics of Respondents

This section presents the demographic profile of respondents, which describes the basic characteristics of the sampled respondents of the study in terms of their gender, ages, educational level, ownership status and legal form of business, among others, in such a manner that allows for easier interpretation and decision-making. These parameters are varied based on each study, whereas those characteristics employed here are keen to spare parts behaviour of the respondents selected for this study.

Gender distribution of respondents shows that more males were captured than their female counterparts, as indicated in Table 6.1. The outcome of the survey revealed that, out of a total of 217 respondents, 169 were males, representing 77.9%, whereas there were 48 females, representing 22.1%. The male dominance in the sector can be attributed to the nature of the spare parts business which sometimes involves lifting heavy metals and some other car parts. The spare parts business is dominated by males compared to their female counterparts because of the technical know-how requirement.

Table 6.1   Socio-demographic Characteristics of Respondents

Gender of Respondents	Frequency	Percent
Male	169	77.9
Female	48	22.1
Age of respondents		
18–25	10	4.6
26–35	49	22.6
36–45	70	32.3
46–55	52	23.9
56 and above	36	16.6
Educational qualification		
No formal education	62	28.6
Basic education	84	38.7
SSCE/WASSCE	43	19.8
Tertiary	28	12.9
Ownership status		
Local	208	95.9
Foreign	8	3.7
Local and foreign	1	0.4
Founder/co-founder		
No	93	42.9
Yes	124	57.1
Legal form of business		
Private company	51	23.5
Sole trader	156	71.8
Partnership	10	4.7

The study captured the age of respondents as actual distinct values. However, the ages of respondents were grouped in the analysis to allow for a concise understanding and presentation. In Table 6.1, the minimum and maximum ages are 18 and 65 years, respectively. The results show that the modal age group of respondents was 36–45 years. Besides, general observation shows that about 79.2% of the total respondents are between the ages of 26 and 55. This implies that most of the spare parts business dealerships are in their prime age of life, which falls within the economic activity age group. Meanwhile, only 16.7% of the total respondents belonging to age 56 and above were captured. The proportion in the age group 36–45 years was 70 out of a total of 216, representing 32.4%, and this takes the highest proportion out of all other age groups.

As part of assessing the influence of marketing strategies on business performance, respondents were asked to state their highest educational qualification among other socio-demographic variables employed in this study. The results revealed that more than half of the respondents had attained secondary education and below. Those without formal educational level but operate a spare parts business are about 62 out of a total of 217, representing 28.6%, whereas those who have attained above secondary level of education (tertiary education) are about 28, representing 13%. The basic level of education seems to be the highest and comprises 84 respondents, representing 38.7%. This is followed immediately by senior high/secondary school education with 43 respondents, representing 19.8%.

The ownership status of the respondents shows that about 3.7% of the spare parts businesses were owned by foreign nationals while 95.8% of the spare parts businesses were owned by local nationals. It implies that the spare parts businesses were dominated by local nationals. In the last decade, the government has put in place policies to protect small local businesses, thus explaining the figures for the ownership status of the businesses. The last category included those with both local and foreign ownership status, which comprised about 0.5% of the total businesses. In terms of how the business was founded, more than half of the respondents indicated that the spare parts business was founded by them in this survey, representing 56.7%, whereas 43.3% indicated that the business was neither founded nor co-foundered by them, which means they were managing the business on behalf of the founder.

The legal form of business shows that out of a total of 217 respondents, about 3.7% of the spare parts businesses were partnerships, 72.6% were sole proprietorships and 23.7% were limited companies. The results show that the sector is dominated by sole proprietorships due to its small nature.

Descriptive Analysis

This section of the study presents descriptive statistics on the key variables of interest. Descriptive statistics intends to provide simple summaries of the sample and the measures that included marketing strategy, environmental dynamism and performance to facilitate the assessment of inferential statistics. Marketing strategy was measured using marketing mix elements; product, price, distribution, promotion and CRM. To effectively appreciate the nature of the results, a discussion was made on the basic parameters of the variables, such as the use of mean and standard deviation values.

To assess marketing strategy and how it influences the performance of spare parts businesses, respondents were requested to rate marketing strategies on a five-point Likert scale with the highest being strong agreement (5) and the lowest being least agreement (1) each to measure the constructs: product, price, place (distribution) and promotion as marketing strategy elements; the moderating variable, environmental dynamism and the dependent variable, performance. The

Table 6.2   Descriptive Statistics

Variables	Mean	Std. Deviation	Rank	N
Product	2.4021	0.91187	Low	217
Price	3.3663	0.46568	Moderate	217
Distribution	2.6796	0.71550	Moderate	217
Promotion	2.7506	0.59797	Moderate	217
Customer relationship management	3.9783	0.51158	High	217
Environmental factors	3.4093	0.50788	High	217
Performance	3.8683	0.43770	High	217
Valid N (listwise)				217

Note: Mean classification: 1.00–1.80 = very low; 1.81–2.60 = low; 2.61–3.40 = moderate; 3.41–4.20 = high; 4.21–5.00 = very high. Where length of the class was calculated by dividing the highest value minus the least value on the number of the class equal 5–1 on 5 = 0.80.

scores were aggregated to obtain the resultant variables or construct in index form for each variable, as presented in Table 6.2.

The descriptive statistics displayed in Table 6.2 is the analysis of the means (average scores), pricing strategy influences business performance (M = 3.13, SD = 0.14), followed by the use of promotion strategy on performance (M = 2.75, SD = 0.59), distribution strategy influences performance (M = 2.68, SD = 0.72) and, finally, product offered by respondents has the least influence on business performance (M = 2.40, SD = 0.91). In all the standard deviation values were close to zero, meaning that most data values of all the variables were close to the mean. The results again indicated that customer relationship management has a higher influence on business performance (M = 3.98, SD = 0.51) than environmental factors do have on the performance of the business (M = 3.41, SD = 0.51). Finally, the average (mean) score of performance stood at 3.86 with a standard deviation of 0.43 measuring the deviation of the data values from the mean score value.

Correlation Analysis

The study examined the relationship between marketing strategies and the business performance of spare parts dealerships. The correlation analysis was performed to show the degree of association between the marketing strategy variables and the business performance of spare parts dealerships. The results are presented in Table 6.3.

The results show that marketing strategy such as the product offered by the spare parts dealerships has a positively significant relationship with the performance of the business (r = 0.493, p < 0.05). Although there was evidence of a linear relationship between product and business performance, the relationship can be described as weak (Cohen, 1988).

The results again showed that the price charged by spare parts dealerships has a positively significant relationship with the performance of the business (r = 0.286, p < 0.05). With evidence of a linear relationship between price and business performance, the relationship can be described as weak (Cohen, 1988). Furthermore, distribution channel as a marketing strategy has a positive

Table 6.3   Correlation Matrix

Variables	Performance	Product	Price	Distribution	Promotion
Performance	1				
Product	0.493***	1			
	(0.000)				
Price	0.286***	0.468***	1		
	(0.000)	(0.000)			
Distribution	0.473***	0.711***	0.384***	1	
	(0.000)	(0.000)	(0.000)		
Promotion	0.419***	0.759***	0.406***	0.674**	1
	(0.000)	(0.000)	(0.000)	(0.000)	

***, ** denote statistical significance at 5% and 10%, respectively.

significant relationship with the performance of the business ($r = 0.473$, $p < 0.05$). Besides the evidence of a linear relationship between distribution and business performance, the relationship is weak (Cohen, 1988). Finally, promotion strategy employed by spare parts dealerships to market their products has a positively significant relationship with performance of the second-hand spare parts business ($r = 0.419$, $p < 0.05$).

Moderation Analysis

The study examined the moderating role of environmental dynamism on the relationship between marketing strategy and the business performance of spare parts dealerships. The results in Table 6.4 reveal that environmental dynamism moderates the association between product as a marketing strategy and performance of the business with a positively significant relationship existing between product and business performance ($r = 0.502$, $p < 0.05$). Likewise, environmental dynamism moderates the association between price as a marketing strategy and performance of the business with a positively significant relationship existing between price and business performance ($r = 0.285$, $p < 0.05$). Furthermore, environmental dynamism moderates the association between distribution as a marketing strategy and performance of the business with a positively significant relationship existing between distribution and business performance ($r = 0.493$, $p < 0.05$). Finally, environmental dynamism moderates the association between promotion as a marketing strategy and performance of the business with a positively significant relationship existing between promotion and business performance ($r = 0.424$, $p < 0.05$).

Regression Analysis

The study assessed the effect of marketing strategy on the business performance of spare parts dealerships in Ghana. The results are presented in Tables 6.5–6.7. From Table 6.5, the results in model 1 of an adjusted R^2 value of 0.262 implies that the marketing strategy adopted or employed by spare parts dealerships explains 26.2% variation in business performance. The findings suggest

Table 6.4 Moderating Matrix

Variables		Performance	Product	Price	Distribution	Promotion
Performance		1				
Product		0.502***	1			
		(0.000)				
Environmental	Price	0.285***	0.484***	1		
		(0.000)	(0.000)			
	Distribution	0.493***	0.692***	0.406***	1	
		(0.000)	(0.000)	(0.000)		
	Promotion	0.424***	0.752***	0.414***	0.664**	1
		(0.000)	(0.000)	(0.000)	(0.000)	

***, ** *denote statistical significance at 1% and 5%, respectively.*

Table 6.5 Model Summary

Model	R	R Square	Adjusted R Square	Std. Error of the Estimate	Durbin–Watson
1	0.525[a]	0.275	0.262	0.37607	
2	0.548[b]	0.300	0.280	0.37134	1.780

Table 6.6 ANOVA[a]

Model		Sum of Squares	df	Mean Square	F	Sig.
1	Regression	11.398	4	2.850	20.148	0.000[b]
	Residual	29.983	212	0.141		
	Total	41.381	216			
2	Regression	12.424	6	2.071	15.016	0.000[c]
	Residual	28.957	210	0.138		
	Total	41.381	216			

[a] Dependent variable: business performance.
[b] Predictors: (constant), promotion, price, distribution, product.
[c] Predictors: (constant), promotion, price, distribution, product, environmental factors, customer relationship management.

that approximately 26% of the variation in business performance was explained jointly by the independent variables (product, price, distribution and promotion), as shown in Table 6.5.

This chapter further assessed the effect of environmental dynamism on the business performance of spare parts dealerships, which was captured by model 2, as presented in Table 6.5, after controlling for marketing strategy and customer relationship management variables. It was evident that environmental dynamism explains variation in business performance with an adjusted R^2 value of 0.28. It, therefore, implies that environmental dynamism explains 28% variation in the business performance of spare parts dealerships.

Furthermore, an analysis of variance was conducted between business performance and marketing strategy, as indicated by model 1, and that of environmental dynamism after controlling for marketing strategy and customer relationship management indicated by model 2 at 95% confidence level. The results in model 1 revealed that the independent variables (product, price, distribution and promotion strategy) were significant joint predictors of business performance of spare parts dealerships ($F_{(4,216)} = 20.15$; $p < 0.05$), while model 2 revealed that the independent variables (product, price, distribution, promotion, environmental dynamism and customer relationship management) were significant joint predictors of business performance of spare parts dealerships in Ghana, ($F_{(6,216)} = 15.02$; $p < 0.05$), as shown in Table 6.6. Furthermore, an individual t-test of significance was performed between business performance and marketing strategy variables, indicated by model 1, and also a further individual t-test of significance was carried out between business performance and environmental dynamism after controlling for marketing strategy and customer relationship management, as indicated by model 2.

Table 6.7 Coefficients

Model 1	Unstandardised Coefficient	Std. Error	Standardised Coefficient	T	Sig.	Tolerance	VIF
	B	Error	Beta				
(Constant)	2.932	0.210		13.967	0.000		
Product	0.135	0.049	0.280	2.763	0.006	0.332	3.010
Price	0.053	0.063	0.056	0.838	0.403	0.766	1.305
Distribution	0.142	0.053	0.232	2.662	0.008	0.450	2.221
Promotion	0.020	0.069	0.028	0.295	0.768	0.387	2.587
Model 2							
(Constant)	2.460	0.318		7.746	0.000		
Product	0.148	0.049	0.308	3.017	0.003	0.320	3.123
Price	0.026	0.065	0.028	0.402	0.688	0.703	1.422
Distribution	0.172	0.055	0.281	3.097	0.002	0.405	2.467
Promotion	0.009	0.069	0.012	0.128	0.899	0.378	2.646
Customer relation management	−0.002	0.070	−0.002	−0.023	0.982	0.494	2.024
Environmental factors	0.143	0.053	0.166	2.706	0.007	0.884	1.131

Model 1 results in Table 6.7 provide evidence that product (β = 0.135; p = 0.006) and distribution (β = 0.142; p = 0.008) were statistically significant independent predictors of business performance at 95% confidence level. The results show that the products offered and the distribution channel employed by spare parts dealerships have a positive and statistically significant effect on business performance such that a unit change in the products offered and distribution channel employed would lead to 0.135 and 0.143 change in business performance, respectively. The results support previous studies that have established that marketing strategies of product and distribution play an important role in enhancing the performance of businesses (Rose & Shoham, 2002; Theodosiou & Leonidou, 2003; Owomoyela, Oyeniyi & Ola, 2013; Kiveu, 2013). Ang, Meng and Kotler (2000) note that new products should be introduced at the same or lower price to induce performance; thus, product and pricing decisions need to be made taking into consideration the complexity of the environment and nature of customers. Our results reveal that price charged (β = 0.053; p = 0.403) and promotion (β = 0.020; p = 0.768) were not statistically significant predictors of business performance. Thus, although a positive influence exists between business performance and price and promotion, it was regarded as statistically not significant. The results contradict the study of Chari et al. (2014) who found that making changes to product, price and promotion plans could be beneficial to firms.

The results in model 2 showed that the environmental dynamism factor (β = 0.143; p = 0.007) was a statistically significant independent predictor of business performance after controlling for marketing strategy and customer relationship management. The implications are that aside from the marketing strategy and customer relationship management employed by spare parts dealerships in Ghana, environmental dynamism had a statistically significant positive effect on business performance such that a unit change in environmental dynamism factors would lead to 0.143 change in performance. This finding supports the other studies (Jiao et al., 2013; Ting, Wang & Wang, 2012) which found that environmental dynamism can significantly influence SME performance. Similarly, the product offered and the distribution channel employed by spare parts dealerships had positive and statistically significant effect on business performance (β = 0.148; p = 0.003; β = 0.172; p = 0.002), respectively. Nevertheless, price charged (β = 0.026; p = 0.688); promotion (β = 0.009; p = 0.899) and customer relationship management (β = −0.002; p = 0.982) were not statistically significant independent predictors of business performance. It can be inferred from the results that, although a positive influence exists between business performance and price and promotion, a negative effect was reported for customer relationship management.

Conclusions and Implications

This chapter examined the influence of marketing strategies on the performance of spare parts dealerships and the moderating role of environmental dynamism. The results showed that marketing strategies were significant joint predictors of performance. Out of the five marketing strategies studied, product and distribution were independent significant predictors of the performance of spare parts dealerships. To gain a competitive advantage over their rivals, the type of product to offer and the quality are very essential when deciding which spare parts to sell. Again, dealerships should emphasise not only the holistic product quality but also the elements of the products that consumers can easily evaluate before purchasing. Additionally, how effectively the spare parts dealerships get their product to consumers and end-users is also relevant. This implies that a firm must distribute its product to the user at the right place at the right time and the distribution strategy must meet the overall marketing objectives of the firm. However, independence, price, promotion and CRM did not have any significant influence on performance. Interaction with some of the dealerships revealed that consumers are less price-sensitive when it comes to spare parts because they are necessities; hence, they are willing to pay no matter what the cost. Even though price did not influence performance significantly, it is important to set realistic prices to increase profitability. For promotion, these spare parts dealerships are found in one location, so it is easy for consumers to locate them. For this reason, they do not see the need to embark on marketing communications activities. It is, however, imperative that they embark on some marketing communications activities when consumers visit their shops as well as when new products are introduced into the market.

Environmental dynamism influenced performance significantly. This implies that knowledge of the relevant macro-environmental factors could cause these spare parts dealerships to adapt to changes when the need arises. The results equally revealed that environmental dynamism moderated the relationship between marketing strategies and the business performance of spare parts dealerships. This implies that changes in the environment can determine the marketing strategy to adopt to ensure higher performance. Hence, there is a need for spare parts dealerships to understand their business environment to know the marketing strategy to adopt at any point in time.

Future Research Directions

Even though the chapter contributes to the literature on the business performance of spare parts dealerships, the study was undertaken in a specific sector and hence could not be generalised to other industries. The validity of our results could be tested by replicating this study in other industries such as the service sector. Again, a quantitative approach was adopted which means that further studies need to use qualitative approaches to better explain the values obtained from the quantitative study.

References

Allwood, C. M. (2012). The distinction between qualitative and quantitative research methods is problematic. *Quality & Quantity*, *46*(5), 1417–1429.

Amit, R., & Zott, C. (2001). Value creation in e-business. *Strategic Management Journal*, *22*(6–7), 493–520.

Ang, H. S., Meng, L. S., & Kotler, P. (2000). The Asian apocalypse: Crisis marketing for consumers and businesses. *Long Range Planning*, *33*(1), 97–119.

Anyika, E. N. (2010). Challenges of implementing sustainable health care delivery in Nigeria under environmental uncertainty. *Journal of Hospital Administration*, *3*(6), 113–125.

Aremu, M. A., & Lawal, A. T. (2012). Exploring marketing strategy as a catalyst for performance in Nigerian telecommunication industry. *International Journal of Multidisciplinarity in Business and Science*, *2*(4), 65–71.

Aryeetey, E. (1998). Informal finance for private sector development in Africa. Economic Research Papers No. 41. The African Development Bank, Abidjan.

Boyd, B. K., & Fulk, J. (1996). Executive scanning and perceived uncertainty: A multidimensional model. *Journal of Management*, *22*(1), 1–21.

Chari, C., Katsikeas, S., Balabanis, G., & Robson, M. J. (2014). Emergent marketing strategies and Performance: The effects of market uncertainty and strategic feedback systems. *British Journal of Management*, *24*, 145–165.

Cohen, J. (1988). *Statistical Power Analysis for the Behavioral Sciences* (2nd ed.). Hillsdale, NJ: Lawrence Erlbaum Associates.

Cravens, D. W., Piercy, N. F., & Baldauf, A. (2009). Management framework guiding strategic thinking in rapidly changing markets. *Journal of Marketing Management, 25*(1–2), 31–49.

Creswell, J. W., Plano Clark, V. L., Gutmann, M. L., & Hanson, W. E. (2003). Advanced mixed methods research designs. In A. Tashakkori & C. Teddlie (Eds.), *Handbook of mixed methods in social and behavioral research* (pp. 209–240). Thousand Oaks: CA Sage.

Dahmiri, Octavia, A., & Fatricia, R. S. (2017). The influence of service marketing mix and service quality on students' satisfaction in Jambi university. Indonesia. *International Journal of Economics, Commerce and Management, 5*(6), 398–414.

David, C. M., Neeraj, A., Derek, K., John, W., Michael, R., Ruba, B., Julia, C., & Julio, B. (2013), *Lessons on technology and growth from small-business leaders,* The Boston Consulting Group, UK. Retrieved from [online]: https://www.bcgperspectives.com/content/articles/technology_software_globalization _ahe ad_curve_lessons_technology_growth_small_business_leaders/ (Posted 5 October 2013).

Duncan, R. B. (1972). Characteristics of organizational environments and perceived environmental uncertainty. *Administrative Science Quarterly,* 17(3), 313–327.

Dzisi, S., & Ofosu, D. (2014). Marketing strategies and the performance of SMEs in Ghana. *Marketing,* 6(5), 102–111.

Green, K. W., Whitten, D., & Inman, A. R. (2012). Aligning marketing strategies throughout the supply chain to enhance performance. *Industrial Marketing Management, 42*(6), 1008–1018.

Haghighinasab, M., Sattari, B., Ebrahimi, M., & Roghanian, P. (2013). Identification of innovative marketing strategies to increase the performance of SMEs in Iran. *International Journal of Fundamental Psychology & Social Sciences, 3*(2), 26–30.

Hamilton, B. H., & Nickerson, J. A. (2003). Correcting for endogeneity in strategic management research. *Strategic Organization, 1*(1), 51–78.

Jiao, H., Alon, I., Koo, C. K., & Cui, Y. (2013). When should organizational change be implemented? The moderating effect of environmental dynamism between dynamic capabilities and new venture performance. *Journal of Engineering and Technology Management, 30*(2), 188–205.

Kadhim, F. A., Abdullah, T. F., & Abdullah, M. F. (2016) Effects of marketing mix on customer satisfaction: Empirical study on tourism industry in Malaysia. *International Journal of Applied Research, 2*(2), 357–360.

Kiveu, D. D. (2013). Determinants of performance of the tourism industry in Kenya: A case of Kakamega County. Unpublished Project, University of Nairobi.

Kohli, A. K., & Jaworski, B. J. (1990). Market orientation: The construct, research propositions, and managerial implications. *Journal of Marketing, 54,* 1–18.

Laanti, R., McDougall, F., & Baume, G. (2009). Evolving value networks and internationalisation of national telecommunication companies from small and open economies. In Lee *Handbook of Research on Telecommunications Planning and Management for Business* (pp. 173–193). IGI Global.

Laura, B. F., Shawnee, K. V., & Cornelia, L. M. D. (1996). The contribution of quality to business performance. *International Journal of Operations & Production Management, 16*(8), 44–62.

Li, H., & Atuahene-Gima, K. (2001). Product innovation strategy and the performance of new technology ventures in China. *Academy of management Journal, 44*(6), 1123–1134.

Lindelöf, P., & Löfsten, H. (2006). Environmental hostility and firm behavior – An empirical examination of new technology-based firms on science parks. *Journal of Small Business Management, 44*(3), 386–406.

Lin-Hung, L. (1993) Consumer product classification, innovation type and new product marketing strategy. National Cheng Chi University Department of Business Administration of PhD Thesis.

Macharia, E. W. (2013). The effects of global financial crisis on the financial performance of commercial banks offering mortgage finance in Kenya. *International Journal of Social Sciences and Entrepreneurship, 1*(2), 688–701.

Marjanova, J. T., & Stojanovski, M. (2012). *Marketing knowledge and strategy for SMEs: Can they live without it?* From: eprints.ugd.edu.mk.

Mohammed, A. A., Rashid, B. B., & Tahir, S. B. (2014). Customer relationship management (CRM) technology and organization performance: Is marketing capability a missing link? An empirical study in the Malaysian hotel industry. *Asian Social Science, 10*(9), 197–212.

Mutambuki, M. K., & Orwa, B. H. (2014). Marketing strategies of commercial fish farming under Economic Stimulus Programme (ESP) in Kenya: An empirical study of Kitui County. *International Journal of Humanities and Social Science, 4*(8), 111–121.

Nishii, L., Gotte, A., & Raver, J. (2007). Upper echelon theory revisited: The relationship between upper echelon diversity, the adoption of diversity practices, and organizational performance. Working Paper, CAHRS WP07–04.

Oloko, M., Anene, E. B., Kiara, P. G., Kathambi, I., & Mutulu, J. (2014). Marketing strategies for profitability: A case of Safaricom Ltd in Kenya Telecommunication Industry. *International Journal of Scientific and Research Publications, 4*(5), 1–5.

Owomoyela, S. K., Oyeniyi, K. O., & Ola, O. S. (2013). Investigating the impact of marketing mix elements on consumer loyalty: An empirical study on Nigerian Breweries Plc. *Interdisciplinary Journal of Contemporary Research in Business, 4*(11), 485–496.

Pett, T. L., & Wolff, J. A. (2011). Examining SME performance: The role of innovation, R&D, and internationalization. *International Journal of Entrepreneurial Venturing, 3*(3), 301–314. http://dx.doi.org /10.1504/IJEV.2011.041277

Rose, G. M., & Shoham, A. (2002). Export performance and market orientation: Establishing an empirical link. *Journal of Business Research, 55*(3), 217–225.

Santos-Vijande, L., Sanzo-Pérez, M., Trespalacios Gutiérrez, J., & Rodríguez, N. (2012). Marketing capabilities development in small and medium enterprises: Implications for performance. *Journal of CENTRUM Cathedra: The Business and Economics Research Journal, 5*(1), 24–42.

Simpson, M., Tuck, N., & Bellamy, S. (2004). Small business success factors: The role of education and training. *Education and Training, 46*(8/9), 481–491.

Taiwo, A. S. (2010). The influence of work environment on workers productivity: A case of selected oil and gas industry in Lagos, Nigeria. *African Journal of Business Management, 4*(3), 299.

Tapia Ruíz, A. L. (2013). *Plan de marketing para el Negocio Soda Bar Mama Julia en el cantón san Juan Bosco.* Bachelor's thesis, Quito: Universidad Israel.

Theng, L. G., & Boon, J. L. W. (1996). An exploratory study of factors affecting the failure of local small and medium enterprises. *Asia Pacific Journal of Management, 13*(2), 47–61.

Theodosiou, M., & Leonidou, L. C. (2003). Standardization versus adaptation of international marketing strategy: An integrative assessment of the empirical research. *International Business Review, 12*(2), 141–171.

Ting, H. F., Wang, H. B., & Wang, D. S. (2012). The moderating role of environmental dynamism on the influence of innovation strategy and firm performance. *International Journal of Innovation, Management and Technology, 3*(5), 517.

Wall, T. D., Michie, J., Patterson, M., Wood, S. J., Sheehan, M., Clegg, C. W., & West, M. (2004). On the validity of subjective measures of company performance. *Personnel Psychology, 57*(1), 95–118.

Williams, C. (2007). Research methods. *Journal of Business & Economics Research, 5*(3),65–72.

Chapter 7

Female Entrepreneurship in the Tourism Industry: A Ghanaian Outlook

Kwame Adom

Contents

Introduction

The global economic downturn and regional uncertainties in 2008 strained tourism (Holden, 2016). The recent COVID-19 pandemic has added more misery to the tourism industry globally (see, Bakar & Rosbi, 2020; Škare, Soriano & Porada-Rochon, 2021; Soliku, Kyiire, Mahama & Kubio, 2021). Consequently, a new word has emerged, "staycation", which means having a vacation in your home country or near home (see Fox, 2009). Regardless of the economic downturn, there is a prediction that the tourism sector will grow or increase over the next decade, given

DOI: 10.4324/9781003302339-7

the changing trends in the business environment (Rate, Moutinho & Ballantyne, 2018; van der Schyff, Meyer & Ferreira, 2019). Changing economic conditions, new technologies and shifting consumer behaviours are likely to alter the work of the tourist population (Rate et al., 2018). The changing cultural trend, the shift from collectivism to individualism, is also expected to emphasise individual and self-determined holidays with vigorous recreational pursuits boosting tourism. According to Gmelch (2018), tourism is one of the world's largest industries. Hence, most governments and entrepreneurs consider it an affirmative force for economic development.

Besides contributing to economic development, the tourism industry also boosts local entrepreneurship (Ateljevic & Page, 2017). Consequently, entrepreneurship is reinforced in the tourism sector, which has received policy support and donor-assisted funding in developing countries. Regardless, understanding the role of entrepreneurship in tourism development needs to be included in academic discourse, as opined by Ateljevic and Page (2017). More so, female entrepreneurs contribute to developing the tourism industry, although few studies are there to prove this (see Kimbu & Ngoasong, 2016; Kimbu, Ngoasong, Adeola & Afenyo-Agbe, 2019; Ngoasong & Kimbu, 2019).

Over the years, it has been challenging to describe the tourism industry. It could be partly due to the lack of a measurable production function or output. Tourism is multifaceted; it transcends several conservative sectors of an economy. Therefore, to thrive in the industry, there is a need to integrate inputs from all the other sectors: economic, social, cultural and environmental (Lickorish & Jenkins, 2007). The outcome could be more precise in conceptualising the term (Middleton, 1994).

Consequently, the definition of the tourism industry is more contextual than a universal concept. No universal industry structure applies in all countries (Middleton, 1994). Whereas restaurants and shopping facilities are key tourist attractions in France, the situation differs in Russia and most developing contexts like Ghana. Reflecting on the Ghanaian situation and for this book chapter, we define tourism in line with the thoughts of Burkart and Medlik (1981). Thus, tourism is the phenomenon that emanates from impermanent visits or stays outside an individual's usual residence for purposes other than advancing an occupation for which one will receive remuneration. Despite the notion that the tourism sector's components differ according to country, it has some sub-sectors. These include accommodation, transport, travel agents, tour operators, catering and creative industries, such as creating handicrafts and entertainment (Middleton, 1994).

The tourism sector in Ghana is growing, presenting the need for more tourism infrastructure (Ghana Investment Promotion Centre -GPIC, n.d). Over ten years (2005–2014), Ghana recorded a 178.5% increase in international tourist arrivals from 392,500 to 1,093,000, representing an annual average growth rate of 11.4% (Ghana Statistical Service, 2017). Resultantly, a wide range of investment opportunities has arisen. Realising the Ghanaian tourism sector's potential, successive governments have made efforts to market the tourism sector. A recent past strategy is the "Year of Return" campaign which encouraged the African-American and Diaspora market to visit Ghana as tourists to mark the 400 years of the first enslaved Africans arriving in Jamestown, Virginia (Ghana Tourism Authority, 2019).

Séraphin, Butler and Vanessa (2013) denote that entrepreneurship is essential to any tourism industry. They identified that female entrepreneurs' role in shaping or developing the tourism sector in Ghana has become imperative. The longing for more female participants in the tourism sector resulted in the World Tourism Organisation's quest to hold the "First Regional Congress on Women Empowerment in the Tourism Sector – Focus on Africa" in November 2019 in Accra, Ghana. The event was hosted by the Government of the Republic of Ghana (United Nations World Tourism Organisation, 2019).

Evidence from literature from developing countries denotes that female entrepreneurs are deemed as "rising stars" and the "new instruments" for the growth of economies (De Vita, Mari &

Poggesi, 2014; Vossenberg, 2013). Reports also show that the tourism sector offers better opportunities for female participation in the workforce, entrepreneurship and leadership than in the alternative sectors of the economy (United Nations Tourism Organization (UNTWO) 2014; World Bank, 2017a). Hence, an analysis of how female entrepreneurs have contributed to the tourism industry in an emerging context like Ghana is timely. Thus, this chapter explores how female entrepreneurs in Ghana have contributed to the tourism industry's development. Hence, the critical research question the study seeks to answer is, "What is the role of female entrepreneurs in the development of the tourism sector of Ghana?" The chapter discusses female entrepreneurship and tourism literature under different relevant headings.

The Tourism Industry at a Glance: An African Perspective

In 2018, Europe was the leader in international tourism, receiving 710 million international tourists and making USD 570 billion. It was followed by Asia and the Pacific, with tourist arrivals of 348 million and a revenue of USD 435 billion. Africa only surpassed the Middle East with tourist arrivals of 67 million and a gain of 38 billion. However, although Africa beat the Middle East regarding the number of international tourist visits, the Middle East made almost twice (USD 73 billion) the revenue Africa mobilised. Hence, globally, Africa made the most negligible revenue from tourism. Forward-looking, the UNWTO predicts that international tourist arrivals in Africa will reach an estimated 134 million by the year 2030 (OSAAS, 2016).

The African continent has witnessed enormous economic growth from tourism in the past decade. The region has mammoth environmental assets, cultural heritage and natural resources, resulting in tourism gains. UNWTO (2014) indicates that globally Africa is one of the fastest-growing destinations for tourism, behind South-East Asia. In 2014, international arrivals to Africa increased by 2%, and the total revenue generated is estimated at USD 56 million. In all, travel and tourism's direct contribution to Africa's GDP hit USD 83 billion in 2014 (World Travel and Tourism Council, 2015). The travel and tourism sector also contributed to approximately nine million direct employees in Africa and is one of the leading employers, exceeding sectors like financial services, banking and mining (World Travel and Tourism Council, 2015).

The statistics for the issues discussed above are captured in Figure 7.1 to create a clearer understanding of Africa's and Ghana's global tourism position. The statistics show that there is still a need for tourism development in the region.

The outlook of the global tourism sector presents several entrepreneurial opportunities for exploits by entrepreneurs and female entrepreneurs. According to the World Bank (2017a), in some countries like Indonesia, Malaysia, Thailand and the Philippines, tourism has almost twice as many women employers/entrepreneurs as other sectors. In Latin America, females own and manage 51% of tourism businesses. An explanation for this phenomenon is that the tourism sector places less emphasis on formal education and training, allows actors to work part-time, is less capital intensive and relies on personal and hospitality skills, hence an attractive sector for females.

Understanding the Composition of the Tourism Industry

The tourism sector, as indicated in the previous section, is multifaceted. "Tourism can raise demand for local products and services, create investment and entrepreneurial opportunities, and improve transportation, infrastructure, and utilities" (World Bank, 2017a, p. 21) as several such

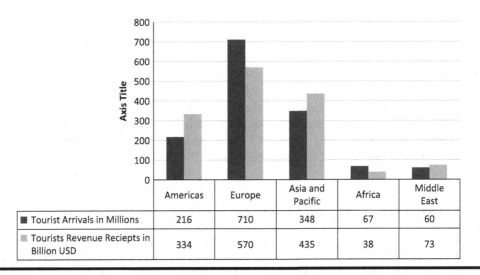

	Americas	Europe	Asia and Pacific	Africa	Middle East
■ Tourist Arrivals in Millions	216	710	348	67	60
▪ Tourists Revenue Reciepts in Billion USD	334	570	435	38	73

Figure 7.1 Tourism arrivals and revenue by the continent. Source: UNWTO (2019).

sub-sectors work together to make up the tourism sector. Scholars such as Middleton (1994) and Lavery (1987a) have identified sub-sectors or components of the tourism sector. Middleton (1994) identifies five sub-sectors of the tourism sector. These are the accommodation, travel, attraction, travel organisation and destination organisation sectors. Lavery (1987a) mentions similar sub-sectors as the tourism industry's components (travel, accommodation, leisure facilities, entertainment and tourism organisations). Whereas Middleton (1994) identifies five sub-sectors, Lavery (1987b) highlights six. The slight difference is that Middleton (1994) emphasises more on tourism organisations and attractions for tourists. Mason (1990) mentions that the tourism activity location and attractions sector is the core of tourism. Figure 7.2 shows the breakdown of these different sub-sectors as Middleton (1994) propagated.

Prosser (1998) also provides an in-depth view of how the tourism sector works. The author illustrates the tourism environment and the interaction of the various actors' activities in the tourism sector. For Prosser (1998), tourist demand attributes, transportation, communication, the destination environment and information, and promotion and direction play critical roles in facilitating tourism. For instance, the characteristics of a tourist destination will attract tourists. However, the desire to see a tourist destination becomes a reality when suitable transportation systems enable tourists to reach the desired destination. Figure 7.3 illustrates Prosser's ideology.

The study adopted the Tourism Environment Framework by Prosser (1998) to discuss female entrepreneurs' contributions to tourism in Ghana. The justification for using the Prosser (1998) framework is that anecdotal evidence reflects how Ghana's tourism industry is structured and works.

The Tourism Industry in Ghana Explained

Over the past decades, the tourism industry has received attention from successive governments in Ghana, with heightened awareness recognised in recent years. The rising attention to the sector results from increased tourist arrivals and mobilised revenue. Hence, there is an increase in both private and public investments in the industry. In recent years, private individuals (entrepreneurs)

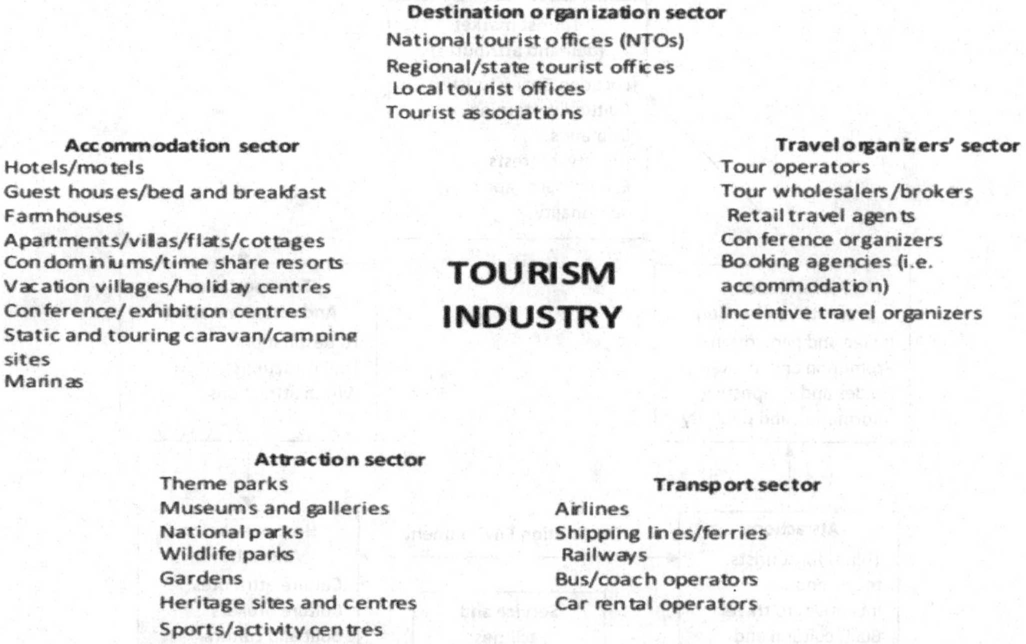

Destination organization sector
National tourist offices (NTOs)
Regional/state tourist offices
Local tourist offices
Tourist associations

Accommodation sector
Hotels/motels
Guest houses/bed and breakfast
Farmhouses
Apartments/villas/flats/cottages
Condominiums/time share resorts
Vacation villages/holiday centres
Conference/exhibition centres
Static and touring caravan/camping
sites
Marinas

**TOURISM
INDUSTRY**

Travel organizers' sector
Tour operators
Tour wholesalers/brokers
Retail travel agents
Conference organizers
Booking agencies (i.e.
accommodation)
Incentive travel organizers

Attraction sector
Theme parks
Museums and galleries
National parks
Wildlife parks
Gardens
Heritage sites and centres
Sports/activity centres

Transport sector
Airlines
Shipping lines/ferries
Railways
Bus/coach operators
Car rental operators

Figure 7.2   The main subsectors of the tourism industry. Source: Adapted from Middleton (1994).

have set up businesses such as travel and tours, catering and craft businesses, and others within the industry. The tourism industry in Ghana can be a significant source of government revenue if the right policies are put in place by all the players in the industry. For example, the government tagged 2019 as "the year of return", which sought to attract African-Americans in the diaspora to visit Ghana to mark the 400 years of the beginning of the slave trade on the Ghanaian coasts (Tetteh, 2019).

Tourism is one of Ghana's critical sectors, which can turn its economic misfortunes around (Akyeampong, 2009). The tourism sector is projected to contribute about 5.20% to GDP in 2022 (Government of Ghana, 2012). Having recognised the tourism sector's potential, Ghana's government, in efforts to develop the tourism sector, developed and implemented a 15-year Integrated Development Programme (1996–2010). After this, upon a review of the mentioned plan, the Tourism Ministry in Ghana collaborated with the United Nations Development Programme (UNDP), United Nations World Tourism Organization (UNTWO) and United Nations Economic Commission for Africa (UNECA) to launch the National Tourism Development Plan (NTDP), which is expected to cover the years 2013–2027 (Government of Ghana, 2012). The NTDP is a blueprint for the development of the sector. The expected revenue via tourism in Ghana may rise to USD 2.5 billion in 2022 and 4.3 billion in 2027. The achievement of these figures will largely depend on both government and private individuals (entrepreneurs).

In recent times, Ghana's tourism sector has witnessed substantial investment. Programmes and projects have been designed to increase the industry's investment, domestic and international tourists and improve present infrastructure. In the last four years, Ghana's tourism sector has attracted over USD 600 million in investments. The sector remains among Ghana's top five foreign exchange earners (GIPC, n.d). In February 2019, CNN International

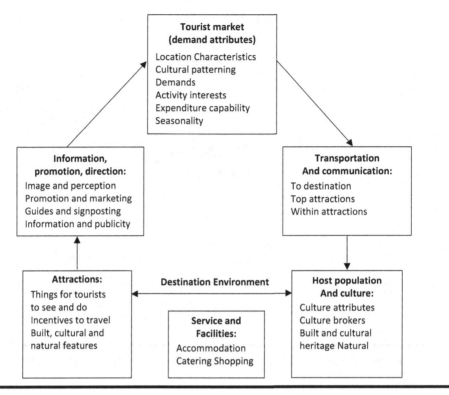

Figure 7.3   The tourism environment. Source: Adapted from Prosser (1998).

identified Ghana as one of the 19 must-visit tourist destinations. This recognition by CNN will likely positively influence the number of international tourist visits to Ghana. Hence, entrepreneurial activities can be pursued by setting up 3–5 stars hotels, restaurants and beach resorts, among others, to handle the rising numbers. Specialised tourism companies could also be created to grow and operate adventure tourism, eco-tourism, cultural tourism and heritage tourism. As part of efforts to develop the tourism sector, the Government of Ghana has instituted incentives to encourage entrepreneurship in the tourism sector. These include a 22% reduced corporate tax rate against the general rate of 25%, a 10% concessionary rate on imported goods for tourist establishments and import duty exemptions for plant and machinery procured for establishing ventures in tourism (GIPC, n.d). These are valuable policies for female entrepreneurs venturing into the tourism sector since studies show that access to finance is difficult for women (Otoo, Fulton, Ibro & Lowenberg-DeBoer, 2011).

Women Entrepreneurship: A Holistic Perspective

Scholars advocate that female entrepreneurship has enormous economic benefits (Adom & Asare-Yeboah, 2016; Knorr, 2011). Franck (2012) believes that female entrepreneurship contributes to economic development, especially in developing countries. Reports indicate that females' participation in entrepreneurship worldwide is lower than that of males (Global Entrepreneurship Monitor (GEM), 2015; 2016). GEM (2011) acknowledged that this gender gap in entrepreneurship could result from inadequate recognition of females' potential and actual contributions to the economies. However, studies identify that female businesses underperform (Modarresi, Arasti, Talebi & Farasatkhah, 2016); Kalnins and Williams (2013) report that female entrepreneurs' ventures consistently perform better than male-owned ones in several industries. The differences in these findings could be a result of contextual differences. For instance, whereas Iran is the study context of Modarresi et al. (2016), Kalnins and Williams (2013) are situated in the United States of America, specifically Texas. Differences in the patriarchal nature of contexts might have birthed differences in findings. Based on the assertion of Kalnis and Williams (2013), female entrepreneurs in the tourism sector are likely to enhance the sector's performance. For Brixiová and Kangoye (2015), the start-up capital for female entrepreneurs is usually small and more likely to be obtained through informal means.

Given the low capital intensiveness of the tourism sector, the sector provides better opportunities for female entrepreneurs. However, Wellalage and Locke (2017) reveal that female entrepreneurs' enterprises are 3% less likely to be credit constrained in South Asia than male entrepreneurs' ventures. The differing views could be attributed to differences in the contexts in which the studies were conducted. A recent study conducted in Cameroon by Ngoasong and Kimbu (2019) revealed that although female entrepreneurs in the tourism sector benefit positively from formal and informal networks for business growth, they still present some hurdles that must be eliminated. Kimbu et al. (2019) examine the collaborative networks that enhance sustainable Human Capital Management (HCM) among women tourism entrepreneurs in Ghana, Nigeria and Cameroon. They propose three determinants of collaborative networks that can enhance sustainable HCM resources, type of network, social capital dimensions and human capital. These studies highlight the essence of networks in running female-owned businesses in the tourism sector.

Female entrepreneurs have faced and continue to face constraints in business venturing (Adom, 2015; Adom, Asare-Yeboa, Quaye & Ampomah, 2017). According to Afza, Hassan and Rashid (2010), the limitations faced by women entrepreneurs cover gender-based discrimination, lack of collective support, limited or lack of access to information, little education and training, lack of trust in one's capabilities as well as the inability to access resources. Additionally, women entrepreneurs are affected by difficult economic conditions and gender stereotypes that compel them primarily to operate in the informal sector (Biernacka, Abu-Rabia-Queder & Kressel, 2017). Gohar and Abrar (2016) state that sociocultural, economic and political factors influence, facilitate and constrain the progress of female entrepreneurship. Further, most female entrepreneurs need more education in business technicalities (Iyiola & Azuh, 2014). Pettersson (2011) posits that programmes aimed at supporting women entrepreneurs in Nomadic countries lead to females' subordination to males.

Moreover, females are generally less likely to become entrepreneurs than males due to gender differences and environmental conditions (Modarresi et al., 2016). Lockyer and George (2012) said that females with entrepreneurial family members or friends are less likely to become entrepreneurs. However, the findings of GEM (2015) contradict the foregone discourse; GEM (2015) espouses that females are more likely to become entrepreneurs if they have an entrepreneurial mother. They are linking this to factors that motivate females to become entrepreneurs; compared to males, females are 20% more likely to cite necessity as a motive for being entrepreneurial. Despite this, opportunity still accounts for significant entrepreneurial reasons among females (GEM, 2016). Akehurst, Simarro and Mas-Tur (2012) mention that fame motivates females. A view shared by Modarresi et al. (2016) states that females are motivated by financial gain, fame, feedback from others and working at home. The tourism sector offers the opportunity for females to achieve the mentioned motivational factors.

Women Entrepreneurship in the Tourism Sector of Africa: An Overview

Over the years, females have undertaken business activities that directly or indirectly support Africa's tourism sector. However, there has yet to be much literature that focuses on female entrepreneurship in the African tourism sector. The few studies on this research issue were predominantly conducted in the South African context, albeit there is a recent interest in the research issue in other countries like Cameroon, Nigeria and Ghana (see Kimbu et al., 2019; Kimbu & Ngoasong, 2016; Ngoasong & Kimbu, 2019). Jiyane, Majanja, Ocholla and Mostert (2012) postulate that in Kwa-Zulu (South Africa), female entrepreneurs in the tourism sector contribute to strengthening the tourism industry, reflecting the economic base of the region. As such, the contributions of females in tourism in Africa must be considered.

Like any entrepreneur in the tourism industry, female entrepreneurs desire business success and work to achieve that. According to Katongole, Ahebwa and Kawere (2013), conscientiousness and extraversion contribute to female-owned ventures in the tourism sector in Uganda. In other words, females in the tourism arena must be reliable and hardworking, tend to persevere and be talkative, outgoing and friendly. However, the authors add that these characteristics are learnable and more essential to female success in business than any other attribute. Considering the industry dynamics, these must be present to ensure success. This study argues that being talkative, outgoing and friendly might not be a critical success factor in a tourism enterprise. Holding on to Katongole et al.'s (2013) views to assert that the tourism sector is a wrong field for introverted females. Also, the need for females in tourism to be talkative, outgoing and friendly to succeed should strongly depend on the size of the females and their businesses. A female entrepreneur with employees may not need to perform the business's marketing and sales function, requiring being outgoing and social. In Ghana, the critical success factors for female-owned ventures in the tourism sector transcend personal traits like being talkative, outgoing and friendly, eliminating gender stereotyping and traditional perceptions.

Scholars who examine the challenges of female tourism entrepreneurs in the African continent find that female entrepreneurs face financial issues, lack the business capability and are affected by traditional norms. For instance, Iwu and Nxopo (2015a) aver that several female entrepreneurs in the Western Cape (South Africa) tourism sector need more financial support, skills and knowledge to operate in the industry. There is, therefore, the need for financial institutions to provide both financial and non-financial support services such as capital provision, mentoring and financial management skills training to females in the sector. These will help to mitigate the challenges identified. Tshabalala and Ezeuduji (2016) identify similar challenges in the same South African context, low business competence, lack of financial capital, issues with size and scope, imperfect business locations, traditional sensitivities and racial issues. Likewise, Chipfuva, Nzonzo and Muchenje (2012) opine that for female entrepreneurs operating in Zimbabwe's tourism industry, the challenges are difficulties securing capital; inadequate business education; and cultural, social and religious barriers. Iwu and Nxopo (2015b) argue that the factors that hinder female entrepreneurs vary according to sub-sectors.

Further, Moswete and Lacey (2015) iterate that in Botswana, females in the tourism sector have low levels of education, lack the founding capital, low potential earnings and face issues regarding the centralised control of protected tourist sites. The authors call for policies promoting females' participation in the tourism sector in Botswana and other developing nations. Ali (2018), focusing on Ghana, also finds a need for more financial resources as a challenge and a bane to the growth of female-owned enterprises in the tourism sector. Interestingly, whereas several authors see a lack of entrepreneurial capability as a challenge in the industry, Ali (2018) finds that female entrepreneurs in tourism believe they can still grow and expand their businesses without "entrepreneurial capabilities". In a drift, the author highlights that business advisory services are less likely to contribute to female entrepreneurs' growth intentions. What is needed is the availability of finance opportunities and finance leveraging, contrary to Iwu and Nxopo (2015a).

These challenges from the foregone discussions are similar to females in Ghana's tourism sector encounter. However, in line with Iwu and Nxopo (2015a), the challenges depend on the sub-sector involved. For instance, rooted in the traditions and perceptions of several citizens in Ghana, females who work or even own and operate hotels and resorts are negative. There have been concerns regarding the morality of such females. Due to their work nature, they tend to contact several hotel lodgers (both male and female), some of whom may be tourists, and their interactions with the males usually send negative signals. The situation has been a bane to the effective participation of Ghanaian females in the tourism sector. There have been several instances where females have had to rescind working in the hotel setting or the tourism industry's temporary accommodation sub-sector. On the contrary, females operating in the attraction as a sub-sector of the tourism industry, like antiques and arts and crafts, tend to face no questions of morality.

On the positive, Tshabalala and Ezeuduji (2016) maintain that although female entrepreneurs in the tourism sector face significant challenges, there are some growth opportunities. According to the authors, these opportunities cover internet marketing and business networks for self-support and business training in South Africa. With current technological advancements, several female tourism entrepreneurs market their activities or services via online marketing platforms, social media sites, and business websites. Evidence shows that several women-owned tourism businesses in Ghana rely on Internet marketing for business promotion. They can contact prospective international and domestic tourists before visiting the destination. Several female tourist entrepreneurs' activities serve as demand attributes, attracting tourists from other countries into the country. Females' participation in arts and crafts like beads-making, painting and fashion attract international tourists. For example, a female entrepreneur who owns and runs "Adu Amani", a fashion business that promotes Ghanaian art and culture by producing shoes, bags and clothes with African-Prints (Afriprints), markets heavily via the internet. As a female entrepreneur who started with no substantial capital and hence no funds for marketing and public relations, the owner of "Adu Amani" had a promotion on social media, putting on a local Ghanaian hairstyle braided with yarn. Her hairstyle went viral on the internet and was named "Adomi Bridge Hairstyle", a name that still markets other tourist destinations in Ghana aside from her business. This act drew local and international attention to her "Adu Amani" brand (Boaso, 2016).

The Role of Female Entrepreneurs in the Tourism Industry in Ghana

Ghana's tourism industry presents extraordinary opportunities for the advancement of females via informal employment, formal employment and supply-chain employment. In Ghana, not all establishments in the tourism sector require colossal start-up capital. Some tourist activities occur in areas that naturally have less economical options, such as small islands, coastlines and the like. Females in these areas have since captured the opportunity to provide services that enhance tourists' experiences. Examples can be made of female dance groups that entertain tourists on the "Dodi" Island in Ghana's Volta Region.

Over the years, females in Ghana have benefitted from the tourism sector in several ways. Firstly, the industry has created self-employment avenues for females more than in other sectors due to the industry's low barriers to entry. It has also provided homegrown entrepreneurial opportunities in hospitality, handicrafts, etc. Irrespective of the unavoidable risks involved in entrepreneurship in the tourism sector, the sector has become a foremost engine for empowering females without denuding the country of its resource base. The subsequent sections illustrate the role female tourism entrepreneurs have played in developing the tourism sector of Ghana in line with Prosser's (1998) Tourism Environment Framework: transportation and communication; service and facilities; attractions; information, promotion and direction.

Methodology

Female tourism entrepreneurship has been an underexplored research phenomenon in the Ghanaian context. For this reason, the study adopts a qualitative approach to collecting and analysing data. The rationale behind this choice is due to the topic's unexploited nature; gaining in-depth knowledge is more beneficial than testing relationships (Queirós, Faria & Almeida, 2017). A vital advantage of the qualitative research approach is its ability to provide deeper insights into research phenomena (Cassell, Bishop, Symon, Johnson & Buehring, 2009). Also, the qualitative approach enhances the interaction between literature and evidence; this is useful in understanding the representativeness across a broader range of issues (Ciao, 2011). The study adopts hermeneutic phenomenology to describe how female entrepreneurs have contributed to developing the tourism industry in Ghana using Prosser (1998) as the study framework. In this case, female tourism entrepreneurs' lived experiences were examined through texts (documents), tweets, audio-visuals and tourism blogs. The hermeneutic phenomenology approach allowed the researcher to explore and observe the activities relating to the context's research issue (Cresswell, 2017).

This research anchors the analysis of both primary and secondary data (Rabianski, 2003). Secondary data were collected from documents, audio-visuals, life stories and diaries, and internet sources (Brewer, 2012). In contemporary times, advancements on the internet have led to data collected, compiled and archived to be readily available for research. According to Johnston (2014), secondary analysis is flexible and can be applied in diverse ways. Thence, secondary data analysis is a viable research method. The formal data-sharing mode of secondary data analysis was adopted as proposed by (Heaton, 2008). Thus, the study reused data that were independently gathered by others. The data used were well documented for archiving purposes and, therefore, could meet ethical and legal requirements regarding research and data-sharing. The study sought to explore female entrepreneurs' contribution to developing Ghana's tourism sector. As such, broader perspectives beyond a single region were needed; hence, the reliance on secondary data, since covering the 16 areas of Ghana would have needed to be revised due to cost imperatives. Considering the research issue's emerging and significant nature, a more extensive section of Ghana needed to be covered.

In addition to the secondary data, the researcher relied on primary data through participant observation. Observations were used as a data collection method because it allows researchers to conduct the studies in a naturalistic environment (Aitken, Marshall, Elliott & McKinley, 2011). The researcher interned for two weeks in two separate enterprises that belonged to females in the tourism sector. The researcher spent one week (five working days) in each enterprise, observing and participating in some enterprises' scheduled activities. In the end, reports were written for this study. The information on the reports was verified by making them available to the two enterprises' owners for confirmation. One of the enterprises where the researcher interned engaged in producing African wear, bags and others; the other was an art business that designs clothes and makes beads. Aside from these two formal enterprises, the researcher also visited tourist routes or areas like "Adobe", "Dodi" and the Koforidua beads market to observe the female entrepreneurs' activities. These places and the two enterprises were purposively selected considering the vibrant nature of tourist activities or related activities at these places. In these observations, the researcher had a list of questions it sought to answer through observation. Therefore, the study conducted assorted analyses, as Heaton (2008) suggested.

The data was analysed by integrating the observational and secondary data to generate specific themes. The analysis was then done following these themes. Ethical issues in the research are taken care of, informing the owners of the firms where the observation was done about the purpose of the data collection. The reports from the observation were presented to the female entrepreneurs to verify if they reflected the actual situations. Both female entrepreneurs involved responded positively.

Assessing Female Entrepreneurs in Transportation and Communication Sector

As Middleton (1994) and Prosser (1998) proposed, the transportation and communication sectors are part of the tourism industry. The activities of transport businesses, such as travel and tour agencies, facilitate tourism. They enable tourists to move from their countries of abode to the land of visit and allow internal movement within the tourism destination. These businesses are necessary for the movement of tourists. Over the years, travel and tour agencies have contributed to the success of the tourism sector; they operate to satisfy different needs of tourists, from history and culture to nature, by offering transportation and communicating with prospective tourists during or before their arrival. Although travel and tour agencies abound in Ghana, the sub-sector has seen minor contributions or female entrepreneurs' participation. Traditionally, the transportation and communication sectors are unattractive to females since it is outbound of the traditional industries that females enjoy operating. According to Dzisi (2008), Ghanaian females are inclined to operate in seven major business sectors: trading (26%), services (21%), agro-processing (16%), manufacturing (12%), textiles and fabrics (12%), agriculture (5%) and construction (4%). The transportation and communication sectors are not an area of interest to female entrepreneurs. However, it does not suggest that no female has ventured into the industry but that the participation of females is limited.

Female Entrepreneurs in Service and Facilities

According to Prosser (1998), the service and facilities sub-sector covers accommodation, catering and shopping. In the Ghanaian context, shopping is not part of the tourism industry. This could be because the country's shopping system needs to be better structured to attract attention from tourists. In some African countries, shopping centres have been strategically positioned as tourist attractions. For instance, Cairo's City Stars shopping mall (Egypt) has become a tourist destination for several domestic and international tourists. Therefore, in Ghana, accommodation and catering are significant components of the service and facilities sub-sector of the tourism industry. A fair number of females operate businesses in the accommodation sector. Although not so predominant, some females own and operate hotels, guesthouses and resorts and facilitate tourism activities.

Nonetheless, the catering sub-sector has witnessed the dominance of female entrepreneurs. This evidence corroborates the assertion of Baum (2013) that females dominate the catering sub-sector. In Ghana, a restaurant is almost synonymous with females. Because females are considered inherently hospitable, caretakers of the home, and burdened with household chores, they tend to excel better in the catering businesses. Many female entrepreneurs in the tourism industry operate in the hospitality or catering sector. Here, they can draw on their strengths and experiences for business success. "Linda Dor" restaurant is one female-owned catering business that has been instrumental in Ghana's developing tourism industry. The restaurant serves domestic and international tourists in the Eastern Region of Ghana. One of the outlets is located on the Accra–Kumasi highway serving travellers and tourists. The dominance of females in the catering business could also be linked to low-entry barriers. As such, more and more females move in, drawing on their experiences and skills to make a living.

More local-based catering businesses can be seen run by women around tourist destinations. Areas like Akosombo in the Eastern region are known for tourism, likewise "Adomi", where the "Adomi bridge" can be found. In these areas are female entrepreneurs in the catering business who sell local delicacies like "adodi" – oysters, "aboboa" – snails and "abodoo" – a locally baked pastry made of maize. These females primarily operate in the informal sector and ply their trade along the roads leading to tourist sites. Their businesses present tourists with the opportunity to taste local Ghanaian dishes. Males are almost missing in this kind of business. Hence, it can be said that female entrepreneurs contribute to having tourists experience Ghanaian culture through local foods.

Female Entrepreneurs in the Attractions Sub-sector

The attraction sub-sector represents things for tourists to see and do, according to Prosser (1998). They usually revolve around arts, crafts and antiques. Female entrepreneurs have been a strong force in the attraction sub-sector. Their crafts' activities, such as beads-making, pottery, basket weaving, art and design, must be considered. The crafts and art female entrepreneurs produce interest in domestic and international tourists. Several tourists travel to the "Koforidua" beads market or the "Odumase- Krobo" beads market in Ghana's Eastern region. Female entrepreneurs dominate these markets. At these markets, tourists learn about Ghanaian culture and heritage through beading. Some buy the beads that come in different designs as a cultural symbol of Ghana. Again, the "Sirigu" pottery and art centre is a female-based organisation. The arts centre serves as a tourism destination, workshop and gift shop. At the centre, tourists learn about the traditional art of the "Gurenes" or "Kasena-Nankanas" (ethnic groups in the Upper East region of Ghana). The female participators of the "Sirigu" pottery and art centre were engaged to create the Navrongo Minor Basilica murals. After registration as a monument with the Ghana Museums and Monuments Board, this building has become a tourist site on its own and is listed as a UNESCO World Heritage Site.

Further, there is no doubt that fabric contributes to the attraction sectors. Over the years, local Ghanaian materials like the "Kente" and Smock have drawn attention in tourism. Tourists who visit Ghana get interested in coming into contact with the local fabrics. As such, females' activities in local material production constitute the contributions of female entrepreneurs in the tourism industry. Although males dominate the "Kente" weaving business, the reverse is the case for the smock industry, also soon as "Fugu", "Montane" or "Zantika". Females actively participate in the smock weaving business, especially in the Northern and

Upper East Regions. Based on this, female entrepreneurs are actively involved in displaying the cultural heritage of Ghana to tourists. A female-owned business that has been instrumental in changing the face of the local fabric (Fugu) industry in Ghana is "Shaaliwud". "Shaaliwud" produces male and female designs using the smock fabric. Traditionally, the locally woven "fugu" or smock was popularly for sewing "Batakari" or "Zantika" – a loosely sewn top for men. Females that bought the fabric used them for "Kaba and slit", – a traditional style for females. "Shaaliwud" went beyond these traditional styles or used the "fugu" to design office wears for women, shirts for men, bags and other traditionally not produced with the local fabric. With this, the business attracted international attention. It became a tourist destination by itself to the extent that some Hollywood stars who visited Ghana (Boris Kodjoe, Michael Jai White) in December 2018 visited the business.

Female Entrepreneurs in Information, Promotion and Direction

The information, promotion and direction as a sub-sector of the tourism industry cover firms that work towards shaping the image and perception of potential tourists towards a tourism destination through promotions and marketing, guides and signposting, and information and publicity (Prosser, 1998). In Ghana, most sub-sector activities are performed by travel and tour agencies like "Kenpong" Travel and Tours, "Emitrade" Travel and Tour, and Dreamland Travel and Tours. They present a positive image of tourism destinations, promote, and market them, and provide information about them. Aside from the travel and tour agencies set up by entrepreneurs, tourist bloggers, who are not necessarily entrepreneurs in the tourism sector, are also instrumental in disseminating tourist information and promoting tourists' destinations through their blogs. The remaining activity, tour guiding, which witnesses entrepreneurs perform for a fee, is male dominated. Most tourist guides are males. However, with the uprising of feminist perspectives in the Ghanaian environment, more females are likely to venture into the tour-guiding sector. In the current sector, more cannot be said about females' role in its development. Evidence shows that the tourist guides at several tourist destinations like the "Pikworo" slave camp, "Kimtampo" waterfalls and "Mole National Park" are male.

Conclusions

The tourism landscape in Ghana is growing, irrespective of changing trends in the business environment. This growth, therefore, presents entrepreneurial opportunities for entrepreneurs. Reports indicate that the tourism industry provides better opportunities for females due to specific inherent characteristics. The tourism sector has lower entry barriers and capital requirements and offers the chance to work part-time. These make the sector attractive to female entrepreneurs. There have been several attempts to empower females in Ghana to be active in Ghana's tourism sector. In June 2019, an association of Women in the tourism business, named "The Women in Business and Tourism" (WIBAT), was set up in Ghana to provide a platform for females in that sector to collaborate and build networks for business success. Despite the growing tourism sector of Ghana, female entrepreneurs' role in its development needs to be better recognised, necessitating this chapter.

The tourism industry comprises several sub-sectors: attractions, transportation and communication, service and facilities, information, promotion, and direction (Prosser, 1998). An analysis of the research phenomenon per the Tourism Environment Framework (Prosser, 1998) indicates that female entrepreneurs dominate hospitality, catering, beading, pottery, and fabric businesses. In other words, female entrepreneurs are very active in the service and facilities sub-sectors and the attractions sub-sector than in transportation and communication and information, promotion, and direction. It shows that female entrepreneurs usually specialise in specific activities in the various sub-sectors of the tourism industry. Female entrepreneurs' dominance in the service and facilities sub-sectors can be attributed to gender stereotyping and capital limitation. For example, only a few females are engaged in the tourism sector in the transportation and communication sub-sector. Transportation businesses are capital intensive, and most females are capital constrained, hence, their inability to venture into such an area. Also, there is prevailing gender stereotyping concerning the kind of businesses males and females should operate. In line with this, the transportation business sector is considered an "unknown water" for females.

Given the tourism industry's happenings concerning female entrepreneurship, it can be concluded that the presence of female entrepreneurs in the tourism sector still needs to be improved. The gender roles carved for both males and females in Ghanaian society reflect the sub-sectors that female and male entrepreneurs operate in the tourism sector. For female entrepreneurs to increasingly participate in the various sub-sectors of the tourism industry, perceptions about gender roles and the business sectors the different genders should operate in need to be dispelled.

Policy Implications

Considering the discussions on the research phenomenon, it has become imperative for societal and governmental actions to support female entrepreneurs in the tourism sector. First, female entrepreneurs must understand that they must undertake certain activities like improved customer service, better facilities and others to enhance the image of the tourism industry. Gender stereotyping concerning what actions should be performed by whom in the business arena, and hence the tourism sector, must be eliminated from society. Eliminating the gender stereotype could be achieved through collaborative efforts by women entrepreneurs themselves on one hand and other stakeholders.

Second, females need support to excel in the tourism industry. Therefore, the need for government-instituted policies or programmes to support females in the tourism sector should be considered. Financial support and business training could be provided for females who venture into tourism sub-sectors outside the traditional hospitality, beading, pottery, and fabric. This financial support will promote the widespread of female entrepreneurs in the tourism sector. In return, their contributions to the development of the tourism sector will increase and be more impactful. Ministries such as the Trade and Industry, Tourism, Gender, the Ghana Enterprise Agency (formerly National Board for Small Scale Industries) and other stakeholders must be involved in making this a reality.

References

Adom, K. (2015). Recognizing the contribution of female entrepreneurs in economic development in sub-Saharan Africa: Some evidence from Ghana. *Journal of Developmental Entrepreneurship*, *20*(01), 1550003.

Adom, K., & Asare-Yeboa, I. (2016). An evaluation of human capital theory and female entrepreneurship in sub-Sahara Africa: Some evidence from Ghana. *International Journal of Gender and Entrepreneurship*, *8*(4). DOI/10.1108/IJGE-12-2015-0048/full/HTML.

Adom, K., Asare-Yeboa, I. T., Quaye, D. M., & Ampomah, A. O. (2017). A critical assessment of work and family life of female entrepreneurs in Sub-Saharan Africa: Some fresh evidence from Ghana. *Journal of Small Business and Enterprise Development.*

Afza, T., Osman, M. H. B. M., & Rashid, M. A. (2010). Enterprising behaviour of enterprise-less rural women entrepreneurs of Khyber Pukhtan Khawa of Pakistan. *European Journal of Social Sciences*, *18*(1), 109–119.

Aitken, L. M., Marshall, A., Elliott, R., & McKinley, S. (2011). Comparison of think aloud and observation as data collection methods in the study of decision making regarding sedation in intensive care patients. *International Journal of Nursing Studies*, *48*(3), 318–325. doi.org/10.1016/j.ijnurstu.2010.07 .014.

Akehurst, G., Simarro, E., & Mas-Tur, A. (2012). Women entrepreneurship in small service firms: Motivations, barriers and performance. *The Service Industries Journal*, *32*(15), 2489–2505. DOI/full/ 10.1080/02642069.2012.677834.

Akyeampong, O. (2009). Tourism development in Ghana, 1957–2007. *Legon Journal of Sociology*, *3*(2), 1–23. legon/3/2/AJA08556261_68.

Ali, R. S. (2018). Determinants of female entrepreneurs growth intentions: A case of female-owned small businesses in Ghana's tourism sector. *Journal of Small Business and Enterprise Development*, *25*(3), 387–404. DOI/10.1108/JSBED-02-2017-0057/full/HTML.

Ateljevic, J., & Page, S. J. (Eds.). (2017). *Tourism and entrepreneurship.* Routledge.

Bakar, N. A., & Rosbi, S. (2020). Effect of Coronavirus disease (COVID-19) to tourism industry. *International Journal of Advanced Engineering Research and Science*, *7*(4), 189–193.

Baum, T. (2013). *International perspectives on women and work in hotels, catering and tourism.* Geneva: International Labour Organization.

Biernacka, A., Abu-Rabia-Queder, S., & Kressel, G. M. (2018). The connective strategies of Bedouin women entrepreneurs in the Negev. *Journal of Arid Environments*, *149*, 62–72.

Boaso, N. J. (2016). Vera Adu Amani: How I found creative ways to build my brand. Retrieved from https:// sheleadsafrica.org/vera-adu-amani/.

Brewer, E. W. (2012). Secondary data analysis. *Sage Secondary Data Analysis*, 165–176.

Brixiová, Z., & Kangoye, T. (2016). Gender and constraints to entrepreneurship in Africa: New evidence from Swaziland. *Journal of Business Venturing Insights*, *5*, 1–8.

Burkart, A. J., & Medlik, S. (1981). *Tourism: Past, present and future* (2nd Ed.). London: William Heinimann Ltd.

Cassell, C., Bishop, V., Symon, G., Johnson, P., & Buehring, A. (2009). Learning to be a qualitative management researcher. *Management Learning*, *40*(5), 513–533.

Chipfuva, T., Nzonzo, J. C., & Muchenje, B. (2012). Challenges faced by women entrepreneurs in the tourism sector in Zimbabwe. *International Journal of Social and Allied Research (IJSAR)*, *1*(1), 25–33.

Ciao, B. (2011). Management studies through qualitative analyses: Epistemological justification, verification of originality, and efforts of conceptualization. *GSTF Business Review (GBR)*, *1*(1), 106.

De Vita, L., Mari, M., & Poggesi, S. (2014). Women entrepreneurs in and from developing countries: Evidences from the literature. *European Management Journal*, *32*(3), 451–460. doi.org/10.1016/j.emj .2013.07.009.

Dzisi, S. (2008). Entrepreneurial activities of indigenous African women: A case of Ghana. *Journal of Enterprising Communities: People and Places in the Global Economy*, *2*(3), 254–264. DOI/10.1108/17506200810897231/full/HTML.

Fox, S. (2009). Vacation or staycation. *The Neumann Business Review*, 1–7.

Franck, A. K. (2012). Factors motivating women's informal micro-entrepreneurship: Experiences from Penang, Malaysia. *International Journal of Gender and Entrepreneurship*, *4*(1), 65–78. DOI/10.1108/17566261211202981/full/HTML.

Ghana Statistical Service. (2017). Trends in the Tourism Industry in Ghana -2004–2014. Retrieved from https://www.statsghana.gov.gh/gssmain/fileUpload/Service/Tourism%20Market%20Trends %20Report%20in%20Ghana1.pdf.

Ghana Tourism Authority. (2019). Year of Return, Ghana 2019. Retrieved from https://visitghana.com/ events/year-of-return-ghana-2019/.

Global Entrepreneurship Monitor. (2011). Global report. Retrieved from https://www.gemconsortium.org/report/gem-2011-global-report.

Global Entrepreneurship Monitor. (2015). Women's report. Retrieved from http://gemconsortium.org/report/49281.

Global Entrepreneurship Monitor. (2016). Global report. Retrieved from https://www.gemconsortium.org/report/gem-2016-2017-global-repor.

Gmelch, S. B., & Kaul, A. (2018). *Tourists and tourism: A reader.* Long Grove: Waveland Press.

Gohar, M., & Abrar, A. (2016). Embedded or constrained informal institutional influences on women entrepreneurship development in Pukhtoon culture. *FWU Journal of Social Sciences, 10*(2).

Government of Ghana. (2012). National Tourism Development Plan (2013–2027). Retrieved from https://www.ghana.travel/wp-content/uploads/2016/11/Ghana-Tourism-Development-Plan.pdf.

Heaton, J. (2008). Secondary analysis of qualitative data: An overview. *Historical Social Research/Historische Sozialforschung, 33*–45.

Holden, A. (2016). *Environment and tourism.* London and New York: Routledge.

Iwu, C. G., & Nxopo, Z. (2015a). The unique obstacles of female entrepreneurship in the tourism industry in Western Cape, South Africa. *Commonwealth Youth and Development, 13*(2), 55–71.

Iwu, C. G., & Nxopo, Z. (2015b). Determining the specific support services required by female entrepreneurs in the South African tourism industry. *African Journal of Hospitality, Tourism and Leisure, 4*(2), 1–13.

Iyiola, O., & Azuh, D. E. (2014). Women entrepreneurs as small-medium enterprise (SME) operators and their roles in socio-economic development in Ota, Nigeria. *International Journal of Economics, Business and Finance, 2*(1), 1–10, ISSN: 2327-8188.

Jhonston, M. P. (2014). Secondary data analysis: A method of which the time has come. *Qualitative and Quantitative Methods in Libraries, 3*, 619–626.

Jiyane, G. V., Majanja, M. K., Ocholla, D. N., & Mostert, B. J. (2012). Contribution of informal sector women entrepreneurs to the tourism industry in eThekwini Metropolitan Municipality, in KwaZulu-Natal: Barriers and issues: Recreation and tourism. *African Journal for Physical Health Education, Recreation and Dance, 18*(Issue 4, Part 1), 709–728.

Kalnins, A., & Williams, M. (2014). When do female-owned businesses out-survive male-owned businesses? A disaggregated approach by industry and geography. *Journal of Business Venturing, 29*(6), 822–835.

Katongole, C., Ahebwa, W. M., & Kawere, R. (2013). Enterprise success and entrepreneur's personality traits: An analysis of micro-and small-scale women-owned enterprises in Uganda's tourism industry. *Tourism and Hospitality Research, 13*(3), 166–177. DOI/full/10.1177/1467358414524979.

Kimbu, A. N., & Ngoasong, M. Z. (2016). Women as vectors of social entrepreneurship. *Annals of Tourism Research, 60*, 63–79. doi.org/10.1016/j.annals.2016.06.002.

Kimbu, A. N., Ngoasong, M. Z., Adeola, O., & Afenyo-Agbe, E. (2019). Collaborative Networks for sustainable human capital management in women's tourism entrepreneurship: The role of tourism policy. *Tourism Planning & Development, 16*(2), 161–172. DOI/full/10.1080/21568316.2018.1556329.

Knorr, H. (2011). From top management to entrepreneurship: Women's next move? *International Journal of Manpower, 32*(1), 99–116. DOI/10.1108/01437721111121251/full/HTML.

Lavery, P. (1987a). The education, training and manpower needs of the tourist industry in Great Britain up to 1990. *Tourism Recreation Research, 12*(1), 19–23.

Lavery, P. (1987b). *Travel and Tourism.* Kings Norton, Cambridge: Elm Publications.

Lickorish, L. J., & Jenkins, C. L. (2007). *Introduction to tourism.* London: Routledge.

Lockyer, J., & George, S. (2012). What women want: Barriers to female entrepreneurship in the West Midlands. *International Journal of Gender and Entrepreneurship, 4*(2), 179–195. DOI/10.1108/17566261211234661/full/HTML.

Mason, P. (1990). *Tourism: Environment and Development Perspectives.* Godalming: World Wide Fund for Nature.

Middleton, V. T. C. (1994). *Marketing in travel and tourism* (2nd ed.). Oxford: Butterworth-Heinemann.

Modarresi, M., Arasti, Z., Talebi, K., & Farasatkhah, M. (2016). Women's entrepreneurship in Iran: How are women owning and managing home-based businesses motivated to grow? *International Journal of Gender and Entrepreneurship, 8*(4), 446–470. DOI/10.1108/IJGE-03-2016-0006/full/HTML.

Moswete, N., & Lacey, G. (2015). "Women cannot lead": Empowering women through cultural tourism in Botswana. *Journal of Sustainable Tourism*, *23*(4), 600–617. DOI/full/10.1080/09669582.2014.98 6488.

Ngoasong, M. Z. & Kimbu, A. N. (2019). Why Hurry? The Slow Process of High Growth in Women-Owned Businesses in a Resource-Scarce Context. *Journal of Small Business Management*, *57*(1), 40–58. DOI/full/10.1111/jsbm.12493.

Office of the Special Adviser to Africa – OSAA. (2016).Promoting Tourism as an Engine of Inclusive Growth and Sustainable Development in Africa, 21 July 2016. Retrieved from https://www.un.org/en/africa/osaa/events/2016/unctad14tourism.shtml.

Otoo, M., Fulton, J., Ibro, G., & Lowenberg-DeBoer, J. (2011). Women entrepreneurship in West Africa: The cowpea street food sector in Niger and Ghana. *Journal of Developmental Entrepreneurship*, *16*(01), 37–63. DOI/abs/10.1142/S1084946711001732.

Prosser, R. (1994). *Societal change and growth in alternative tourism* (pp. 19–38). Chichester: John Wiley & Sons.

Prosser, R. (1998). Tourism. *Encyclopaedia of Ethics*, *4*, 373–411.

Queirós, A., Faria, D., & Almeida, F. (2017). Strengths and limitations of qualitative and quantitative research methods. *European Journal of Education Studies*, *3*(9), 369–387. DOI/10.5281/zenodo.887089.SVG.

Rabianski, J. S. (2003). Primary and secondary data: Concepts, concerns, errors, and issues. *The Appraisal Journal*, *71*(1), 43.

Rate, S., Moutinho, L., & Ballantyne, R. (2018). The new business environment and trends in tourism. In L. Moutinho & A. Vargas-Sanchez (Eds.), *Strategic management in tourism, CABI tourism texts* (pp. 1–15). Boston: Cabi. doi.org/10.4324/9780429200694.

Séraphin, H., Butler, C., & Vanessa, G. (2013). Entrepreneurship in the tourism sector: A comparative approach of Haiti, coastal Kenya and Mauritius. *Journal of Hospitality and Tourism*, *11*(2), 72–92.

Škare, M., Soriano, D. R., & Porada-Rochoń, M. (2021). Impact of COVID-19 on the travel and tourism industry. *Technological Forecasting and Social Change*, *163*, 120469.

Soliku, O., Kyiire, B., Mahama, A., & Kubio, C. (2021). Tourism amid COVID-19 pandemic: Impacts and implications for building resilience in the eco-tourism sector in Ghana's Savannah region. *Heliyon*, *7*(9), e07892.

Tetteh, B. (2019). 2019: Year of return for African Diaspora. Retrieved https://www.un.org/africarenewal/magazine/december-2018-march-2019/2019-year-return-african-diaspora.

Tshabalala, S. P., & Ezeuduji, I. O. (2016). Women tourism entrepreneurs in KwaZulu-Natal, South Africa: Any way forward?. *Acta Universitatis Danubius. Œconomica*, *12*(5).

United Nations World Tourism Organisation (2014). UNWTO tourism highlights. Retrieved from chrome-extension://efaidnbmnnnibpcajpcglclefindmkaj/https://www.e-unwto.org/doi/pdf/10.18111/9789284416226.

United Nations World Tourism Organisation – UNWTO. (2019). International tourism highlights. Retrieved from https://www.e-unwto.org/doi/pdf/10.18111/9789284421152.

van der Schyff, T., Meyer, D., & Ferreira, L. (2019). Analysis of the impact of the tourism sector as a viable response to South Africa's growth and development challenges. *Journal of International Studies*, *1*, 168–183.

Vossenberg, S. (2013). Women entrepreneurship promotion in developing countries: What explains the gender gap in entrepreneurship and how to close it. *Maastricht School of Management Working Paper Series*, *8*, 1–27.

Wellalage, N., & Locke, S. (2017). Access to credit by SMEs in South Asia: Do women entrepreneurs face discrimination. *Research in International Business and Finance*, *41*, 336–346. doi.org/10.1016/j.ribaf.2017.04.053.

World Bank. (2017a). Tourism for development. Retrieved from http://documents.worldbank.org/curated/en/401321508245393514/pdf/120477-WP-PUBLIC-Weds-oct-18-9am-ADD-SERIES-36p-IFCWomenandTourismfinal.pdf.

World Bank. (2017b). Women and tourism: Designing for inclusion. Retrieved From http://documents.worldbank.org/curated/en/401321508245393514/pdf/120477-WP-PUBLIC-Weds-oct-18-9am-ADD-SERIES-36p-IFCWomenandTourismfinal.pdf.

World Travel and Tourism Council –WTTC. (2015). A year in review: Travel & tourism in 2015. Retrieved from https://medium.com/@WTTC/a-year-in-review-travel-tourism-in-2015-8537ae351e40.

Chapter 8

Gender Perspectives of African SMEs: The Role of Formal and Informal Institutional Contexts

Oyedele Martins Ogundana, Amon Simba
and Ugbede Umoru

Contents

Introduction

The entrepreneurial activities of women-owned small and medium enterprises (SMEs) play a crucial role in Africa's economic development and prosperity (Bulanova et al., 2016; Costin, 2012; Kiviluoto, 2013). In agriculture, sub-Saharan Africa's (SSA) most vital economic sector, women contribute 60–80% of labour in food production, both for household consumption and for sale (United Nations, 2005). The Global Entrepreneurship Monitor's (GEM) report on women's entrepreneurship in Africa found that women-owned SMEs contribute over 1 million jobs in Angola, 4 million in Nigeria, 1.08 million in Burkina Faso and 1.64 million

DOI: 10.4324/9781003302339-8

in Zambia (GEM, 2014; 2015). Moreover, GEM's report (2017) estimated that women-owned SMEs in East, North and sub-Saharan Africa would create more jobs as women in those regions are projected to each hire six or more employees between the years 2017 and 2023. The employment projection within GEM's report indicates that women-owned SMEs could reduce unemployment in Africa by an average of 6% before the end of 2023 (GEM, 2017). Aside from their contribution to the reduction of unemployment, entrepreneurial activities amongst women have reduced the number of child trafficking and prostitution in Nigeria (Ogundana et al., 2018); improved the rate of child education in Ghana and the Republic of Niger (Chea, 2008; Otoo et al., 2012); improved family nutritional rates by 33% in Botswana (Ama et al., 2014); reduced the level of crime by 23.3% in Ogun State Nigeria (Iyiola and Azuh, 2014; Ogundana et al., 2022b); and played a crucial role in alleviating hunger and poverty in Kenya (IFC, 2014; Misango and Ongiti, 2013). In other words, the activities of women-owned SMEs are crucial within the African society. However, the context within Africa plays a tremendous role in determining the extent of economic benefits that the nations could benefit from the activities of women-owned SMEs (Simba et al., 2022; Welter, 2011).

Context refers to those circumstances, conditions, situations and environments that are external to women-owned SMEs (Amoako, 2018; Scott et al., 2014; Welter, 2011). This chapter offers detailed insights into the circumstances, conditions, situations and environments in which female owners of SMEs operate their businesses within the African context. This is necessary, especially as several studies have acknowledged that women-owned SMEs in Africa are inextricably linked to their contexts (Aldrich and Cliff, 2003; Igwe et al., 2018; Ogundana et al., 2022a). Besides, Amine and Staub (2009) explained that to understand women's entrepreneurship in Africa, one must also understand the context within which they work and live. As such, contextualisation of women entrepreneurship in this chapter is useful for enriching the understanding of readers (Welter, 2011; Zahra et al., 2014); to unravel what makes women-owned SMEs in Africa unique; and to reveal how they might differ from those in the developed countries (Madichie, 2009; Scott et al., 2014; Welter and Gartner, 2016). Therefore, in the sub-section hereafter, the formal (i.e., government policies, legal/judicial system and financial institutions) and informal institutional contexts (i.e., culture, religion, family and trade associations) within Africa are discussed. Additionally, we discussed how both formal and informal institutional contexts interconnect to influence women's entrepreneurship in the African context.

Women-Owned SMEs and Africa's Institutional Context

Institutional contexts are generally described as the set of rules that articulate and organise the economic, social and political interactions between individuals and social groups, with consequences for women entrepreneurial activities (Gimenez-Jimenez, et al., 2020; Thornton et al., 2011; Webb et al., 2020). It is well acknowledged in the gender and entrepreneurship literature that women's entrepreneurship can be better understood within their institutional contexts as it is difficult to separate the two phenomena from one another (Brush et al., 2009; Ogundana, 2020; Rugina, 2018; Welter, 2011). Besides, the institutional contexts produce opportunities and challenges that influence and shape women's entrepreneurial activities and performances (Igwe et al., 2018; Madichie, 2009; Ogundana et al., 2022b). Thus, women entrepreneurship is significantly sensitive to its institutional context which is generally categorised into formal and informal institutions discussed thereafter.

Formal Institutional Context

The formal institutional context includes government policies, legal/judicial system and financial institutions (Amoako, 2018; Amoako and Lyon, 2014; World Bank 2018). It is generally believed that, especially through the establishment of policy instruments, the government is one of the best-equipped stakeholders to support women-owned SMEs (Dionco-Adetayo et al., 2005; Iyiola and Azuh, 2014; Lincoln, 2012). Regardless of this widely held view, African female business owners are not well represented in the policymaking process, especially in issues of business and manpower development (Adom and Asare-Yeboa, 2016; Okafor and Mordi, 2010). Thus, government policies developed for women-owned SMEs in the African context are primarily described as gender-insensitive, unsupportive, unreliable and weak (Iyiola and Azuh, 2014; Lincoln, 2012; Okafor and Mordi, 2010). However recently, there have been some levels of improvements in the effectiveness of policies developed in several African countries including Ghana, Nigeria, Angola, Rwanda, Tanzania, Zambia and Ethiopia (Amoako, 2018). The 2017 Edelman Trust Barometer still indicated that the success levels of government policies in developing countries were still very low with South Africa at 15%, Nigeria 31% and Liberia 32% (Edelman, 2017). Government policies in Africa are mainly unsupportive because of weak institutional environmental factors including political instability, bureaucracy, regulations and corruption (Andrews, 2018; Amoako, 2018; Madichie and Nkamnebe, 2010). Corruption constrains the growth of women-owned SMEs by deterring women entrepreneurs that are unwilling to engage in corrupt practices (Igwe et al., 2018).

Many African countries, including Nigeria, Zimbabwe, Congo, Burundi and Somalia, are ranked one of the most corrupt nations and fewer peaceful countries around the world (Transparency International, 2018; Institute for Economics and Peace, 2020). Regionalism, tribalism, sectionalism and ethnicity are other significant problems facing sub-Saharan Africa political development (Ochulor, 2011). This is a sharp difference to the developed nations (such as the United Kingdom, the United States, Germany and Iceland) where the government instituted effective policies to support women-owned SMEs including low interest on borrowing, reduced imports and exports tariffs, efficient markets, enforcing property law and promoting exports (Amoako, 2018; Bridge and O'Neill, 2012; Igwe and Icha-Ituma, 2020). Taking that into account, Madichie and Nkamnebe (2010) concluded that two key features epitomise government policies in Africa's operating environment. First, the poor state of road networks especially the connecting roads from the rural areas to the urban centres makes movement to and from rural/urban markets particularly difficult resulting in extra costs, wastages of perishable items in transit, losses arising from avoidable accident, time wastages and attacks from hoodlums (Igwe et al., 2018; Lincoln, 2012). Second, electricity supply is highly unstable in nature (Igwe et al., 2018; Iyiola and Azuh, 2014; Oke, 2013). According to Ado and Josiah (2015), 41% of women-owned SMEs stay without the public supply of electricity for an average of 11–15 days in a month. This makes women-owned SMEs that depend on electricity, especially those that belong to the manufacturing sector, to suffer (Madichie and Nkamnebe, 2010). As a survival strategy, these women will typically buy power-generating sets, which could raise operating costs by between 40% and 60% (Lincoln, 2012; Madichie and Nkamnebe, 2010). This proportion will typically increase their overhead expenditure by an average of $255–$388 for fuelling and generator maintenance. Consequently, this unavoidable cost often decreases their profit margins by a significant proportion (Ado and Josiah, 2015; Madichie and Nkamnebe, 2010).

The legal/judicial system within the African region is described mainly as being weak (Amoako and Lyon, 2014; Amoako and Matalay, 2015) and women-owned SMEs are not recognised (Adom and Asare-Yeboa, 2016). For example, Amoako and Lyon (2014) found that Ghanaian women entrepreneurs owning and managing internationally trading SMEs avoid the courts due to the weaknesses of the legal systems. This is different in the developed country context such as the United States and the United Kingdom, where the legal/judicial systems are reliable and ensure compliance with contractual relationships regardless of the gender of the owner (Dionco-Adetayo et al., 2005). Additionally, the legal/judicial systems in Africa are mostly described as a vain attempt, due partly to their expensive cost, long processes involved and corruption within the judicial system (Amoako and Lyon, 2014). The weak and unreliable legal/judicial system creates an institutional void which often weighs heavily on women-owned SMEs in Africa (Igwe et al., 2018; Ogundana, 2020). For instance, Gao et al. (2017) observed how the burden of managing against political risks and regulatory uncertainty in the absence of institutions required dedicating significant organisational resources and constant attention. This is unlikely to occur in developed markets where credible information analysers and verifiers, as well as stable and independent regulatory, political and legal institutions, help mitigate such concerns (Gao et al., 2017). Another issue that makes the African contexts unique and different is the issue of women's rights. Unlike the developed contexts (including the United Kingdom, the United States, Canada and Germany) where women's right is primarily upheld; most of the African countries (including Sudan, Nigeria, Tanzania and the Niger Republic) lack women's right (World Bank, 2013). For instance, the World Bank (2013) revealed that in the majority of sub-Saharan countries including Niger, Kenya, Madagascar, Sudan and Nigeria, there is an absence of law or criminal sanctions explicitly addressing sexual harassment in business; absence of legislation ensuring that married women and men have equal property ownership rights; absence of laws mandating equal pay for work of equal value; and the presence of laws requiring married women to obey their husbands. This evidence suggests that women entrepreneurship in the African and indeed the developing contexts may likely play out differently from their counterparts in the developed countries' context where women's rights are more potent and effective (Azmat and Fujimoto, 2016; World Bank, 2013).

The financial service landscape of most African countries is one that shows a lack of access to a range of affordable, safe and reliable financial services (Amoako and Matlay, 2015; Igwe et al., 2018; Ogundana, 2022). Women entrepreneurs are more likely to encounter limited access to money in developing nations such as Nigeria (Ogundana et al., 2022b; Woldie and Adersua, 2004). Besides, the negative attitudes of financial institutions and investors towards women entrepreneurs (such as doubt regarding women's ability) are often not encouraging (De Vita et al., 2014; Ibidunni et al., 2021; Lincoln, 2012). One of the reasons for women's inability to access financial services is their lack of a formal bank account which is a necessary precursor required by financial institutions for granting credit facility. For instance, the Gender–GEDI (2014) index revealed that 50% or more of the women population in Uganda and Nigeria do not have a bank account or use banks or banking institutions in any capacity. Because women entrepreneurs have smaller businesses in comparison to their male counterparts, women-owned businesses are usually considered risky (Treichel and Scott, 2006). Therefore, financial institutions often decline women's application for loans or make the terms more stringent to avoid the more significant cost of monitoring and evaluating women-owned SMEs (Treichel and Scott, 2006). This is not the same in developed countries such as the United States and the United Kingdom, where women entrepreneurs have access to excellent financial services and multiple sources of finance (Gender–GEDI index, 2014). This is unlike the African nations, including Zimbabwe, Niger Republic and Cameroon, where the sources of venture capital available to women-owned businesses are minimal. For instance, the Gender–GEDI index (2014) revealed that multiple sources of finance are still very limited in developing countries including Morocco, Ghana, Egypt, Nigeria and Uganda, which are all nations that mainly possess one investing platform.

Furthermore, lending institutions in Africa often turned down women entrepreneurs' applications for credit finance more often than their male counterparts (Jamali, 2009; Ogundana, 2022). Bank officers in Africa are more likely to differentiate between men- and women-owned SMEs during the consideration of whether to approve loan facilities (Iakovleva et al., 2013). The traditional gender stereotype is embedded within the banking sector as women entrepreneurs are refused finances because entrepreneurship is mainly considered a man's job in some African contexts such as Zimbabwe (Tlaiss, 2013). Besides, women entrepreneurs are more likely to be granted loans if they can provide a male guarantor and also agree to pay a very high-interest cost (Jamali, 2009; Mazonde and Carmichael, 2016). This may be due to a lack of creditworthiness or lack of personal assets for use as collateral (Jamali, 2009). In many African nations including Nigeria, women entrepreneurs will usually lack personal assets to use for collateral because family properties are usually registered in the name of the husband (Klapper and Parker, 2011). In many African countries, there are also legal restrictions to women's ownership of property (Gender–GEDI, 2014). In patriarchal societies such as Zimbabwe, men have more rights (social) to ownership of assets and decision-making authority (Mazonde and Carmichael, 2016). Consequently, women need to gain the permission of their husbands before such assets can be used as collateral for external finance. However, their husbands will usually disagree with using the family's property as security for a loan; as the men will instead look down on their wives' entrepreneurial activities (Azmat and Fujimoto, 2016). Thus, women from the African region will often rely more on their savings or co-run their businesses with their spouses, in order to access finance from the family's savings or banks (Mazonde and Carmichael, 2016).

Informal Institutional Context

The informal institutional context relies heavily on culture, family relationships, religion and trade associations (Amoako and Matlay, 2015; Welter, 2011; Welter and Smallbone, 2008). Many African countries are primarily religious, and they strictly adhere to norms, beliefs and folkways (Igbanugo et al., 2016; Mazonde and Carmichael, 2016; Woldie and Adersua, 2004). For example, Nigeria is rated as the ninth country in the world with the most active religious views (PEW research centre, 2019) and over 500 cultural groups (WorldAtlas, 2019). However, the religious and cultural philosophy within many African countries (such as Nigeria, Ghana, Angola, Cameron and Ethiopia) is based on the patriarchal thought system, more so than the developed countries (Aliyu, 2013; Okafor and Mordi, 2010; Olawepo and Fatulu, 2012). This patriarchal system which is evident in the sociocultural practices in the African regions has often made women subordinate to men (Igbanugo et al., 2016; Lincoln, 2012; Madichie and Nkamnebe, 2010; Woldie and Adersua, 2004). The implication of that is that women entrepreneurs are unlikely to have equal opportunities as their male counterparts (Adom and Asare-Yeboa, 2016; Aliyu, 2013; Okafor and Mordi, 2010).

The African patriarchal socio-culture also moulded and shaped women's roles and responsibilities in their family (Baughn et al., 2006; Lincoln, 2012). Thus, the patriarchal socio-culture in many African nations prescribes men as breadwinners, while women are expected to support their spouse's career in addition to their primary responsibility of childcare and housework (Igwe et al., 2018; Madichie, 2011; Ogundana et al., 2018; Yang and Triana, 2019). This is different in the developed country context such as the United Kingdom where women and men can play one another's role or switch responsibilities altogether (Nel et al., 2010). For instance, in the United Kingdom, there are stay at home men who are primarily responsible for childcare and household duties; while women play the role of the breadwinners (Doucet, 2016). Many scholars associate the prevalence of gender equality to a country's level of development (Pinillos and Reyes, 2011). Thus, in Africa where a majority of the countries (including Nigeria, Zimbabwe and Ghana) are still considered to be developing countries, women entrepreneurs are expected to operate their businesses in addition to their home-making responsibilities (Lincoln, 2012; Madichie and Nkamnebe, 2010; Mazonde and Carmichael, 2016; Ogundana et al., 2018). Unlike developed countries such as the United Kingdom where men can take up childcare responsibilities; women in developing countries such as Nigeria are less likely to be supported by their spouses to undertake household chores and childcare responsibilities while they focus on their businesses (Madichie and Nkamnebe, 2010; Yang and Triana, 2019). Nevertheless, in order to supplement the family income, women must strive to balance work and household responsibilities, especially with raising children in the African context (Lincoln, 2012; Nel et al., 2010). Thus, women entrepreneurs are often considered "double burdened" when they perform the role of mother and worker concurrently (Adom and Asare-Yeboa, 2016; Ogundana et al., 2018; Ogundana et al., 2022a).

In the context of Africa, men are often considered imprudent for letting their wives start and grow a business (Jamali, 2009; Madichie and Nkamnebe, 2010; Mazonde and Carmichael, 2016). In instances when women can obtain spousal support, they would jointly identify business opportunities with their husbands (Jamali, 2009). However, as the business grows and the woman spend more time at work, the husband becomes unsupportive and quarrelsome; leading to domestic disputes (Lincoln, 2012; Madichie and Nkamnebe, 2010; Nel et al., 2010). Consequently, the spouse withdraws his supports, and the lack of this spousal support is very detrimental to women entrepreneurs, as women are often less optimistic and confident about their abilities (Brush et al., 2017; Devine et al., 2019; Oke, 2013; Ogundana et al., 2022a). However, women do not want to displease their husbands or go against cultural norms; they consequently try to appease their husbands by spending more time performing their prescribed caregiving role and living the business to suffer (Igbanugo et al., 2016; Madichie, 2011; Madichie and Nkamnebe, 2010). On the contrary, Nel et al. (2010) provided strong evidence that women entrepreneurs in developed countries, such as Australia, are encouraged to own and grow their businesses while still maintaining allegiance to their family.

Trade association represents another informal institutional context that many women entrepreneurs in Africa are affiliated to (Amoako and Matlay, 2015; Andrae and Beckman, 2013; Oke, 2013). According to Amoako (2018), the trade associations in Africa often make the rules, mediate in disputes and enforce business contracts between women entrepreneurs and their customers. Trade associations also function as parallel institutions to the courts and fill the institutional void left by the weak and unsupportive legal institutions in Africa (Amoako and Matlay, 2015). In addition to that, the vast majority of the trade associations in Africa often provide training programmes that include soft skills development training (Andrae and Beckman, 2013; Ogundana et al., 2022a). For example, the Ethiopian Women Exporters' Association (EWEA), whose mission is to inspire and support members to become successful exporters, organise business development forums designed to support their members in their application for an export license as well as for providing them with essential shipping information (EWEA, 2018). The Ethiopian Women Exporters' Association also provides workshops and specific training for its members in order to strengthen their compatibility with both local and global markets (EWEA, 2018). Another example is the Network of African Women in Agribusiness (AWAN) which support its members by sharing information about new markets, organising trade fairs and organising buyers and seller's market (AWAN, 2019). However, there are political-related studies (see, for instance, Faseke, 2004; Madichie, 2011) that recognise that African women leaders consciously or unconsciously may not support fellow women within a social group. In order words, any trade association that is constituted of women in its leadership structure are unlikely to support female members of the trade association. Mama and Okazawa-Rey (2012) concluded that the lack of mutual support for each other is the most vital ingredient militating against women's emergence as political leaders in the Nigerian political scene. Amid these formal and informal institutional contexts, African women entrepreneurs pursue their business ventures with the marked determination to succeed.

The Interconnectedness between Women's SMEs, Formal and Informal Institutional Contexts in SSA

The discussions about the interconnections between the formal and informal institutional contexts in developing economies are inconclusive in women's entrepreneurship literature. The informal institutional contexts frequently play the dominant role in the interrelationship with the formal institutional context (Rugina, 2018). The informal institutional contexts often mediate, moderate and interact with formal institutions to affect individual behaviours of women entrepreneurs (Gimenez-Jimenez et al., 2020). For instance, informal institutions (including masculinity, individualism and indulgence) could mediate the degree of influence of formal institutions (including public expenditure on childcare) on women's likelihood of starting new ventures (Gimenez-Jimenez, et al., 2020). This is largely because informal institutional contexts have a stronger influence on women's entrepreneurship than formal institutions (Alvarez et al., 2011; Noguera et al., 2013). This is perhaps applicable to the developing country context, including those within the SSA, where the formal institutional contexts are mostly weak and unreliable (Andrews, 2018; Amoako, 2018; Madichie and Nkamnebe, 2010). Besides, informal institutions play a major role in determining how the formal institutional context influences women's entrepreneurship. For instance, the cultural perspective that perceives women as second-class citizens plays a major role in limiting women's participation in policy development – formal institutional contexts (Mazonde and Carmichael, 2016; Ogundana et al., 2022b). Besides, women's second-class citizenship also limits their access to resources and supports mechanisms deriving from the formal institutional contexts (Lincoln, 2012; Mazonde and Carmichael, 2016). The institutional contexts (including culture and religion) shape the decision-making processes of gatekeepers of resources and powerholders (Iakovleva et al., 2013; Mazonde and Carmichael, 2016). Women entrepreneurs would sometimes require a male guarantor for their loan applications to get approved because of the culturally birthed occupational stereotype that assumes that entrepreneurship is not for women (Jamali, 2009; Mazonde and Carmichael, 2016).

Formal institutions continue to generate a reverse impact, although minimal in comparison to the impact of the informal institutions, on informal institutional contexts. For instance, players within the formal institutional context (including policymakers) have started to implement laws and policies with the aim of impacting and reshaping the informal institutions, especially those characterised by issues contrary to women (Ogundana et al., 2022a; Ojong et al., 2021; Omodara et al., 2020). In the past decade, there have been over 274 laws and regulations passed with the aim of reshaping the chauvinistic attitude towards women in 131 economies (United Nations Foundation, 2020). In the African region, Malawi and Namibia both instituted policies to revise discriminatory informal institutions that govern inheritance and property rights, and in the decade that followed, female labour force participation increased substantially in those two countries (United Nations Foundation, 2020). Similarly, laws and regulations instilled in other African regions have in the last two decades improved gender parity in Kenya, Tunisia, Nigeria and South Africa (PEW Research Centre, 2019). In the political arena, which in the past was often stereotyped as male domain, policymakers have taken steps to reduce this occupational stereotype often induced by sociocultural beliefs and norms (United Nations, 2005). In Africa, the African Union (AU) promoted gender parity in its top decision-making positions by electing three women and three men as AU Commissioners (African Union, 2021). Despite these reverse impacts demonstrated by formal institutions in the SSA regions, the informal institutional contexts continue to exercise a significant impact on the formal institutional context that women entrepreneurship operates within (Gimenez-Jimenez et al., 2020).

Women entrepreneurs have little or no influence on the informal institutional contexts (such as culture and religion) which is often described as exogenous in that the women entrepreneurs by themselves have very little or no control over it and limited means of directly changing it (Brush et al., 2009; Ogundana, 2022). Howbeit, women entrepreneurs and their enterprises are influencing the formal institutional contexts within the SSA region and indeed the world (Berger and Kuckertz, 2016; Ettl and Welter, 2012; Ogundana, 2020). In other words, women's entrepreneurship has a mutual and intertwined relationship with the formal institutional contexts (Munkejord, 2017; Waterhouse et al., 2017). According to Munkejord (2017), women are changing the places where they live (formal institutional contexts). For instance, to protect female entrepreneurs, women parliamentarians in Uganda helped instituted legislations that made rape a capital offence in Uganda (United Nations, 2005). Similarly, the presence of women in parliaments increased the adoption of gender-sensitive policies in South Africa, Rwanda and Mozambique (United Nations, 2005). However, the influence that women entrepreneurs have on the formal institutional contexts within SSA is still very limited. This is so especially as the proportion of women in the place of authority is still very small in comparison to their male counterparts (McKinsey Global Institute, 2019). In 2021, women constituted 24% of the 12,113 parliamentarians in Africa (see Figure 8.1) (International IDEA, 2021). As such, many quarters have suggested that it might take a long time for women to have significant influence over the formal institutional contexts (McKinsey Global Institute, 2019).

Summary and Conclusions

This chapter exposed the formal and informal institutional contexts within the SSA regions. Both formal and informal institutional contexts offer support and hindrances to women entrepreneurs and their enterprises (Brush et al., 2009). The informal institutional contexts have a stronger impact on women entrepreneurship than the formal institutions. This is largely because the formal institutional contexts are weak and ineffective (Amoako and Matlay, 2015; Simba et al., 2022). In terms of the interrelationships between women entrepreneurship and the institutional contexts, the formal and informal institutional contexts shape one another in influencing women's entrepreneurship in the SSA region (see Figure 8.2). Presently, the informal institutional contexts have a more significant influence on the formal institutional contexts which is mainly weak and oftentimes non-existent (McKinsey Global Institute, 2019). Women entrepreneurs in the SSA region possess a reverse influence on the formal institutional contexts, especially through

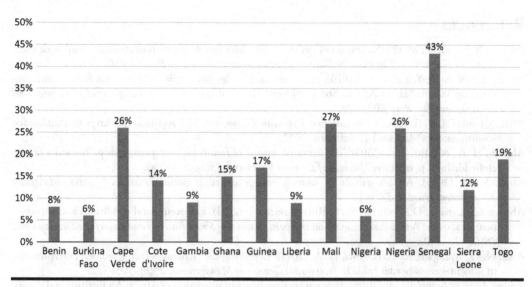

Figure 8.1 Proportion of women in SSA parliament. Source: International Institute for Democracy and Electoral Assistance (International IDEA) 2021 – Women's Political Participation: Africa Barometer 2021.

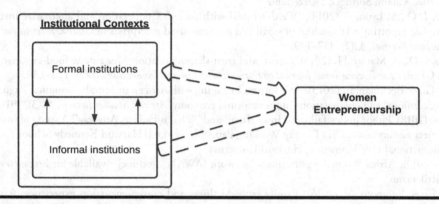

Figure 8.2 Interconnection between formal, informal institutions and women entrepreneurship. Source: Authors' idea.

their participation in policy developments and trade union activism (see Figure 8.2) (Andrae and Beckman, 2013; Ogundana et al., 2022b). Women entrepreneurs and their enterprises still maintain very little and inconsequential influence on the informal institutions especially as they are mainly exogenous forces (see Figure 8.2) (Brush et al., 2009). However, women entrepreneurs are still able to indirectly mitigate the adverse influence of informal institutions through formal institutional contexts (including policies). To further improve the contribution of women entrepreneurship to the SSA region, it is important to improve the proportion of women involved in policy development. Doing that would enable women to further utilise the formal and informal institutional contexts to better support the performance of their enterprises. In conclusion, future studies should consider conducting empirical investigation of how various formal and informal institutional contexts influence women entrepreneurship in the SSA region. Doing this will further enrich studies in women entrepreneurship from developing economies.

References

Ado, A., & Josiah, M. M. (2015). Impact of deficient electricity supply on the operations of small-scale businesses in North East Nigeria. *The Business & Management Review*, 6(2), 240–250.

Adom, K., & Asare-Yeboa, I. T. (2016). An evaluation of human capital theory and female entrepreneurship in sub-Sahara Africa: Some evidence from Ghana. *International Journal of Gender and Entrepreneurship*, 8(4), 402–423.

African Union. (2021). *AUC Commissioners | African Union*. [online] Available at: https://au.int/en/auc-commissioners (Accessed 17 February 2022).

Aldrich, H. E., & Cliff, J. E. (2003). The pervasive effects of family on entrepreneurship: Toward a family embeddedness perspective. *Journal of Business Venturing*, 18(5), 573–596.

Aliyu, S. M. (2013). An assessment of women entrepreneurship performance in Nigeria. *Malaysian Management Journal*, 17, 1–12.

Alvarez, C., Urbano, D., Coduras, A., & Ruiz-Navarro, J. (2011). Environmental conditions and entrepreneurial activity: A regional comparison in Spain. *Journal of Small Business and Enterprise Development*, 18(1), 120–140.

Ama, N. O., Mangadi, K. T., & Ama, H. A. (2014). Exploring the challenges facing women entrepreneurs in informal cross-border trade in Botswana. *Gender in Management*, 29(8), 505–522.

Amine, L. S., & Staub, K. M. (2009). Women entrepreneurs in sub-Saharan Africa: An institutional theory analysis from a social marketing point of view. *Entrepreneurship and Regional Development*, 21(2), 183–211.

Amoako, I. O. (2018). *Trust, institutions and managing entrepreneurial relationships in Africa: An SME perspective*. Cham: Springer, Switzerland

Amoako, I. O., & Lyon, F. (2014). 'We don't deal with courts': Cooperation and alternative institutions shaping exporting relationships of small and medium-sized enterprises in Ghana. *International Small Business Journal*, 32(2), 117–139.

Amoako, I. O., & Matlay, H. (2015). Norms and trust-shaping relationships among food-exporting SMEs in Ghana. *The International Journal of Entrepreneurship and Innovation*, 16(2), 123–134.

Andrae, G., & Beckman, B. (2013). ASR forum: Engaging with African informal economies: Lagos tailors, trade unions, and organizations in the informal economy. *African Studies Review*, 56(3), 191–208.

Andrews. (2018). Public policy failure: 'How Often?' and 'What is Failure, Anyway'? A study of world bank project performance. CID Faculty Working Paper No. 344 ed. Harvard Kennedy School: Center for International Development at Harvard University.

AWAN. (2019). Africa Women Agribusiness Network (AWAN). [online] Available at: https://www.awanafrika.com/.

Azmat, F., & Fujimoto, Y. (2016). Family embeddedness and entrepreneurship experience: A study of Indian migrant women entrepreneurs in Australia. *Entrepreneurship & Regional Development*, 28(9–10), 630–656.

Baughn, C. C., Chua, B. L., & Neupert, K. E. (2006). The normative context for women's participation in entrepreneruship: A multicountry study. *Entrepreneurship Theory and Practice*, 30(5), 687–708.

Berger, E. S., & Kuckertz, A. (2016). Female entrepreneurship in startup ecosystems worldwide. *Journal of Business Research*, 69(11), 5163–5168.

Bridge, S., & O'Neill, K. (2012). *Understanding enterprise: Entrepreneurship and small business*. Macmillan International Higher Education.

Brush, C., Ali, A., Kelley, D., & Greene, P. (2017). The influence of human capital factors and context on women's entrepreneurship: Which matters more?. *Journal of Business Venturing Insights*, 8, 105–113.

Brush, C., De Bruin, A., & Welter, F. (2009). A gender-aware framework for women's entrepreneurship. *International Journal of Gender and Entrepreneurship*, 1(1), 8–24.

Bulanova, O., Isaksen, E. J., & Kolvereid, L. (2016). Growth aspirations among women entrepreneurs in high growth firms. *Baltic Journal of Management*, 11(2), 187–206.

Chea, A. C. (2008). Entrepreneurial venture creation: The application of pattern identification theory to the entrepreneurial opportunity-identification process. *International Journal of Business and Management*, 3(2), 37–53.

Costin, Y. (2012). In pursuit of growth: An insight into the experience of female entrepreneurs. *International Journal of Gender and Entrepreneurship, 4*(2), 108–127.

De Vita, L., Mari, M., & Poggesi, S. (2014). Women entrepreneurs in and from developing countries: Evidences from the literature. *European Management Journal, 32*(3), 451–460.

Devine, R. A., Molina-Sieiro, G., Holmes Jr., R. M., & Terjesen, S. A. (2019). Female-Led high-growth: Examining the role of human and financial resource management. *Journal of Small Business Management, 57*(1), 81–109.

Dionco-Adetayo, E., Makinde, J., & Adetayo, J. (2005). Evaluation of policy implementation in women entrepreneurship development. In: *ICSB-2005 Conference*, Washington, D.C.

Doucet, A. (2016). The ethics of care and the radical potential of fathers 'Home Alone on Leave': Care as practice, relational ontology, and social justice. *Comparative Perspectives on Work-Life Balance and Gender Equality: Fathers on Leave Alone, 6*, 11.

Edelman. (2017). *Edelman trust barometer global results*. Edelman Insights.

Ettl, K., & Welter, F. (2012). Women entrepreneurs and success. In *Women's entrepreneurship and economics* (pp. 73–88). New York: Springer.

EWEA. (2018). Ethiopian Women Exporters' Association. [online] Available at: https://amp.what-this.com /28935888/1/ethiopian-women-exporters-association.html (Accessed 17 February 2022).

Faseke, M. (2004). Women and governance in Nigeria. In *Governance: Nigeria and the World* (pp. 282-297). Lagos: Centre for Constitutionalism and Demilitarization (CENCOD).

Gao, C., Zuzul, T., Jones, G., & Khanna, T. (2017). Overcoming institutional voids: A reputation-based view of long-run survival. *Strategic Management Journal, 38*(11), 2147–2167.

GEM. (2014). Global Report. Global Entrepreneurship Monitor. [online] Available at: http://www.bab-son.edu/Academics/centers/blank-center/globalresearch/gem/Documents/GEM%202014%20Global %20Report.pdf.

GEM. (2015). Special Report Women's Entrepreneurship. Global Entrepreneurship Monitor. [online] Available at: http://www.babson.edu/Academics/centers/blank-center/globalresearch/gem/ Documents/GEM%202015%20Womens%20Report.pdf.

GEM. (2017). Women's Entrepreneurship Report. Global Entrepreneurship Monitor. [online] Available at: https://www.gemconsortium.org/report/gem-20162017-womens-entrepreneurship-report.

Gender-GEDI. (2014). *The Gender Global Entrepreneurship and Development Index (GEDI)*. Global Entrepreneurship and Development Institute.

Gimenez-Jimenez, D., Calabrò, A., & Urbano, D. (2020). The neglected role of formal and informal institutions in women's entrepreneurship: A multi-level analysis. *Journal of International Entrepreneurship, 18*(2), 196–226.

Iakovleva, T., Solesvik, M., & Trifilova, A. (2013). Financial availability and government support for women entrepreneurs in transitional economies. *Journal of Small Business and Enterprise Development, 20*(2), 314–340.

Ibidunni, A. S., Ogundana, O. M., & Okonkwo, A. (2021). Entrepreneurial competencies and the performance of informal SMEs: The contingent role of business environment. *Journal of African Business, 22*(4), 468–490.

IFC. (2014). Women-Owned SNEs: A business opportunity for financial institutions. International Finance Corporation. [online] Available at: http//www.ifc.org.

Igbanugo, I. C., Uzonwanne, M. C., & Ezenekwe, R. U. (2016). Small and medium scale enterprises in African setting: The place of women. *International Journal of Economics, Commerce and Management, 4*(3), 762–778.

Igwe, P. A., & Icha-Ituma, A. (2020). A review of ten years of African entrepreneurship research. In M. E. M. Akoorie, J. Gibb, J. M. Scott, & P. Sinha (Eds.), *Research handbook on entrepreneurship in emerging economies: A Contextualized Approach (pp. 325-353) Cheltenham*: Edward Elgar, England

Igwe, P. A., Amarachi, N. A., Ogundana, O. M., Egere, O. M., & Anigbo, J. A. (2018). Factors affecting the investment climate, SMEs productivity and entrepreneurship in Nigeria. *European Journal of Sustainable Development, 7*(1), 182–182.

Institute for Economics and Peace. (2020). Global peace index. Available: http://visionofhumanity.org/ indexes/global-peace-index/ (Accessed 17 February 2022).

International IDEA. (2021). Women's political participation: Africa Barometer 2021. International IDEA. [online] Available at: https://www.idea.int/publications/catalogue/womens-political-participation -africa-barometer-2021 (Accessed 18 February 2022).

Iyiola, O., & Azuh, D. E. (2014). Women entrepreneurs as small-medium enterprise (SME) operators and their roles in socio-economic development in Ota. *Nigeria. International Journal of Economics, Business and Finance*, 2(1), 1–10.

Jamali, D. (2009). Constraints and opportunities facing women entrepreneurs in developing countries: A relational perspective. *Women In Management Review*, 24(4), 232–251.

Kiviluoto, N. (2013). Growth as evidence of firm success: Myth or reality?. *Entrepreneurship & Regional Development*, 25(7–8), 569–586.

Klapper, L. F., & Parker, S. C. (2011). Gender and the business environment for new firm creation. *The World Bank Research Observer*, 26(2), 237–257.

Lincoln, A. (2012). Prospects and challenges of women entrepreneurs in Nigeria. *Cardiff School of Management, Cardiff Metropolitan University UK, Western Avenue Llandaff Cardiff, CF5 2YB.Tel*, 44(0), 29.

Madichie, N. O. (2009). Breaking the glass ceiling in Nigeria: A review of women's entrepreneurship. *Journal of African Business*, 10(1), 51–66.

Madichie, N. O. (2011). Setting an agenda for women entrepreneurship in Nigeria. *Gender in Management*, 26(3), 212.

Madichie, N. O., & Nkamnebe, A. D. (2010). Micro-credit for microenterprises? A study of women. *Gender in Management: An International Journal*, 25(4), 301–319.

Mama, A., & Okazawa-Rey, M. (2012). Militarism, conflict, and women's activism in the global era: Challenges and prospects for women in three West African contexts. *Feminist Review*, 101(1), 97–123.

Mazonde, N. B., & Carmichael, T. (2016). The influence of culture on female entrepreneurs in Zimbabwe. *The Southern African Journal of Entrepreneurship and Small Business Management*, 8(1), 1–10.

McKinsey Global Institute. (2019). *The power of parity: Advancing women's equality in Africa*. [online] Available at: https://www.mckinsey.com/featured-insights/gender-equality/the-power-of-parity -advancing-womens-equality-in-africa.

Misango, S. B., & Ongiti, O. K. (2013). Do women entrepreneurs play a role in reducing poverty? A case in Kenya. *International Review of Management and Business Research*, 2(1), 87.

Munkejord, M. C. (2017). Local and transnational networking among female immigrant entrepreneurs in peripheral rural contexts: Perspectives on Russians in Finnmark, Norway. *European Urban and Regional Studies*, 24(1), 7–20.

Nel, P., Maritz, A., & Thongpravati, O. (2010). Motherhood and entrepreneurship: The mumpreneur phenomenon. *International Journal of Organizational Innovation*, 3(1), 6–34.

Noguera, M., Alvarez, C., & Urbano, D. (2013). Socio-cultural factors and female entrepreneurship. *International Entrepreneurship and Management Journal*, 9(2), 183–197.

Ochulor, C. L. (2011). Ethical and moral implications of corruption. *Canadian Social Science*, 7(5), 223–228.

Ogundana, O. (2020). *Factors influencing the business growth of women-owned sewing businesses (WOSBs) in Lagos-State, Nigeria: A gender-aware growth framework*. Nottingham Trent University.

Ogundana, O. (2022). Obstacles facing women-owned enterprises: A case for sub-Sahara African women. *World Review of Entrepreneurship, Management and Sustainable Development*, 18(5–6), 529–544.

Ogundana, O., Galanakis, K., Simba, A., & Oxborrow, L. (2018). Factors influencing the business growth of women-owned sewing businesses in Lagos-State, Nigeria: A pilot study. *Organisational Studies and Innovation Review*, 4(2), 25–36.

Ogundana, O., Galanakis, K., Simba, A., & Oxborrow, L. (2022a). Growth perception amongst women entrepreneurs: An emerging economy perspective. *International Journal of Entrepreneurship and Small Business*, 47(1), 109–127.

Ogundana, O., Simba, A., Dana, L. P., & Liguori, E. (2022b). A growth model for understanding female-owned enterprises. *Journal of the International Council for Small Business*, 1–10.

Ojong, N., Simba, A., & Dana, L. P. (2021). Female entrepreneurship in Africa: A review, trends, and future research directions. *Journal of Business Research*, 132, 233–248.

Okafor, C., & Mordi, C. (2010). Women entrepreneurship development in Nigeria: The effect of environmental factors. *Petroleum-Gas University of Ploiesti Bulletin, Economic Sciences Series*, 62(4), 43–52.

Oke, D. F. (2013). The effect of social network on women entrepreneurs in Nigeria: A case study of Ado-Ekiti Small scale Enterprise. *International Journal of Education and Research*, 1(11), 1–14.

Olawepo, R. A., & Fatulu, B. (2012). Rural women farmers and food productivity in Nigeria: An example from Ekiti Kwara, Nigeria. *Asian Social Science*, 8(10), 108.

Omodara, D., Ikhile, D., Ogundana, O., & Akin-Akinyosoye, K. (2020). Global pandemic and business performance: Impacts and responses. *International Journal of Research in Business and Social Science*, 9(6), 1–11.

Otoo, M., Ibro, G., Fulton, J., & Lowenberg-Deboer, J. (2012). Micro-entrepreneurship in Niger: Factors affecting the success of women street food vendors. *Journal of African Business*, 13(1), 16–28.

Pew Research Center. (2019). *How people around the world view gender equality in their countries.* [online] Available at: https://www.pewresearch.org/global/2019/04/22/how-people-around-the-world-view -gender-equality-in-their-countries/.

Pinillos, M. J., & Reyes, L. (2011). Relationship between individualist–collectivist culture and entrepreneurial activity: Evidence from Global Entrepreneurship Monitor data. *Small Business Economics*, 37(1), 23–37.

Rugina, S. (2018). Women entrepreneurship in Estonia: Formal and informal institutional context. In *Women's entrepreneurship in Europe* (pp. 105–135). Cham: Springer.

Scott, J., Harrison, R., Hussain, J., & Millman, C. (2014). The role of guanxi networks in the performance of women-led firms in China. *International Journal of Gender and Entrepreneurship*, 6(1), 68–82.

Simba, A., Kalu, E. U., Onodugo, V., Okoyeuzu, C. R., & Ogundana, O. M. (2022). Women entrepreneurs in Nigeria. In *Women entrepreneurs in Sub-Saharan Africa* (pp. 155–172). Cham: Springer.

Thornton, P. H., Ribeiro-Soriano, D., & Urbano, D. (2011). Socio-cultural factors and entrepreneurial activity: An overview. *International Small Business Journal*, 29(2), 105–118.

Tlaiss, H. A. (2013). Women managers in the United Arab Emirates: Successful careers or what?. *Equality, Diversity and Inclusion: An International Journal*, 32(8), 756.

Transparency International. (2018). Corruption perceptions index. Available: https://www.transparency .org/en/cpi/2018 (Accessed 17 February 2022).

Treichel, M. Z., & Scott, J. A. (2006). Women-owned businesses and access to bank credit: Evidence from three surveys since 1987. *Venture Capital*, 8(1), 51–67.

United Nations. (2005). *African women battle for equality | Africa Renewal.* [online] Available at: https:// www.un.org/africarenewal/magazine/july-2005/african-women-battle-equality.

United Nations Foundation. (2020). *Five things world leaders can do right now to advance gender equality.* [online] Available at: https://unfoundation.org/blog/post/five-things-world-leaders-can-do-right-now -to-advance-gender-equality/.

Waterhouse, P., Hill, A. G., & Hinde, A. (2017). Combining work and childcare: The experiences of mothers in Accra, Ghana. *Development Southern Africa*, 34(6), 771–786.

Webb, J. W., Khoury, T. A., & Hitt, M. A. (2020). The influence of formal and informal institutional voids on entrepreneurship. *Entrepreneurship Theory and Practice*, 44(3), 504–526.

Welter, F. (2011). Contextualizing entrepreneurship—Conceptual challenges and ways forward. *Entrepreneurship Theory and Practice*, 35(1), 165–184.

Welter, F., & Gartner, W. B. (2016). Advancing our research agenda for entrepreneurship and contexts. In *A research agenda for entrepreneurship and context.* Edward Elgar Publishing.

Welter, F., & Smallbone, D. (2008). Women's entrepreneurship from an institutional perspective: The case of Uzbekistan. *International Entrepreneurship and Management Journal*, 4(4), 505–520.

Woldie, A., & Adersua, A (2004). Female entrepreneurs in a transitional economy: Businesswomen in Nigeria. *International Journal of Social Economics*, 31(1–2), 78–93.

World Bank. (2013). *Women, business and the law.* Washington D.C., USA: The World Bank. [online] Available at: https://wbl.worldbank.org/en/reports.

World Bank. (2018). *Enterprise surveys from developing economies 2009–2017.* Washington D.C., USA: The World Bank.

WorldAtlas. (2019). *Nigeria maps & facts*. [online] Available at: https://www.worldatlas.com/maps/nigeria.

Yang, T., & del Carmen Triana, M. (2019). Set up to fail: Explaining when women-led businesses are more likely to fail. *Journal of Management, 45*(3), 926–954.

Zahra, S. A., Wright, M., & Abdelgawad, S. G. (2014). Contextualization and the advancement of entrepreneurship research. *International Small Business Journal, 32*(5), 479–500.

Chapter 9

Women's Access to Financial Capital and High-Growth Enterprises

Rebecca C. Emeordi, Paul Agu Igwe and Nnamdi O. Madichie

Contents

Introduction

Financial inclusion or access to financial resource is a major challenge to ease of doing business, limiting the rate of entrepreneurship and enterprise growth in many developing countries. Financial inclusion has been described as "a process that ensures the ease of access, availability, and usage of formal financial services by all members of the society" (Govindapuram et al., 2022). To overcome the challenge of financial exclusion, government and international agencies have promoted several programmes and policies for several decades. Despite the efforts of governments and local and international agencies, access to finance remains the most common obstacle in many regions of the Global South. Besides, when compared to men's or men-owned enterprises, women's

DOI: 10.4324/9781003302339-9

or women-owned enterprises are more affected by the problem of access to financial capital. Only a few studies have attempted to study the impediments that women face when trying to access finance (Morsy & Youssef, 2017).

Arguably, women are more likely to be excluded from financial services in societies where there are gaps in educational attainment between women and men (Morsy, 2020). More so, there is a disparity between the sizes of firms (small, medium and large enterprises) regarding access to financial capital across many regions. Large firms have more access to financing and more internal resources, thus making large firms grow faster than small and medium enterprises (SMEs) (Hashmi et al., 2020). The effect of the lack of access to finance is that many small firms remain informal and lack the capacity to generate employment opportunities. As a feature of informality, the modal firm size in many developing countries is one worker, consisting of only the owner of the firm and family member(s). Khavul et al. (2009) posit that most family businesses in Africa are informal enterprises, and they have fewer than five employees, are unregistered and unlicensed and typically do not pay taxes. Informal firms that do hire additional workers hire fewer than ten employees.

In Nigeria, survey data indicate that 99.6 per cent of firms have fewer than ten workers (World Bank, 2015). Similarly, in India and Indonesia, the fraction of firms with less than ten employees is nearly 100 per cent (Hsieh & Olken, 2014). More so, most firms in African countries are informal and family businesses (Igwe, Newbery & Icha-Ituma, 2018; International Labour Organisation, 2014; African Development Bank, 2013). Arguably, there may be some association between informality and business exits or failure (GEM, 2021). To address this imbalance, many governments and international agencies have embarked on policies aimed at promoting and supporting SMEs and women's enterprises.

This chapter adds to various types of literature on women entrepreneurship in developing countries and examines the challenges and barriers facing women entrepreneurship in the context of contemporary African economies. First is by exploring the role of capital access to high-growth firms, types of women in high-growth firms and employment capacity. Several studies show evidence from developing countries, highlighting the importance of business start-ups and young firms in job creation (World Bank, 2015; Ayyagari et al., 2014). Also, several findings show that "high-growth entrepreneurs" or "high-impact firms" represent a tiny fraction of the overall firm population but make a disproportionally large contribution to job growth (World Bank, 2015; Henrekson & Johannsson, 2010). Second, it helps increase awareness about the gender gaps, social, cultural and size of firms' impediments to entrepreneurship. It contributes to addressing a bias in the entrepreneurship literature towards the developed world (Ariyo et al., 2015; Newbery et al., 2017).

Institutional and Resource-Based Theories

Finance is a major resource of the firm and ease of doing business depends on the effectiveness of institutions.[1] Within the framework of the resource-based view (RBV), entrepreneurship researchers have explored in-depth the determinants of entrepreneurial venture performance (Kellermanns et al., 2016; Wiklund & Shepherd, 2003; Alvarez & Busenitz, 2001). Some scholars attribute women's lower levels of participation in growth-oriented entrepreneurship to gender differences in key resource inputs including human, social and financial capital (Coleman & Robb, 2009 & 2014; Madichie & Gallant, 2012; Fairlie & Robb, 2009; Robb & Coleman 2010).

Similarly, several studies have examined access to capital as a possible impediment to the growth of women-owned firms (Coleman & Robb, 2009; Katwalo & Madichie, 2008). Recent studies indicate that women-owned entrepreneurs raise smaller amounts of capital to finance their firms and are more reliant on personal rather than external sources of financing (Coleman & Robb, 2009; Robb & Coleman 2010). Access to capital depends heavily on the institutional structure prevalent in a location.

Here, institution refers to political, social and legal ground rules within which businesses operate, including stable government, the time it takes in dealing with government procedures, property rights and taxation. Within the context of growth-oriented entrepreneurship, there is a consensus that a good business environment fosters firms' growth, productivity and development, while an adverse business environment increases firms' transaction costs and constraints on its development (Herrera & Kouamé, 2017). Africa is still at its earliest stage of economic development and this process is held back by several socio-economic, political, and environmental constraints (Igwe, Onjewu & Nwibo, 2018). Among these constraints are low-skilled labour, lack of market information, poor access to financial services and technology, and weak demand for goods and services due to widespread poverty, leaving SMEs at a competitive disadvantage in the global marketplace according to International Finance Corporation (IFC, 2008).

Ease of Doing Business in Africa

The now withdrawn World Bank "Ease of Doing Business" once revealed that economic reforms in some African countries such as Benin, Kenya, Mauritania, Senegal and Uganda have enabled Africa to comprise half of the world's top ten improvers (that is, countries that implemented at least three fiscal reforms) and move up the global ranking for ease of doing business (World Bank, 2016). Similarly, out of the 189 countries, South Africa fared the best on the continent ranking number 73 (relegated from 69 in 2015), followed by Uganda at 122 (up from 135 in 2015), Burkina Faso at 143 (up from 149 in 2015), Nigeria 169 (ranked 170 in 2015) and Angola 181 (ranked 183 in 2015), as shown in Table 9.1.

Table 9.1 Doing Business Ranking of Selected Sub-Saharan African Countries

Indicator/Ranking	Nigeria	Angola	Burkina Faso	Uganda	South Africa
GNI per capita (US$)	2,950	5,300	710	660	6,800
Ease of doing business (1–189)	169	181	143	122	73
Starting a business	139	141	78	168	120
Time (days)	30.8	36	13	27	46
Cost (% of income per capita)	31.7	22.5	43.5	39.7	0.3
Obtaining credit	60	181	133	42	59
Power supply	182	166	183	167	168
Time (days)	181.2	145	158	86	226

Source: Igwe, Onjewu & Nwibo (2018).

To explain the shifts in these rankings, the World Bank (2016) provided a list of reforms in sub-Saharan Africa (SSA) as follows:

- Thirty-five of 47 economies in SSA implemented at least one reform, making it easier to do business in the past year.
- SSA accounted for 14 of the 32 reforms globally in obtaining credit. Of the 14 reforms, 12 focused on improving the availability of credit information – more than in any other region.
- The region accounts for five of the ten top improvers in 2015. These five are Benin, Kenya, Mauritania, Senegal and Uganda.
- Rwanda implemented the most reforms in SSA (with six reforms), and Kenya, Madagascar and Senegal followed (with four reforms each). These reforms include credit-scoring services, business pre-registration services and power connection process, reducing costs of security deposits etc.
- Fourteen of the 17 economies implemented business regulation reforms (29 reforms in total). Twenty-four of these reforms reduced the complexity and cost of regulatory processes, while the other five strengthened legal institutions.

Nigeria was not listed among the world's top ten improvers. Successive Nigerian governments face major challenges in policymaking and implementation of their economic reform agenda on how to boost entrepreneurial activities and economic development. Those challenges include weak policy implementation, weak government agencies, weak institutions, and adverse cultural norms. Culture is directly associated with institutions in the sense that culture, like formal institutions as defined by North (1990), governs individual behaviour. A major challenge that has impeded sustainable entrepreneurial growth in Nigeria is corruption. The problem of corruption appears embedded in the culture (Igwe, Onjewu & Nwibo, 2018; Faleye, 2013; Keeper, 2012). Aidis et al. (2012) argue that corruption constrains entrepreneurship by deterring entrepreneurs unwilling to engage in corrupt practices and encouraging unproductive forms of entrepreneurship.

Determinants of Productivity and Firm Growth

Several studies have revealed determinants of productivity which include age and size of firms, access to capital, access to infrastructure and education of the labour force (Igwe, Onjewu & Nwibo, 2018; Fabusoro et al., 2010). The age of owners and the age of firms are important determinants of growth and can have a major influence on the type of activities in which they can participate (Gordon & Craig, 2001). Younger people may have more energy and drive and may be more familiar with the technology and trends required to benefit from entrepreneurship than older people (GEM, 2021). Furthermore, younger firms are more likely to grow faster than older firms (Haltiwanger, Jarmin and Miranda, 2013; Coad & Rao, 2008). The "Learning-by-doing models" (Chang et al., 2002) suggest that older firms may benefit from their greater business experience, and therefore have more growth persistence than younger firms. On the other hand, older firms might suffer from a "liability of obsolescence" and a "liability of senescence" (Coad, 2014). Coad posits lower growth persistence for old firms since they have problems adapting their strategies to changing or current business conditions.

Access to capital is another major business concern and youth-specific obstacle in Africa (GEM, 2014). Financial exclusion refers to a situation where the poor and other disadvantaged groups are unable to access formal financial services, owing to their perceived vulnerability (Mishra et al.,

2014; Katwalo & Madichie, 2008). The Nigerian financial services landscape shows a lack of access to a range of affordable, safe and reliable financial services (Igwe, Newbury & Icha-Ituma, 2018; Madichie & Nkamnebe, 2010). The Central Bank of Nigeria (CBN, 2005) indicates that the formal financial system provides services to about 35 per cent of the economically active population while the remaining 65 per cent are excluded from access to financial services in Nigeria. As a result, households have traditionally patronised informal credit lenders some of whom charge higher interest rates and give short-term small credit.

There is a positive association between education and lifetime income and the ability to spot opportunities (GEM, 2021). Aikaeli (2010) maintains that education allows people to adapt more easily to social-economic, cultural and technical changes in the economy with associated changes in the demand for labour. Nigeria is noted for its poor quality of primary education as well as low levels of tertiary enrolment (GEM, 2014). About 40 per cent of Nigerian children aged 6–11 years (about 4.7 million children of primary school age) do not attend any primary school with the Northern region recording the lowest school attendance rate in the country, particularly for girls according to the United Nations International Children's Emergency Fund (UNICEF, 2005). The problem in Nigeria is not just poor levels of school completion rates but that of skills mismatch (GEM, 2014).

Several studies cite the high rate of inefficient and unsustainable transport systems in most countries in the SSA region as the most important factor affecting women in business (Madichie & Hinson, 2014; Porter, 2013; Starkey & Njenga, 2010). Also, the relationship between infrastructure and economic growth is a major focus of development literature Krishna & Shariff, 2011; Ayogu, 2007). These studies support the idea that under the right conditions, infrastructure development plays a major role in increasing productivity, promoting economic growth and reducing poverty. Onyeiwu & Liu (2011) found that in Bangladesh, a 1 per cent increase in households with access to electricity and paved roads in the villages led to 0.8 per cent increase and 33 per cent in total per capita income, respectively.

In this study, the primary focus is on the role of capital access, and institutional and cultural impediments to women's entrepreneurial activities and ease of doing business. Gender issues have long been a major concern in recent years in light of the role of women in new business venture creation for economic growth. The failure of transport policies and planning to effectively integrate women into the mainstream of economic activities in SSA has long been a cause for policy concern. The World Bank (2013) maintains that after decades of progress towards the equality of women, almost 90 per cent of countries continue to have laws or regulations that prevent women from fully participating in economic life as entrepreneurs or employees. Jamali (2009) maintains that for many women entrepreneurs in Africa, the choice of self-employment may reflect the restricted structure of opportunities in the labour market, labour market discrimination or glass ceiling career problems, with self-employment often perceived as a survival strategy or as means of providing flexibility in work scheduling and reconciling multiple roles.

Economic Growth and Level of Entrepreneurial Activity

Starting a new business or growing an existing business requires resources, including access to finance. The Global Entrepreneurship Monitor (GEM) programme initiated by Babson College and London Business School measures the differences in the level of entrepreneurial activity between countries since 1999. GEM data have been used in a variety of research and studies.

GEM studies show the disparity in Total Entrepreneurial Activity (TEA) between males and women across the world. In the United States, the female TEA rate is 11.2 per cent (two-thirds of males), indicating a much lower UK women rate and a wider relative gender difference (GEM, 2014). In Africa, male and female entrepreneurial activity is at near parity, but there is a vast gender gap in the Middle East and Asia (Kelley et al., 2012). As of 2010, the share of women business owners in Africa was about 65 per cent in Ethiopia, 45 percent in Kenya and 43 per cent in Tanzania, 73 per cent in Lesotho, 84 per cent in Swaziland, 62 per cent in South Africa and 67 per cent in Zimbabwe according to studies carried out by the United States Agency for International Development (USAID, 2010).

The Organisation for Economic Co-operation and Development (OECD) Eurostat Manual on Business Demography Statistics (2007, p. 3) defines a high-growth enterprise as;

> *"all enterprises with average annualized growth greater than twenty per cent per annum, over a three-year period, and with ten or more employees at the beginning of the observation period. Growth is thus measured by the number of employees and by turnover."*

Given the increasing interest in women entrepreneurs and enterprises in academic and policy domains, this chapter contributes to closing the gap between what we know and what we don't know about the challenges facing female high-growth firms in the context of Africa.

"Business Plan Competitions" have become one popular tool that seeks to foster high-growth entrepreneurship in many parts of the world. The World Bank (2017) notes that the competitions seek to identify individuals with promising ideas and aspirations to grow their enterprises, by helping them to formalise these ideas. Practically, the individuals get further assistance by getting them to develop detailed business plans, and then spur the development of some of these potentially high-growth firms through providing financing to the winners. In 2011, the government of Nigeria started a nationwide contest to give out $60 million to young Nigerians trying to start or grow their business tagged "Youth Enterprise with Innovation in Nigeria" (YouWiN). According to the World Bank, "YouWiN" is a large-scale national business plan competition and a collaboration project between Nigeria's Ministry of Finance, Ministry of Communication Technology and Ministry of Youth Development with support from the Department for International Development (DFID) and the World Bank.

In the second year of the competition, PricewaterhouseCooper's accounting firm was brought in to do part of the scoring, while Plymouth University, UK, provided the quality assurance. The programme's aim is to encourage innovation and job creation through the establishment of new businesses and the expansion of existing businesses. Some of the objectives of "YouWiN" include increasing firm growth by 20 per cent; encouraging expansion, specialisation and spin-offs of existing businesses; and targeting growth in the Agriculture/Agro-processing, Construction, ICT, Fashion, Manufacturing and Retail sectors, etc (YouWiN Connect, 2017). The competition attracted almost 24,000 entrants and random assignment was used to select some of the winners from a pool of semi-finalists, with each winner allocated grant funding of almost US$50,000 (World Bank, 2017). The World Bank analysed the competition impact over three years. The report examined the 1,200 winners and found they had created 7,000 jobs, real jobs that stuck around three years later.

"YouWiN" competition calls for online submission of initial concepts (for both new and existing businesses), these are then marked to some set criteria, with 1,500 national merit winners and 750 zonal merit winners (from six regions) being invited to participate in training. The 6,000 applicants then undergo further training before submitting a final business plan to a set template.

The "YouWiN" applications were further screened, and 1,500 winners selected. These winners are provided with further training, mentoring and allocated grant money in line with their achievement of various developmental milestones. Between 2011 and 2016, "YouWiN" generated data on more than 18,000 detailed business plans: a dataset of entrepreneurial aspirations, perceived opportunities, business experience, qualifications and funding requirements.

Institutional Challenges and the Ease of Doing Business Narrative

An institution is a system of rules, norms, customs and actors. Institutions are sets or systems of rules that determine and constrain social behaviour and interaction (Farkas, 2019). Different types of regulation (formal and informal) encourage or discourage the efficiency and effectiveness of doing business. Also, institutions determine how resources are allocated, including access to financial resources. Therefore, there is a causal relationship between a firm's growth and its institution. In the World Bank Enterprise Survey (2014), business owners and top managers were presented with a list of ten business environmental obstacles and asked to choose the biggest obstacle to their business. Access to finance, access to electricity and the level of corruption were the most ranked obstacles for firms registering at 33.1 per cent, 27.2 per cent and 12.7 per cent, respectively.

Previous studies reveal that there is a consensus that a good business environment fosters firms' growth, productivity and development, while an adverse business environment increases firms' transaction costs and constraints on their development (Herrera & Kouamé, 2017). Arguably, the institutional void also contributes positively to driving entrepreneurship in some parts of Nigeria. The findings in much of the ethnic entrepreneurship literature (Ojiaku, 2015; Olakunle, Iseolorunkanmi & Segun, 2016; Igwe et al., 2017) suggest that the Igbos in Nigeria in the face of institutional disadvantage engage in business to create economic power and fill the institutional voids. The Igbos, when compared to the other major ethnic groups in Nigeria, are at the forefront of entrepreneurial activities (Igwe et al., 2017; Olakunle, Iseolorunkanmi & Segun, 2016).

Social Cultural Barriers

Gender, social and cultural barriers reflect the exclusion, discrimination and inequality posed by the gender divide that exists in developing countries where women are mostly affected as reflected in many studies (World Bank, 2013; Porter, 2013; Jamali, 2009). Corruption constrains entrepreneurship by deterring entrepreneurs unwilling to engage in corrupt practices and encouraging unproductive forms of entrepreneurship (Aidis et al., 2012). The World Bank (2013) maintains that after decades of progress towards the equality for women, almost 90 per cent of countries continue to have laws or regulations that prevent women from fully participating in economic life as entrepreneurs or employees.

It has been suggested by some scholars that from the perspective of diversity, equality and inclusion, entrepreneurship can be viewed as a means of inclusion for women and other marginalised groups in low-income countries, in which they suffer from a lack of equal opportunities and social exclusion (Pines et al., 2010). Several studies show perceive gender bias as a very real obstacle in raising resources for entrepreneurship. Akhalwaya and Havenga (2012) maintain that women must cope with negative prevailing social and cultural attitudes, lack of education and training, as well as gender discrimination.

Chinomona and Maziriri (2015) note that sex discrimination, gender bias or gender stereo-typing is a challenge, which is faced by most women entrepreneurs and that being discriminated against in a male-dominated society hinders women entrepreneurs from being successful. In many parts of Nigeria, culture and traditions constrain entrepreneurship by deterring women willing to engage in entrepreneurship and those who wish to expand their businesses. On the other hand, some authors believe that sexual stereotyping and discrimination against women less suited for managerial roles pushed women into entrepreneurship (Buttner & Rosen, 1988). Others report of "glass ceiling" (barriers that prevent female mid-managers from moving up to the executive suite) as a factor that influence women into business (Madichie, 2009).

Infrastructural Challenges

Physical infrastructure such as roads, railways, airports, schools, hospitals, sources of power, technology and markets enhance or facilitate the exploitation of entrepreneurial opportunities. It has been suggested that closing the infrastructural gaps will foster entrepreneurial opportunities, reduce African unemployment and boost the firm's productivity (Ajide, 2020; Igwe & Icha-Ituma, 2020; Igwe et al. 2022). Transport barriers refer to the challenges that women face regarding avail-ability, suitability and transport policies that discriminate against women using public transport. The existence of inadequate transportation impacts negatively the competitiveness of businesses. However, the transport problem is more challenging to women than to men and even more pres-ent in agricultural or rural communities. Where there are poor transport facilities, this limits trade and market flows between rural communities and rural–urban centres as well as reducing social contact and interaction.

Adequate and efficient transport system enables entrepreneurs to respond to new types of opportunities in different locations and provides opportunities for women to combine domestic work with business activities. It has been suggested that mobility promotes entrepreneurship and intrapreneurship by acting as a catalyst for socio-economic development and growth (Aceituno-Aceituno et al., 2018). In distinguishing between mobility and accessibility, Bryceson et al. (2003) note that accessibility depends on infrastructure and availability of affordable modes of transport for the movement of people and their products and/or services. Accessibility, or the perceived proximity of desired location destinations, is heavily influenced by the transport mode being used (ibid, p. 179). One of the pillars for promoting economic growth and entrepreneurship is techno-logical and digital innovation. The process of discovering and applying new technological systems has become the most important driver of economic and social change in the last 50 years (Lucas et al., 2013).

Access to Financial Capital and Women Entrepreneurship

At multiple levels (micro, meso and macro), several factors contribute to women's exclusion in access to finance (Table 9.2). For instance, there are rural–urban location differences, informal gender norms that govern women's mobility and economic activity, and the ability to have access to finance or financial services (Govindapuram et al., 2022). There have been difficulties in draft-ing legislation to protect women's access to critical entrepreneurial resources (such as land and capital), thereby limiting the achievement of financial inclusion and the Sustainable Development Goal (SDG 1) that focuses on ending poverty (Manji, 2010). Using data from 80 nations,

Table 9.2 Challenges That Women-Owned Enterprises and Entrepreneurs Face

Findings	Sources	Critical Factors
Women entrepreneurs are less likely to obtain formal loan approval due to formalities and requirements associated with formal lending	Mascia & Rossi (2017), Bellucci et al. (2010) Chundakkadan & Sasidharan (2022)	Regulations and bureaucracy
Women entrepreneurs are more likely to encounter credit market discrimination due to lenders' preferences and prejudice against women	Blanchard et al. (2008), Chundakkadan & Sasidharan (2022)	Prejudicial discrimination
Lenders are prejudiced about the skills, knowledge and managerial capabilities of women entrepreneurs	Chundakkadan & Sasidharan (2022)	
Inequal access to education, unequal pay, unequal opportunity and political inequality between men and women	Chundakkadan & Sasidharan (2022)	Institutional gender inequality
Financial institutions are mostly male-dominated	Chundakkadan & Sasidharan (2022)	
Socio-economic differences between men and women	Ghosh & Chaudhury (2022)	
Significant between rural and urban and gender	Senou & Manda (2022)	
Gender gap in lending markets can be explained by firms' characteristics and selection bias	Senou & Manda (2022)	
Networks are homogeneous, small or poorly developed when compared to men in developing economies	Jaim (2021) & Minniti (2010)	
Lack of information access and support system for their disadvantaged positions in society	Jaim (2021), Hersby et al. (2009) & Santos et al. (2019)	

Source: Compiled by authors.

Chundakkadan and Sasidharan (2022) found that women-owned and managed enterprises are more likely to be discouraged from applying for formal finance or loans.

The review of the literature (Table 9.2) highlights several challenges that women-owned enterprises and entrepreneurs face including (i) regulations and bureaucracy, (ii) prejudicial discrimination and (iii) institutional gender inequality. It is important to focus on the policies, eligibility conditions, rules and regulations of practices governing access and availability of financial capital to overcome the differences between gender (women–men), rural–urban, youths–adults and small–large enterprises.

Discussion, Conclusion and Implications

Although the highest levels of women entrepreneurship globally as reported by GEM report are in the Middle East and Africa with more women starting or running a new business (GEM, 2021, p. 53), several challenges prevent women from growing their firms. This chapter assessed the challenges faced by high-growth women enterprises in a developing world context. It was observed that the contribution of YouWiN to the growth of women's high-growth enterprises in Nigeria was still constrained by a myriad of factors ranging from the "gender liability" to other social and cultural barriers, which require targeted interventions.

Policies must focus on enhancing the legitimacy of a more diverse array of women entrepreneurs and increasing their access to financial capital. Nigeria's business environment is characterised by corruption, lack of access to capital and the poor state of the country's infrastructure, which has stifled the growth of the country's 17.3 million micro, small and medium enterprises (MSMEs). This study reveals institutional, social, cultural and gender biases that women must overcome to be able to not only establish new businesses but more importantly scale up existing ones (Madichie & Agu, 2022; Madichie, 2011). Some cultures in Nigeria assign domestic roles to women and proscribe certain trades from women's participation. We also find unfavourable transport policies to support women entrepreneurs as one of the challenges hampering the success of high-growth women entrepreneurs.

The results of this study are in consistence with the literature (Porter, 2013; Starkey & Njenga, 2010; Katwalo & Madichie, 2008), which maintain that inadequate and unsustainable transport systems are the most important factors affecting women in business in many SSA countries. The study also reveals that women entrepreneurs still experienced gender discrimination, and this limits women from starting new businesses or expanding their existing businesses. These range from inferiority complex, self-esteem and societal expectations. Other problems include sexual harassment, corruption, crime and insecurity which mostly affect women in developing world contexts – not the least, in Nigeria.

There are several implications for policy and practice emerging from this study. Financial inclusion helps to enhance the capabilities of vulnerable groups (Morsy, 2020). First, the identification of wider gender, social and cultural barriers, and especially transport barriers could provide policymakers with information on transport policy that is required to support women's entrepreneurship. Second, the focus of policies designed to support women's entrepreneurship should recognise the traditional gendered role of women that contributes to the double burden of responsibilities. Third, in order to address the gender challenges, capacity building in entrepreneurship should be complemented by access to social interventions to relieve the burden of multiple roles that businesswomen perform.

Given the impact of access to finance on poverty and economic growth, more research is required to map out strategies for tackling the barriers to financing high-growth women entrepreneurs in developing countries. There may also be the need to focus on examining the determinants of women's high-growth firms' productivity through modelling firm growth (using a stochastic process). Ultimately the use of mixed-methods research designs would go a long way towards tracking and reversing the impediments to the growth of women's businesses in the country.

Note

1. It is worth acknowledging the suspension of the World Bank's "Ease of Doing Business" reports following some methodological irregularities. As the statement reads, "After data irregularities on Doing Business 2018 and 2020 were reported internally in June 2020, World Bank management paused the next Doing Business report and initiated a series of reviews and audits of the report and its methodology" (World Bank, 2021).

References

Aceituno-Aceituno, P., Danvila-Del-Valle, J., González García, A., & Bousoño-Calzón, C. (2018). Entrepreneurship, intrapreneurship and scientific mobility: The Spanish case. *PLoS One*, *13*(9), e0201893. doi: 10.1371/journal.pone.0201893

African Development Bank (2013). Recognizing Africa's informal sector. https://www.afdb.org/en/blogs/afdb-championing-inclusive-growth-across-africa/post/recognizing-africas-informal-sector-11645/ (Accessed 17 March 2017).

Aidis, R., Estrin, S., & Mickiewicz, T. (2012). Size matters: Entrepreneurial entry and government. *Small Business Economics*, *39*, 119–139.

Aikaeli, J. (2010). Determinants of rural income in Tanzania. 'An Empirical Approach'. Research on Poverty Alleviation REPOA, 10/4.

Ajide, F. M. (2020). Infrastructure and entrepreneurship: Evidence from Africa. *Journal of Developmental Entrepreneurship*, *25*(03), 2050015. https://doi.org/10.1142/S1084946720500156

Akhalwaya, A., & Havenga, W. (2012). The Barriers that hinder the success of Women Entrepreneurs in Gauteng - South Africa. *International Journal of Sustainable Development*, *3*(5), 11–22.

Alvarez, S. A., & Busenitz, L. W. (2001). The entrepreneurship of resource-based theory. *Journal of Management*, *27*(6), 755–775. doi: 10.1177/014920630102700609

Ariyo, A., Lee, J., & McCalman, D. (2015). Entrepreneurship in India: The challenges ahead. *Journal of International Business Disciplines*, *10*(1), 1–17.

Ayogu, M. (2007). Infrastructure and economic development in Africa: A review. *Journal of African Economies*, *16*, 75–126. https://doi.org/10.1093/jae/ejm024

Ayyagari, M., Demirguc-Kunt, A., & Maksimovic, V. (2014). Who creates jobs in developing countries? *Small Business Economics*, *43*(1), 75–99. http://www.jstor.org/stable/43553735

Bellucci, A., Borisov, A., & Zazzaro, A. (2010). Does gender matter in bank–firm relationships? Evidence from small business lending. *Journal of Banking & Finance*, *34*(12), 2968–2984.

Blanchard, L., Zhao, B., & Yinger, J. (2008). Do lenders discriminate against minority and woman entrepreneurs? *Journal of Urban Economics*, *63*(2), 467–497. https://doi.org/10.1016/j.jue.2007.03.001

Bryceson, D. F., Mbara, T. C., & Maunder, D. (2003). Livelihoods, daily mobility and poverty in sub-Saharan Africa. *A Transnational Transdisciplinary Journal*, *23*(2), 177–196.

Buttner, E. H., & Rosen, B. (1988). Bank loan officers' perceptions of the characteristics of men, women, and successful entrepreneurs. *Journal of Business Venturing*, *3*(3), 249–258.

Central Bank of Nigeria (CBN, 2005). Micro Finance Policy, Regulatory & Supervisory Framework for Nigeria. http://www.cenbank.org/Out/publications/guidelines/DFD/2006/MICROFINANCE%20POLICY.pdf

Chang, Y., Gomes, J. F., & Schorfheide, F. (2002). Learning-by-doing as a propagation mechanism. *American Economic Review*, *92*, 1498–1520.

Chinomona, E., & Maziriri, E. T. (2015). Women in action: Challenges facing women entrepreneurs in the Gauteng province of South Africa. *International Business & Economics Research Journal (IBER)*, *14*(6), 835–850.

Chundakkadan, R., & Sasidharan, S. (2022). Gender gap and access to finance: A cross-country analysis. *Review of Development Economics*, *26*, 180–207. https://doi.org/10.1111/rode.12830

Coad, A. (2014). *Firm age and growth persistence, innovation forum VI-2014, crisis, innovation and transition*, 1–3 October 2014, University of Paris Quest, Nanterre, La Defense.

Coad, A., & Rao, R. (2008). Innovation and firm growth in high-tech sectors: A quantile regression approach. *Research Policy*, *37*(4), 633–648.

Coleman, S. & Robb, A. (2009). A comparison of new firm financing by gender: evidence from the Kauffman firm survey data. *Small Business Economics*, 33: 397–411.

Coleman, S., & Robb, A. (2014). Access to capital by high-growth women-owned businesses. The National Women's Business Council. SBAHQ-13-Q-0A63.

Fabusoro, E., Omotayo, A. M., Apantaku, S. O., & Okuneye, P. A. (2010). Forms and determinants of rural livelihoods diversification in Ogun State, Nigeria. *Journal of Sustainable Agriculture*, *34*(4), 417–438.

Fairlie, R., & Robb, A. (2009). Gender differences in business performance: Evidence from the characteristics of business owners survey. *Small Business Economics*, *33*, 375–395.

Faleye, O. A. (2013). Religious corruption: A dilemma of the Nigerian State. *Journal of Sustainable Development in Africa, 15*(1), 1520–5509.

Farkas, Z. (2019). The concept and coverage of institution. *Rationality and Society, 31*(1), 70–97. https://doi .org/10.1177/1043463118821654

GEM (2014). Africa's young entrepreneurs: Unlocking the potential for a better future. Global Entrepreneurship Monitor, UK. United Kingdom Monitoring Report.

Ghosh, C., & Chaudhury, R. H. (2022). A comparative study of saving behaviour between India and China. *Millennial Asia*. https://doi.org/10.1177/09763996221087049

Global Entrepreneurship Monitor (GEM, 2021). 2020/2021 Global Report. The World Bank. file:///C:/ Users/pauli/Downloads/gem-global-report-2020-21-web-1620064317.pdf

Gordon, A., & Craig, C. (2001). *Rural non-farm activities and poverty alleviation in Sub-Saharan Africa.* Policy Series 14. Chatham: Natural Resources Institute.

Govindapuram, S., Bhupatiraju, S., & Sirohi, R. A. (2022). Determinants of women's financial inclusion: Evidence from India. *Annals of Public and Cooperative Economics*, 1–28. https://doi.org/10.1111/apce .12376

Haltiwanger J., Jarmin, R. S., & Miranda, J. (2013). Who creates jobs? Small versus large versus young. *Review of Economics and Statistics, 95*(2), 347–361.

Hashmi, S. D., Gulzar, S., Ghafoor, Z. et al. (2020). Sensitivity of firm size measures to practices of corporate finance: Evidence from BRICS. *Future Business Journal, 6*, 9. https://doi.org/10.1186/s43093 -020-00015-y

Henrekson, M., & Johansson, D. (2010). Gazelles as job creators: A survey and interpretation of the evidence. *Small Business Economics, 35*, 227–244. https://doi.org/10.1007/s11187-009-9172-z

Herrera, S., & Kouamé, W. (2017). Productivity in the non-oil sector in Nigeria: Firm-level evidence. Policy Research Working Paper, 8145. Macroeconomics and Fiscal Management Global Practice Group, the World Bank Group, July 2017.

Hersby, M. D., Ryan, M. K., & Jetten, J. (2009), Getting together to get ahead: The impact of social structure on women's networking. *British Journal of Management, 20*(4), 415–430.

Hsieh, Chang-Tai, & Oklen, P. (2014). The life cycle of plants in India and Mexico. *Quarterly Journal of Economics, 129*(3), 1035–1084. http://klenow.com/HsiehKlenow_LifeCycle.pdf

Igwe, P. A., & Icha-Ituma, A. (2020). A review of ten years of African entrepreneurship research, 325-353, Edited by Sinha, P., Gibb, J., Akoorie, M. & Scott, J. M. (2020), *Research handbook on entrepreneurship in emerging economies*, Edward Elgar Publishing. https://doi.org/10.4337/9781788973717.00027

Igwe, P. A., Madichie, N. O., Chukwuemeka, O., Rahman, M., Ochinanwata, N., & Uzuegbunam, I. (2022). Pedagogical approaches to responsible entrepreneurship education. *Sustainability, 14*(15), 9440. https://doi.org/10.3390/su14159440

Igwe, P., Newbery, R., & Icha-Ituma, A. (2018). Entrepreneurship challenges and gender issues in the African informal rural economy. In *Knowledge, learning and innovation, Research insights into Cross Sector Collaboration*. Springer. ISBN 978-3-319-59282-4. https://books.google.co.uk/books?id =z4M0DwAAQBAJ&pg=PA92&lpg=PA92&dq

Igwe, P.A., Newbery, R., Amoncar, N., White, G.R.T. and Madichie, N.O. (2020), Keeping it in the family: exploring Igbo ethnic entrepreneurial behaviour in Nigeria. International Journal of Entrepreneurial Behavior & Research, 26(1), 34-53. https://doi.org/10.1108/IJEBR-12-2017-0492.

Igwe, P. A., Onjewu, A. E., & Nwibo, S. U. (2018). Entrepreneurship and SMEs' productivity challenges in the Sub-Saharan Africa, 189-221, Edited by Dana, L-P., Ratten, V. & Honyenuga, B. Q (2018), *African Entrepreneurship: Challenges and Opportunities for Doing Business*. Palgrave Macmillan Cham.

International Finance Corporation (IFC) (2008). Supporting entrepreneurship at the base of the pyramid through business linkages. IFC.

International Labour Organisation (ILO) (2014). Transitioning from the informal to the formal economy, 103rd Session, Report V (1), International Labour Office, Geneva.

Jaim, J. (2021). Does network work? Women business-owners' access to information regarding financial support from development programme in Bangladesh. *Business Strategy and Development, 4*, 148–158. https://doi.org/10.1002/bsd2.135

Jamali, D. (2009). Constraints and opportunities facing women entrepreneurs in developing countries. *Gender in Management: An International Journal, 24*(4), 232–251.

Katwalo, A., & Madichie, N. O. (2008). Entrepreneurial and cultural dynamics: A gender kaleidoscope of Ugandan microenterprise. *International Journal of Entrepreneurship and Small Business, 5*(3/4), 337–348.

Keeper, D. G. (2012). Systemic corruption in Nigeria: A threat to sustainable development. Proceedings of the 1st International Technology, Education, Environment Conference. *A Journal of African Society for Scientific Research, 1*(1), 172–179.

Kellermanns, F., Walter, J., Crook, T. R., Kemmerer, B., & Narayanan, V. (2016). 'The Resource-Based View in Entrepreneurship': A content-analytical comparison of researchers' and entrepreneurs' views. *Journal of Small Business Management, 54*, 26–48.

Kelley, D., Roberts, A., Goff, L., Pertea, G., Kim, D., Trapnell, C., Pimentel, H., Salzberg, S., Rinn, J., & Pachter, L. (2012). Differential gene and transcript expression analysis of RNA-seq experiments with TopHat and Cufflinks. *Nature Protocols, 7*(3), 562–578.

Khavul, S., Bruton, G., & Wood, E. (2009). Informal family business in Africa. *Entrepreneurship Theory and Practice, 33*(6), 1217–1236.

Krishna, A. and Shariff, A., 2011. The Irrelevance of National Strategies? Rural Poverty Dynamics in States and Regions of India, 1993–2005. *World Development, 39*(4), pp.533–549.

Lucas, H. C., Agarwal, R., Clemons, E. K., El Sawy, O. A., & Weber, B. (2013). Impactful research on transformational it: An. opportunity to inform new audiences. *MIS Q, 37*, 371–382. doi: 10.1098/rsif.2009.0564

Madichie, N. O. (2009). Breaking the glass ceiling in Nigeria: A review of women's entrepreneurship. *Journal of African Business, 10*(1), 51–66.

Madichie, N. O. (2011). Setting an agenda for women entrepreneurship in Nigeria: A commentary on Faseke's journey through time for The Nigerian Woman. *Gender in Management, 26*(3), 212–219.

Madichie, N. O., & Agu, A. G. (2022). The role of universities in scaling up informal entrepreneurship. *Industry and Higher Education*, 09504222221101548. https://doi.org/10.1177/09504222221101548

Madichie, N. O., & Gallant, M. (2012). Broken silence: A commentary on women's entrepreneurship in the United Arab Emirates. *The International Journal of Entrepreneurship and Innovation, 13*(2), 81–92.

Madichie, N. O., & Hinson, R. E. (2014). Women entrepreneurship in sub-Saharan Africa. *The Routledge Companion to Business in Africa*, pages 175-196.

Madichie, N. O., & Nkamnebe, A. D. (2010). Micro-credit for Micro-enterprises? A study of women 'petty' traders in Eastern Nigeria. *Gender in Management, 25*(4), 301–319.

Manji, A. (2010). Eliminating poverty? 'Financial Inclusion,' access to land, and gender equality in international development. *The Modern Law Review, 73*, 985–1004. https://doi.org/10.1111/j.1468-2230.2010.00827.x

Mascia, D. V., & Rossi, S. P. (2017). Is there a gender effect on the cost of bank financing? *Journal of Financial Stability, 31*, 136–153.

Minniti, M. (2010). Female entrepreneurship and economic activity. *The European Journal of Development Research, 22*(3), 294–312.

Mishra, A., Igwe, P. A, Lean, J. et al. (2014) Supporting micro and small enterprises. In *The Routledge companion to financial services marketing*. Routledge Companions in Business, Management and Accounting (vol. 28, pp. 1–576). London: Routledge. ISBN 9780415829144.

Morsy, H. (2020). Access to finance – Mind the gender gap. *The Quarterly Review of Economics and Finance, 78*, 12–21. https://doi.org/10.1016/j.qref.2020.02.005

Morsy, H., & Youssef, H. (2017). Access to finance – Mind the gender gap. European Bank for Reconstruction and Development (EBRD). Working Paper No. 202 Prepared in July 2017. file:///C:/Users/pauli/Downloads/WP_202.pdf

Newbery, R., Siwale, J., & Henley, A. (2017). Rural entrepreneurship theory in the developed and developing context. *International Journal of Entrepreneurship and Innovation, 18*(1), 3–4.

North, D. C. (1990). *Institutions, institutional change, and economic performance.* New York: Cambridge University Press.

Ojiaku, O. (2015). *Textbook on Igbo people, culture and character* (pp. 1–178). Bradenton: Booklucker.com. http://assets.booklocker.com/pdfs/8047s.pdf (Accessed October 07, 2017).

Olakunle, O., Iseolorunkanmi, J., & Segun, O. (2016). Indigene-settler relationship in Nigeria: A case study of the Igbo community in Lagos. *Afro Asian Journal of Social Sciences, VII*(III), 2229–5313.

Onyeiwu, S., & Liu, J. (2011). Determinants of income poverty in rural Africa: Empirical evidence from Kenya and Nigeria. Paper Presented at the African Economic Conference, Addis Ababa, October 26–28.

Organization for Economic Co-operation and Development (OECD) Eurostat Manual on Business Demography Statistics (2007). Eurostat-OECD manual on business demography statistics. https://www.oecd.org/sdd/business-stats/eurostat-oecdmanualonbusinessdemographystatistics.htm

Pines, M. A., Lerner, M. & Schwartz, D. (2010). Gender differences in entrepreneurship: Equality, diversity and inclusion in times of global crisis. *Equality, Diversity and Inclusion, 29*(2), 186–198. https://doi.org/10.1108/02610151011024493.

Porter, G. (2013). Transport services and their impact on poverty and growth in rural sub-Saharan Africa. Crown Agents /AFCAP/Durham University, UK. http://www.ifrtd.org/files/uploads/AFCAP%20TS%20POVERTY%20AND%20GROWTH%20COMBINED%20DOC%20Jan%207%202013[1].pdf (Accessed January 10, 2013).

Robb, A., & Coleman, S. (2010). Financing strategies of new technology-based firms: A comparison of women-and men-owned firms. *Journal of Technology Management & Innovation, 5*(1), 1-50.

Robb, A., Coleman, S., & Stangler, D. (2014). Sources of economic hope: Women's entrepreneurship. SSRN. Elsevier. http://dx.doi.org/10.2139/ssrn.2529094

Santos, G., Marques Carla, S., & Ratten, V. (2019). Entrepreneurial women's networks: The case of D'Uva—Portugal wine girls. *International Journal of Entrepreneurial Behavior & Research, 25*, 298–322.

Senou, M. M., & Manda, J. (2022). Access to finance and rural youth entrepreneurship in Benin: Is there a gender gap? *African Development Review, 34*, 29–41. https://doi.org/10.1111/1467-8268.12623

Starkey, P. C., & Njenga, P. (2010). Improving sustainable rural transport services, constraints, opportunities and research needs. AFCAP Practitioners Conference paper, November. www.ifrtd.org

United Nations International Children's Emergency Fund (2005). Education in Nigeria. https://www.unicef.org/nigeria/children_1937.html (Accessed March 10, 2017).

United States Agency for International Development (2010). Constraints to female entrepreneurship in sub-Saharan Africa. USAID Knowledge Services Centre, June 17, 2010.

Wiklund, J., & Shepherd, D. (2003). Knowledge-based resources, entrepreneurial orientation, and the performance of small and medium-sized businesses. *Strategic Management Journal, 24*, 1307–1314. https://doi.org/10.1002/smj.360

World Bank (2008). Agriculture for development. World Development Report, Washington, DC.

World Bank (2013). Gender and transport. Washington, D.C.: The World Bank. http://www.worldbank.org/en/news/press-release/2013/09/24/societies-dismantle-gender-discrimination-world-bank-group-president-jim-yong-kim (Accessed December 17, 2017).

World Bank (2015). Fact sheet: Doing business 2016 in sub-Saharan Africa, October 27, 2015. http://www.worldbank.org/en/region/afr/brief/fact-sheet-doing-business-2016-in-sub-saharan-africa (Accessed March 9, 2017).

World Bank (2016). Doing business report. https://www.doingbusiness.org/content/dam/doingBusiness/media/Annual-Reports/English/DB16-Full-Report.pdf

World Bank (2017). Nigeria - youth enterprise with innovation in Nigeria (YouWiN!) program impact evaluation 2011–2016, March 30. http://microdata.worldbank.org/index.php/catalog/2329/study-description (Accessed December 15, 2017).

World Bank (2021, September 16). World bank group to discontinue doing business report. https://www.worldbank.org/en/news/statement/2021/09/16/world-bank-group-to-discontinue-doing-business-report

World Bank Enterprise Surveys (2014). Nigerian country profile. http://www.enterprisesurveys.org/ (Accessed January 12, 2017).

YouWiN Connect (2017). Aims and Objectives. https://www.youwinconnect.org.ng/about/about.php

Chapter 10

Policy and Managerial Implications for Entrepreneurial Practice in Africa

Patient Rambe, Doreen Anyamesem Odame,
Kojo Kakra Twum, Paul Agu Igwe, Robert E. Hinson
and David Gamariel Rugara

Contents

Introduction

This book provides evidence-led multi-perspective review of the role that entrepreneurship can play in the execution of entrepreneurship and small business development ideas under national export promotion agencies like the Ghana Export Promotion Agency and their counterparts in places like Nigeria and South Africa. Whilst there has been long-held belief that an entrepreneurship-centred approach would relieve Sub-Saharan Africa of challenges to emerge from low employment and high-poverty stress levels, the book challenges these epistemic commitments through a problem-atisation of terms of commitment. Some of the terms employed focus on customer retention and attraction strategies, thinking further than the size of the firm and leveraging local know-how least employed by big business. It can also be argued that there is space for small and medium enterprises (SMEs) to build customer-intelligent agile responsiveness by utilising digital platforms to enhance their Corporate Responsibility Management (CRM). Chapter 3 offers evidence of how the responsive and innovative use of existing digital platforms such as WhatsApp and Facebook has been employed improve competitive advantage, albeit at little cost to "Koko" King and "Cookhouse" Ghana.

For the reader, the book highlights the necessity of the role that continental bodies such as the African Development Bank (AfDB), the African Union (AU) and African Continental Free Trade Area (AfCFTA) have in reinforcing Afro-centric trade priorities in view of the conceptualisation of the consumer and the service provider. One of the key objectives of the AfCFTA is to "create a single market for goods, services, facilitated by movement of persons in order to deepen the economic integration of the African continent" (Igwe, Ochinanwata & Madichie, 2021, p. 291). It can be argued that the Business-to-Business (B2B) and Business-to-Customer (B2C) theoretical frameworks in both consumer and business orientation tend to be framed on multinational corporations' (MNCs) CRM programmes at the expense of the small and medium enterprises landscape dominating African entrepreneurship. Incumbently, the argument inevitably posits itself in the resurgent demands for decolonial approaches to business and academic enterprise. As such, the conclusion of the book will take a deliberate detour to bring in decolonial argumentation as both the purpose and anchorage of such bodies as AfCFTA and other regional politico-economic bodies.

It has been argued that for Sub-Saharan Africa, entrepreneurship and small business development have been recognised as major techniques for alleviating income poverty (Igwe, Okolie, & Nwokoro, 2019). The early development literature reveals that the growth path of most nations was accompanied by a process of agricultural and industrial transformation (Diao, Magalhaes & Mcmillan, 2018; Diao et al., 2017 Mason & Brown, 2013). Since the beginning of the 21st century, internet of things, digital platforms, Robotics and Big Data have become the main drivers of development shaping industries and services. The economic transformation of Southern Africa is no exception. Eastern and Southern Africa boost about 60% of Africa's population with an estimated gross domestic product of $1,917,904 million in 2021 (World Bank, 2022). Southern African biggest exports are precious metals, minerals, gold, diamonds and platinum. Also, entrepreneurship and free trade have become Africa's catalysts for a new era of economic prosperity and transformation (African Development Bank, 2021). Therefore, entrepreneurship has been a driver of South African economic growth. The growth of entrepreneurial ventures results from the interaction between internal and external environment and resources. The role of the national and regional trade institutions creates the structure of the ecosystem and thus determines the entrepreneurial capacity of an economy.

Despite the leverage trade institutions have for regional and national economies, there is evidence that Eastern and Northern African. This is because Ethiopia and Kenya are not Southern African countries' entrepreneurs still face some of the world's toughest business conditions and are ranked poorly in the World Bank's Ease of Doing Business surveys, for example, Kenya and Ethiopia – both ranked 136 and 132 (World Economic Forum, 2015). In their study Sutter, Burton and Chen, (2019) used a three-lens approach to entrepreneurship development starting with Remediation (resource-based); Reform (institutional forces) and Revolution (agent-based factors) as a solution for alleviating extreme poverty. Institutional drivers of entrepreneurship comprise macro-, meso- and micro-level forces (formal, informal, cultural, legal, political and social norms). Macro-level defines the national rules and enforcement mechanisms. Meso-level represents organisational ecology and dynamics. Micro-level represents the reasons and conditions for undertaking economic activities (What to produce? How to produce and whom to produce?). Despite the successes created by entrepreneurship, there are several challenges such as the legacies of apartheid, containing crime, fostering acceptable business ethics, dealing with diversity and facilitating reconciliation (Robinson, 2004). In the past few decades, government policies and socio-cultural elements encouraged entrepreneurship; however, the support was not enough to contribute positively towards economic growth (Madzikanda, Li & Dabuo, 2022).

More so, unhealthy entrepreneurial ecosystems block access to resources and opportunities, limiting entrepreneurial activity and economic output (Madzikanda, Li & Dabuo, 2022).

Other critical pressing issues for entrepreneurial development in Africa include the development and enhancement of marketing capabilities, international entrepreneurship in all its forms and development of more women entrepreneurs for the growth of Africa. The political, cultural, social, economic and technological environments have not been effective in supporting international entrepreneurship and innovation. Most of the Southern economies are dominated by micro-informal activities. These are businesses that employ fewer than five individuals and mostly family members (Igwe, Newbery & Icha-Ituma, 2018). Informal enterprises do not usually register with the government, hence do not pay taxes. They are limited by resource access, productivity and marketing capability. These firms are dominated by women entrepreneurs. Most of the enterprises are seasonal and micro-businesses where there is no guarantee of income or wage receipts (World Economic Forum, 2015). African women enterprises are rooted in culture and their businesses are organised with strong family influence, and the women entrepreneurs lack entrepreneurial skills such as buying, selling, negotiation, customer relations, networking, funds management, innovations, market trends analysis, etc (Okolie et al., 2021).

In the light of increasing globalisation of the world economy, international marketing is a necessity for the survival of all organisations, whether big or small, rather than a luxury traditionally reserved for multinational corporations (Lee & Carter, 2012). Therefore, SMEs are constantly seeking sustainable competitive advantages that create superior performance in their international markets (Johansen & Knight, 2010). This is because operating on the international market serves as an opportunity for firms to diversify the various risks involved in their operations, to take advantage of foreign market opportunities, to extend sales of seasonal products, to take advantage of opportunities that come with economies of scale and to serve as a solution to stagnant or declining home market (Albaum, Duerr & Strandskov, 2005).

For decades, it has been contended that African economies and firms are closed to international business activity, and this may have been justified to some extent by notable cases of some African nations temporarily closing their national borders to foreign investors and multinational enterprises (Babarinde, 2009; Boso, Debrah & Amankwah-Amoah, 2018). Indeed, poor enforcement of private property rights (leading to widespread nationalisation and confiscation of private properties) has discouraged local and international entrepreneurial activities on the continent. Driven by socialist and nationalistic mindsets, the entrepreneurial activities of individuals and businesses were replaced by state-owned enterprises. Despite the many benefits of the global market, most SMEs shy away from engaging in international marketing because of the numerous challenges related to ease of doing business, institutional, cultural and informal attribute challenges. Albaum, Duerr and Strandskov (2005) echoed this argument when they opined that an obstacle that affect many firms has to do with the greater operational effort involved in foreign market operations and the perceived high level of risk involved in international marketing operations. However, SMEs that strive to engage in international marketing encounter different challenges such as limited access to the Internet of Things, network and experience. Hence, the international market is dominated by medium and large organisations that have the capability, experience and resources.

To that end, regional joint ventures between firms can become an innovative means of engaging in the international market or doing business. To overcome the challenges of lack of capability, experience and resources, entrepreneurs can, through their firms, engage in joint ventures or alliances to access new markets and distribution networks. Joint venturing offers an opportunity for each partner to benefit significantly from the comparative advantages of the other. Some of the benefits of the joint venturing arrangement are that local partners bring knowledge of the domestic market; familiarity with government bureaucracies and regulations; understanding of local labour markets; and, possibly, existing manufacturing facilities. On the other hand, foreign partners offer advanced process and product technologies, management know-how and access to export and to advanced technology (Miller et al., 1997; Safina, 2020). Joint partnerships also allow firms to build stronger partnerships to fend off competition (Safina, 2020). Therefore, several firms prefer to engage in joint ventures as a springboard to international markets as a medium to learn, gain experience and reduce risks.

To be able to participate in joint ventures, it is critically important for entrepreneurs to be aware of their enterprise's identity. Indeed, the definitions of SMEs and micro, small and medium enterprises (MSMEs) are disputed mostly according to context, and economic activity is an interesting point that requires further critical interrogation. As explored in the book, there are different ways of defining small to medium enterprises, with different contexts applying varied definitional and conceptual understanding. However, equally important is the concept of enterprise's organisational identity which we break down into five domains with critical implications for how enterprises are perceived. The five domains are Shared Identity, Lived Identity, Attraction Identity, Perceived Identity and Regulatory Identity (SLAPR).

Domain 1: Shared Identity: a shared identity by people leading an organisation and shaping its vision and mission. This identity is shared by organisational members from the top down. Critically, organisational leadership enforces an identity through organisational policies and directives.

Domain 2: Lived Identity: this is an identity shaped by and through the experiences of people working within an organisation (Internal Identity).

Domain 3: Attraction Identity: this is an identity that thrives on organisational esteem against local perceptions of value, by the organisation (external but internally served stakeholder) and investors, that is, those that can derive value through investment or aligning to the organisational brand.

Domain 4: Perception Projected Identity: People working within the organisation project the values as carriers of organisational shared identity (1). We also suggest the fourth domain as a challenged forte due to brand dominance by MNC's marketing budgets, pre- and post-colonial resonance which has given a competitive advantage to local producers, manufacturers and service providers.

Domain 5: Regulatory Identity: This is an identity that is shaped by regulatory guidelines and constraints for monitoring and compliance with governmental and local authority levies. Indeed, as this identity carries liabilities to levies/taxes, it disincentivises local entrepreneurs from formalising their trade. As addressed in the preceding chapters of the book, the regulatory identity varies according to national and regional descriptions of SMEs.

The development of entrepreneurship and the growth of small businesses in Africa are top of the agenda for almost all governments. In view of this, many aspects of entrepreneurial development must be well researched to serve as a guide to stakeholders, business managers and policymakers. The theoretical and practical implications of research findings on the African continent are crucial considering the urgency to develop the continent through entrepreneurship. This book provides a concise description of the challenges of small businesses, marketing aspect of entrepreneurship, internationalisation, women and gender-based approach to entrepreneurship, and the role of regional integration in enhancing entrepreneurship in Africa. This book opens up the reader to studiously challenge the mainstream conceptualisation of African entrepreneurship outside of mainstream and Euro-American ways of business development. It is a welcome point to ask pointed questions about what internationalisation and globalisation mean for sub-Saharan Africans. Most pointedly, the book opens up a platform and adds to the voices of scholars concerned with contextualising entrepreneurship from the perspectives of the Global South.

The COVID-19 pandemic has affected the business of small entrepreneurship in Africa. To respond to this threat, many businesses have adopted a digital approach to doing business. A typical small business is making good use of digital platforms to organise their operations to achieve sales goals. The role of social entrepreneurs during the COVID-19 pandemic took the form of businesses providing services to help fight the pandemic. Social entrepreneurs promoted the provision of hand sanitisers, nose and face masks and other protective equipment. The role of the government in supporting small businesses to mitigate the effect of COVID-19 also presents lessons for public policy makers. Small businesses were provided with business support loans, tax holidays by governments. The financial sector also introduced some innovative financial services to reduce the financial burden on businesses and citizens.

The marketing implications on entrepreneurship are best described in the literature as the marketing entrepreneurship interface (MEI). These disciplines have a history of adopting concepts and practices that create value for customers and organisations through the identification of opportunities, innovation, risk-taking, proactiveness and customer-centric activities. The market orientation and entrepreneurial orientation concepts must be aggressively pursued by small businesses in developing economies. The success of small businesses depends on the ability to exploit limited resources through risk-taking, proactiveness and innovation. Similarly, developing small business market orientation, thus strategically focusing the entire business around the customer, is key to delivering superior value, building profitable customer relationships and improving firm performance.

Another strong position this book takes is the promotion of small businesses through internationalisation. Taking part in global trade by African countries is necessary to gain competitiveness and promote economic development. Apart from internal factors such as firm characteristics and resources, external environmental factors are seen as crucial in determining the success of small businesses on the international stage. In this book, a careful look at the external factors affecting internationalisation identified that political, economic/financial and technological factors are significant factors affecting small businesses.

A gender-based approach to entrepreneurship is also discussed in this book. The chapter on the role of women in entrepreneurship argues that women are considered a major part of entrepreneurial success in Africa. In the tourism sector, for instance, women have provided self-employment avenues and home-grown hospitality services. Another chapter in this book makes a case for supporting women entrepreneurs using formal and informal institutions. However, the chapter acknowledges that information institutions are able to provide more support to women entrepreneurs in Africa. This book also dedicated a chapter to the challenges in financing women entrepreneurs in Africa.

Conclusions on the Role of Marketing on Entrepreneurial Success of SMEs

The role of marketing in entrepreneurship cannot be underestimated. Two decades ago, Carson and Coviello (1996) acknowledged that the interface between marketing and entrepreneurship has increased. Collinson (2002) asserts that the initial search for the interface between entrepreneurship and marketing was conceived when researchers from the US and the UK worked on a project in 1999 through a Special Interest Group (SIG). Hisrich (1992) had earlier asserted that marketing and entrepreneurship each play a role in innovation, new product introduction economic development and new venture creation. Even though entrepreneurship is not a business function like marketing, Hisrich (1992) admits that the two disciplines are all management functions that are closely related.

Collinson (2002) reports that the SIG project found that the interface between marketing and entrepreneurship focuses on three key areas:

Change Focused: Entrepreneurship and marketing are focused on economic and social change. The marketing discipline has constantly been shaped by changes related to technological trends, socioeconomic trends and geopolitical trends (Rust, 2020). Technological changes have increased the ability to communicate with customers, the ability to collect, share and analyse customer information. The marketing discipline has introduced some changes in how goods and services are marketed. The contemporary marketing discipline has been introduced. The changing role of marketing in behaviour change campaigns seeks to change the behaviour of people creating social marketing (Lahtinen, Dietrich & Rundle-Thiele, 2020). In recent times, customers' growing concern for sustainable business has propelled the practice of environmental marketing (Taherdangkoo, Mona & Ghasemi, 2019).

On the entrepreneurial aspect as a change-focused endeavour, small businesses play a critical role as change agents (Betta, Jones & Latham, 2010; Partzsch & Ziegler, 2011). Betta, Jones and Latham (2010) assert that the Schumpeter notion of entrepreneurship is based on the assumption that effective economic change occurs among actors that have resources already within the context they operate. Entrepreneurship as a social change factor ensures that individuals with the ability to see new opportunities are able to adjust societies to their directions (Betta, Jones & Latham, 2010). A typical example of entrepreneurs creating societal change is social entrepreneurs who use resources in the immediate environment to promote social well-being.

Opportunistic in Nature: Entrepreneurship and marketing disciplines attempt to take advantage of opportunities in the environment. Chell (2000) posits that entrepreneurial behaviours entail a relentless pursuit of opportunity regardless of available resources. In effect, entrepreneurs have the ability to recognise and proactively pursue opportunities for business development and growth and also have the confidence to exploit resources to take advantage of the opportunities (Chell, 2000). Marketing managers also continuously seek growth opportunities to increase sales (Hanssens et al., 2016). Sarkees (2011) posits that the capability of firms to sense and respond to changes in technologies referred to as technological opportunism is necessary to gain competitive advantage and impact sales, profits and market value.

Innovative in Approach: Entrepreneurship and marketing are arguably the two disciplines that have been benefiting from innovative practices. The early work of Schumpeter has strongly related to the concept of entrepreneurship and innovation (Autio et al., 2014). Entrepreneurship has introduced some destructive products, services and processes to the marketplace (Autio et al., 2014). In marketing, there are many forms of innovation that aid in the marketing of goods and services. Design innovation plays a crucial role in marketing as it involves the development of new products through research and development (Hsu, 2011). Also, marketing innovation involves changes in product design, packaging, promotions and pricing (Moreira et al., 2012).

From a review of the literature, scholars were still in search of the interface between entrepreneurship and marketing. Hansen et al. (2019) identified four components of the interface between entrepreneurship and marketing:

Antecedents: the antecedents that enable the performance of entrepreneurship and marketing duties include actors, firm characteristics and resources. The actors refer to the individuals, teams and organisations that are involved in the marketing and entrepreneurship process. In relation to the firm characteristics, two main concepts namely Entrepreneurial Orientation and Market Orientation are at the centre of the interface between the two disciplines.

Entrepreneurial Orientation: this is the propensity for organisation management to take calculated risk, to be innovative and be proactive.

Market Orientation: this refers to the organisational culture of truly adopting a marketing approach that focuses strategically on the customer.

The resources that have been identified in the literature that links entrepreneurship and marketing include networks, knowledge, human and financial.

Functions and Processes: the various antecedents of the marketing and entrepreneurship interface will feed into the various functions and processes that exist in performing these activities. On the marketing side, the key functions and processes that are needed include new product development, supply chain management and customer relationship management. The entrepreneurial concepts that have promoted marketing are entrepreneurial marketing. Entrepreneurial marketing is the proactive identification and exploitation of opportunities for acquiring and retaining profitable customers through innovative approaches. The dimensions of entrepreneurial marketing include proactiveness, innovativeness, customer intensity, risk-taking, opportunity focus and value creation.

Outcomes and Environmental Context: the outcomes of marketing and entrepreneurial processes involve change. These changes may not be limited to business growth: strategy, target customers and markets. Also, the value created through entrepreneurial and marketing activities for firms, customers, stakeholders and employees is an important outcome. In the literature, an important outcome of marketing and entrepreneurship is new product creation.

In this book, the role of marketing in promoting entrepreneurship has been highlighted. The interface between marketing and entrepreneurship is evident among small businesses in Africa. From a Ghanaian perspective, marketing has been influential in the success of small businesses in the sense that it offers the opportunity to create value with the little resources they have. Marketing strategies using the traditional marketing mix elements of product development, pricing, promotion and distribution. One important marketing concept that small businesses must implement is customer relationship management. Small business managers must consciously build relationships with customers using innovative techniques such as information management systems. A good relationship with customers can be established by having information about customers regarding their interests and needs. Also, environmental dynamism which entails the knowledge of the relevant macro-environmental factors can promote marketing performance. Finally, this book collaborates with the literature on the outcomes of the entrepreneurship and marketing interface. The results highlighted in this book suggest that view.

Conclusions on Internationalisation of SMEs

The marketing of small businesses in international markets can be promoted through internationalisation. Internationalisation is a process that is manifested in a number of ways including setting up foreign subsidiaries, joint ventures, international advertising campaigns, licensing agreements, internal trade, exhibitions among others (Johanson & Vahlne, 1990). The process of internationalisation happens within the internal environment and the external examination (Fletcher, 2001). The internal environment entails management and organisational characteristics as factors promoting internationalisation. A holistic approach to understanding internationalisation also involves the external environment impediments and incentives. However, the external environment in relation to the barriers and incentives has been a major concern for researchers since SMEs in developing countries are very vulnerable to participating in international business. Igwe and Kanyembo (2019) acknowledge that SMEs in developing countries are faced with external barriers in seeking internationalisation. This book, therefore, focuses on factors in the external environment that affect the internationalisation of small business in Africa.

The external barriers to internationalisation according to Rahman et al. (2020) include economic, technological, cultural differences, political systems and institutional systems: theoretically, the Diffussion of Innovation Theory and the PESTEL Framework (Political, Economic, Social, Technological, Environmental and Legal) provide useful theoretical lens and analytical frameworks.

The economic barriers that have been identified go a long way to affect assets, finance and capital. In developing economies, financial constraints that hinder internationalisation have been identified as the greatest barrier, with factors such as economic growth, interest rates, income distribution and inflation rate. It is worth noting that even though economic barriers affect large and small firms, this barrier has a greater effect on small firms due to their vulnerability and limited resources. In this book, the results indicate that financial and economic barriers have a significant effect on the internationalisation of SMEs in Nigeria. These results present an implication for small businesses in developing economies. Therefore, government must work on preferential custom levies and reduce foreign exchange risk. These two factors were found to be the most significant economic barriers affecting internationalisation from a developing country perspective. The AfCFTA as an economic union can be used to promote trade among African countries and also create a bargaining power on the international market.

The technological factors affecting small businesses in developing countries were found to have a significant effect on internationalisation. The issues relating to underdeveloped information technology, lack of electricity, underdeveloped telecommunication system and lack of warehouse were identified as major constraints to business growth. The implications are that small businesses are disadvantaged in the absence of technological development that is available in advanced economies. Therefore, governments must invest in infrastructure and technology that enable small businesses to partake in internationalisation.

On the political front, governments in Africa must work towards eliminating corruption and striving for political stability. This is because political instability has created insecurity among small businesses. Ensuring a stable political environment will foster collaboration between local firms and foreign firms since there is the assurance that political instabilities will not result in the loss of investment. In Africa, there is a potential for countries that are democratic to attract foreign businesses that may partner with local firms to internationalise.

A Discussion of Gendered (Women) Perspectives in Promoting Entrepreneurship

Although the broad field of entrepreneurship has been examined from historical, temporal, institutional spatial and social contextual perspectives (Welter, 2011), the appreciation of context as founded in uniqueness and differences is critical to preventing the generalisation of patterns of specific entrepreneurial behaviours (Welter and Gartner, 2016). As such, the proper conception, operationalisation and application of the gendered context of entrepreneurship are critical as institutional, social and spatial contexts are not the sole explanatory variables for the development and sustenance of entrepreneurship, especially in the understudied African contexts.

The inclusion of a gendered context of entrepreneurship is particularly fundamental in the emerging African context where individuals especially women are called upon to overcome resource constraints and institutional hurdles to pursue entrepreneurship (Lim et al., 2016). For women entrepreneurs, there is a wide configuration of factors that coalesce in explaining their success and failure in the institution and thriving of entrepreneurial ventures. These include inter alia, the dominant patriarchal norms (Ndhlovu, 2009), social stereotypes that project women as inferior (Bobrowska & Conrad, 2017) to their male counterparts and whose roles are reduced to procreation and consumption in domestic circles, the prevalence of social norms that undermine the social autonomy of women to pursue entrepreneurship due to burdensome family responsibilities and social norms that shape the demand for maintaining a good balance between work and family unit (Nxopo & Iwu, 2015).

Moreover, female entrepreneurs are confronted with culturally imposed constraints that psychologically and physically impede their autonomy, aspirations and priorities (Siba, 2019). Second, a gendered perspective on entrepreneurship has been credited with facilitating a deeper understanding of the motivations and reasons for men and women acting differently in entrepreneurship: such as the role of womanhood and how gender plays out in the enactment of entrepreneurship and founding of new ventures (Welter et al., 2014). To advance a gender-sensitive framework (Brush et al., 2009), it is critical to acknowledge that male and female entrepreneurs face inherently different constraints to the growth and development of their ventures (Siba, 2019). For instance, female entrepreneurs are often confronted with a lack of access to capital, which impedes the growth of their firms.

Third, female entrepreneurs with human capital including soft skills such as leadership (Siba, 2019) and limited expertise and experience may be forced to divert scarce resources away from operations to establish credibility and legitimacy among external stakeholders such as suppliers and customers (Amankwah-Amoah, 2016). As such, firms (including those that are women-owned) are required to access new knowledge, resources and skills to ensure their long-term survival (Ahmadi and O'Cass, 2018).

The chapter makes three main contributions. First, the study provides a fresh gender perspective to the study of entrepreneurship by not only pointing out the circumstances that female entrepreneurs are situated but also demonstrating the specific psychological traits that they possess that make them well positioned to compete with their male counterparts. This is particularly critical given the paucity of theoretical perspectives explaining the growth factors of businesses owned by females in the developing world. This under-theorisation is worsened by an apparent lack of scholarship on women's entrepreneurship in developing countries. This theoretical vacuum has contributed to a lack of knowledge on the activities of women entrepreneurs (Jamali, 2009), especially in the developing world.

Second, the chapter demonstrates that the gender issue as it relates to entrepreneurship cannot be treated independently but coalesces with a constellation of other factors such as access to funding and human capital. As literature suggests, grasping the resources, strategies and institutions that female entrepreneurs in Africa grapple with necessitates a multi-level and multi-pronged approach that accommodates institutional, political, economic, social and cultural contexts and their implications for entrepreneurial activities and outcomes (Ojong, Simba & Dana, 2021).

Third, given the potential of female entrepreneurs to contribute directly to the growth and development of their enterprises, Cornwall (2016) emphasises the need to challenge cultural beliefs about gender and power that perpetuate their subordination to men. For instance, as more female entrepreneurs engage in entrepreneurship, their contribution has positively impacted economic productivity affirming their economic value (Nwagu and Onwuatuegwu, 2021). For instance, across many African countries such as Nigeria, Ghana, Kenya and Zimbabwe, the majority of entrepreneurs who engage in informal and survivalist entrepreneurship are women.

Discussion on the execution of the entrepreneurship and small business development ideas under national export promotion agencies like the Ghana Export Promotion Agency and their counterparts in places like Nigeria and South Africa

The striving export markets in many parts of Africa present an opportunity to intensify internationalisation. A decade ago, Lederman, Olarreaga and Payton (2010) indicated that national export promotion agencies have tripled and have been made part of national export strategy. In Africa, export agencies undertake export promotion programmes to enhance the attractiveness of foreign markets and export performance (Sharma, Sraha & Crick, 2018). The Department of Trade, Industry, and Competition is mandated by the government of South Africa to promote value-added goods and services abroad by broadening the export base and targeting high-growth markets (http://www.thedtic.gov.za). The department is responsible for providing an enabling environment, increasing the demand for the country's products, enhancing the value position and branding, and initiating export financing (http://www.thedtic.gov.za). Similarly, the Ghana Export Promotion Authority (GEPA) is mandated to diversify exports from traditional exports. These export promotion objectives in Africa can be realised with a clearer understanding of the challenges of internationalisation, the marketing of small export businesses and export financing.

Considering the role played by national export agencies and the criticisms about the efficacy of these institutions in developing countries (Lederman, Olarreaga & Payton, 2010), this book proposes some novel ideas that can guide export promotions. First, the promotional and marketing mix that drives internationalisation thrust of SMEs dovetails with this book's authors' thrust to reflect on research fundings in a critical sense to the future of entrepreneurship and marketing. Chapters 6 not only presents and well captures the backdrop of an evolving business environment with contemporary market conditions becoming influenced by chaos, complexity ambiguity (Fillis & Telford, 2020) but projects an appealing exemplar of how marketing strategies drive better economic outcomes for firms in emerging contexts. The market-driven approach that the book advocates, transcends and addresses the growing critique against a customer-centric perspective in marketing which has culminated in the lack of innovation and truly innovative products, services and experiences that have constrained SME growth (Eggers et al., 2013).

Second, export promotion agencies must foster internationalisation through a number of innovative ideas. There is a need to seek strategic collaboration with players within industries. The export performance agenda must be in line with the current trends in many industries. Industry players such as those in the financial sector must be highly involved. For instance, the Exim Guaranty model in Ghana is a typical example of providing financial information to enable access to finance. Also, the establishment of business incubators, seminars, training sections on marketing and business management, and assistance in the development of strategic plans are all ways to enhance the competitiveness of small businesses.

References

African Development Bank (AfDB) (2021). Entrepreneurship is critical to Africa's transformation - African Development Bank, 21 June 2021. https://www.afdb.org/en/news-and-events/entrepreneurship-critical-africas-transformation-african-development-bank-44309

Ahmadi, H., & O'Cass, A. (2018). Transforming entrepreneurial posture into a superior first product market position via dynamic capabilities and TMT prior start-up experience. *Industrial Marketing Management, 68*, 95–105.

Albaum, G. S., Duerr, E., & Strandskov, J. (2005). *International Marketing and Export Management.* Pearson Education.

Amankwah-Amoah, J. (2016). Coming of age, seeking legitimacy: The historical trajectory of African management research. *Critical Perspectives on International Business, 12*(1), 22–39.

Autio, E., Kenney, M., Mustar, P., Siegel, D., & Wright, M. (2014). Entrepreneurial innovation: The importance of context. *Research Policy, 43*(7), 1097–1108.

Babarinde, O. A. (2009). Africa is open for business: A continent on the move. *Thunderbird International Business Review, 51*(4), 319–328.

Betta, M., Jones, R., & Latham, J. (2010). Entrepreneurship and the innovative self: A Schumpeterian reflection. *International Journal of Entrepreneurial Behavior & Research, 16*(3), 229–244.

Bobrowska, S., & Conrad, H. (2017). Discourses of female entrepreneurship in the Japanese business press– 25 years and little progress. *Japanese Studies, 37*(1), 1–22.

Boso, N., Debrah, Y. A., & Amankwah-Amoah, J. (2018). (How) does Africa matter for international business scholarship? *AIB Insights, 18*(4), 6–9.

Carson, D., & Coviello, N. (1996). Qualitative research issues at the marketing/entrepreneurship interface. *Marketing Intelligence & Planning, 14*(6), 51–58.

Chell, E. (2000). Towards researching the 'opportunistic entrepreneur': A social constructionist approach and research agenda. *European Journal of Work and Organizational Psychology, 9*(1), 63–80.

Collinson, E. (2002). The marketing/entrepreneurship interface. *Marketing Management, 18*(3–4), 337–340.

Cornwall, A. (2016). Women's empowerment: What works?. *Journal of International Development, 28*(3), 342–359.

Department of Trade. Industry, and Competition. Export Promotion. http://www.thedtic.gov.za/sectors-and-services-2/1-4-2-trade-and-export/export-development-and-promotion/export-promotion/#:~:text=The%20directorate%20is%20mandated%20to,market%20share%20in%20traditional%20markets.

Diao, X., Kweka, J., McMillan, M., & Qureshi, Z. (2017). *Economic transformation from the bottom up: Evidence from Tanzania* (IFPRI Discussion Paper 1603). Washington, DC: International Food Policy Research Institute.

Diao, X., Magalhaes, E., & Mcmillan, M. (2018) Understanding the role of rural non-farm enterprises in Africa's economic transformation: Evidence from Tanzania. *The Journal of Development Studies, 54*(5), 833–855.

Eggers, F., Kraus, S., Hughes, M., Laraway, S., & Snycerski, S. (2013). Implications of customer and entrepreneurial orientations for SME growth. *Management Decision, 51*(3), 534–546.

Fillis, I., & Telford, N. (Eds.). (2020). *Handbook of Entrepreneurship and Marketing.* Edward Elgar Publishing.

Fletcher, R. (2001). A holistic approach to internationalisation. *International Business Review, 10*(1), 25–49.

Hisrich, R. D. (1992). The need for marketing in entrepreneurship. *Journal of Business & Industrial Marketing, 7*(3), 53–57.

Hsu, Y. (2011). Design innovation and marketing strategy in successful product competition. *Journal of Business & Industrial Marketing, 26*(4), 233–236.

Igwe, P. A., & Kanyembo, F. (2019). The cage around internationalisation of SMEs and the role of government. *International entrepreneurship in emerging markets: Nature, drivers, barriers and determinants, 10*, 161–176).

Igwe, P. A, Newbery, R., & Icha-Ituma, A. (2018). Entrepreneurship challenges and gender issues in the African informal rural economy. In *Knowledge, learning and innovation: Research insights into cross sector collaboration* (pp. 91–111). Springer. ISBN 9783319592824

Igwe, P. A., Ochinanwata, C., & Madichie, N. O. (2021). The 'Isms' of regional integration: What do underlying interstate preferences hold for the ECOWAS union? *Politics Policy, 49*: 280–308. https://doi.org/10.1111/polp.12396

Igwe, P. A., Okolie, U. C., & Nwokoro, C. V. (2021). Towards a responsible entrepreneurship education and the future of the workforce. *The International Journal of Management Education*, *19*(1), 100300 https://doi.org/10.1016/j.ijme.2019.05.001

Jamali, D. (2009). Constraints and opportunities facing women entrepreneurs in developing countries: A relational perspective. *Gender in Management: an International Journal*, *24*(4), 232–251.

Johansen, D., & Knight, G. (2010). Entrepreneurial and market-oriented SME'S fit to international environments, dynamic capabilities and competencies. *International Business: Research*, Teaching and Practice, *4*(1), 38–55.

Johanson, J., & Vahlne, J. E. (1990). The mechanism of internationalisation. *International Marketing Review*, *7*(4). https://doi.org/10.1108/02651339010137414.

Lahtinen, V., Dietrich, T., & Rundle-Thiele, S. (2020). Long live the marketing mix. Testing the effectiveness of the commercial marketing mix in a social marketing context. *Journal of Social Marketing*, *10*(3), 357–375.

Lederman, D., Olarreaga, M., & Payton, L. (2010). Export promotion agencies: Do they work?. *Journal of Development Economics*, *91*(2), 257–265.

Lee, K., & Carter, S. (2012). *Global marketing management: Changes, new challenges and strategies*. Oxford: Oxford University Press.

Lim, D. S., Oh, C. H., & De Clercq, D. (2016). Engagement in entrepreneurship in emerging economies: Interactive effects of individual-level factors and institutional conditions. *International Business Review*, *25*(4), 933–945.

Madzikanda, B., Li, C., & Dabuo, F. T. (2022). Barriers to development of entrepreneurial ecosystems and economic performance in Southern Africa. *African Journal of Science, Technology, Innovation and Development*, *14*(4), 936–946 https://doi.org/10.1080/20421338.2021.1918316

Mason, C., & Brown, R. (2013). Creating good public policy to support high-growth firms. *Small Business Economics*, *40*(2): 211–225.

Miller, R., Glen, J., Jaspersen, F., & Karmokolias, Y. (1997). International joint ventures in developing countries. International Monetary Fund, IMF. https://www.imf.org/external/pubs/ft/fandd/1997/03/pdf/miller.pdf

Moreira, J., Silva, M. J., Simoes, J., & Sousa, G. (2012). Marketing innovation: Study of determinants of innovation in the design and packaging of goods and services—Application to Portuguese firms. *Contemporary Management Research*, *8*(2), 117–130.

Nwagu, N. B., & Onwuatuegwu, I. N. (2021). Women entrepreneurship in Africa and implications on development: Obstacles and remedies. *Journal of African Interdisciplinary Studies*, *5*(6), 56–67.

Nxopo, Z., & Iwu, C. G. (2015). The unique obstacles of female entrepreneurship in the tourism industry in Western Cape, South Africa. *Commonwealth Youth and Development*, *13*(2), 55–71.

Ojong, N., Simba, A., & Dana, L. P. (2021). Female entrepreneurship in Africa: A review, trends, and future research directions. *Journal of Business Research*, *132*, 233–248.

Okolie, U. C., Ehiobuche, C., Igwe, P. A., Agha-Okoro, M. A., & Onwe, C. C. (2021) Women entrepreneurship and poverty alleviation: Understanding the economic and socio-cultural context of the Igbo women's basket weaving enterprise in Nigeria. *Journal of African Business*. https://doi.org/10.1080/15228916.2021.1874781

Partzsch, L., & Ziegler, R. (2011). Social entrepreneurs as change agents: A case study on power and authority in the water sector. *International Environmental Agreements: Politics, Law and Economics*, *11*(1), 63–83.

Rahman, M., Akter, M., Odunukan, K., & Haque, S. E. (2020). Examining economic and technology-related barriers of small-and medium-sized enterprises internationalisation: An emerging economy context. *Business Strategy & Development*, *3*(1), 16–27.

Robinson, D. A. (2004) Entrepreneurial challenges in South Africa. *Journal of African Business*, *5*(2), 173–185. DOI: 10.1300/J156v05n02_10

Safina, J. (2020). How to form a successful global joint venture? *Forbes*, October 01, 2020. https://www.forbes.com/sites/forbesfinancecouncil/2020/10/01/how-to-form-a-successful-global-joint-venture/?sh=3aa78d827906

Sarkees, M. (2011). Understanding the links between technological opportunism, marketing emphasis and firm performance: Implications for B2B. *Industrial Marketing Management, 40*(5), 785–795.

Sharma, R. R., Sraha, G., & Crick, D. (2018). Export promotion programmes and the export performance of Ghanaian firms: The mediating role of foreign market attractiveness. *International Marketing Review, 36*(4), 661–682.

Siba, E. (2019). *Empowering women entrepreneurs in developing countries: Why current programs fall short* (Policy Brief, pp. 1–9). Africa Growth Initiative.

Sutter, C. J., Burton, G. D., & Chen, J. (2019). Entrepreneurship as a solution to extreme poverty: A review and future research directions. *Journal of Business Venturing, 34*: 197–214.

Taherdangkoo, M., Mona, B., & Ghasemi, K. (2019). The role of industries' environmental reputation and competitive intensity on sustainability marketing strategy: Customers' environmental concern approach. *Spanish Journal of Marketing-ESIC, 23*(1), 3–24.

Welter, F. (2011). Contextualizing entrepreneurship—Conceptual challenges and ways forward. *Entrepreneurship Theory and Practice, 35*(1), 165–184.

Welter, F., & Gartner, W. B. (2016). Advancing our research agenda for entrepreneurship and contexts. In *A research agenda for entrepreneurship and context* (pp. 156–160). https://doi.org/10.4337/9781784716844.00017.

World Bank (2022). The World Bank in Eastern and Southern Africa. https://www.worldbank.org/en/region/afr/eastern-and-southern-africa

World Economic Forum (2015). What are the biggest challenges for Africa's entrepreneurs? https://www.weforum.org/agenda/2015/08/what-are-the-biggest-challenges-for-africas-entrepreneurs/.

Index

Printed in the United States
by Baker & Taylor Publisher Services